# NEW PERSPECTIVES
## ON RACIAL IDENTITY DEVELOPMENT

# New Perspectives
# on Racial Identity Development

*Integrating Emerging Frameworks*

SECOND EDITION

*Edited by Charmaine L. Wijeyesinghe*
*and Bailey W. Jackson III*

NEW YORK UNIVERSITY PRESS
*New York and London*

NEW YORK UNIVERSITY PRESS
New York and London
www.nyupress.org

Library of Congress Cataloging-in-Publication Data
New perspectives on racial identity development : integrating emerging frameworks / edited
by Charmaine L. Wijeyesinghe and Bailey W. Jackson III. -- 2nd ed.
p. cm.
Includes bibliographical references and index.
ISBN 978-0-8147-9479-1 (cl : alk. paper) -- ISBN 978-0-8147-9480-7 (pb : alk. paper) -- ISBN
978-0-8147-2453-8 (ebook) -- ISBN 978-0-8147-2452-1 (ebook)
1. Ethnicity. 2. Race awareness. 3. Identity (Psychology) 4. Race awareness--United States.
I. Wijeyesinghe, Charmaine, 1958- II. Jackson, Bailey W.
GN495.6.N49 2012
305.8--dc23
2011052291

*This book is dedicated to our parents:*
*Bailey W. Jackson, Jr. and Theodora G. Jackson,*
*and*
*Oscar R. Wijeyesinghe and Barbara J. Wijeyesinghe*

CONTENTS

## ACKNOWLEDGMENTS

We are thankful and indebted to the many people who helped us complete this book. First, we wish to thank the chapter authors, many of whom contributed to the first edition of *New Perspectives* and offered their time, energy, patience, and wisdom to us a second time. We were fortunate to also have new colleagues contribute to this edition. Their voices, perspectives, and words enrich the book immensely. We also wish to acknowledge and thank the extended network of people who supported the individual authors as they wrote their chapters.

At all phases of the project, Jennifer Hammer, our editor at NYU Press, was available to offer guidance and encouragement. Her perspective was especially useful when this project was in the early proposal phase and undergoing outside review. We also appreciate Jennifer's flexibility—which allowed us, and all the contributors, the time needed to produce chapters that reached their fullest potential. In addition, we thank Usha Sanyal and Despina Papazoglou Gimbel for their careful attention and diligence during the copyediting and production phases of this manuscript.

We again used the professional skills of Mary McClintock to develop a properly formatted and copyedited manuscript. Mary was accessible, knowledgeable, and patient. We very much relied on and appreciated her willingness and ability to accept, research, and respond to our inquiries concerning format, often at short notice. Her efforts relieved us of a significant burden, for which we are very thankful.

As individual authors and editors, we relied on the love and support of several individuals. For their work, patience, and encouragement, Bailey Jackson acknowledges Lenore Reilly, Maya Jackson, and Amber Jackson; Charmaine Wijeyesinghe acknowledges Christian Lietzau, Andreas and Rebecca Wijeyesinghe Lietzau, Diane Goodman, Katja Hahn D'Errico, James Bonilla, and a very special group of Delmar Moms.

# INTRODUCTION

CHARMAINE L. WIJEYESINGHE AND BAILEY W. JACKSON III

From initial theories influenced by the experience of African Americans during the civil rights movement, the study of racial identity development has expanded to encompass a range of racial groups, including Whites, Asian Americans, Latinos, Native Americans, and people with multiple racial backgrounds. Models of racial identity development are tools for understanding how individuals achieve an awareness of their sense of self in relation to race within a larger social, cultural, and historical context. Faculty members, counselors, organizational consultants, and mediators have integrated aspects of racial identity development theory into their teaching and practice—having found that the models provide insight into many aspects of individual, interpersonal, and intergroup dynamics. As campuses and communities become increasingly diverse, models of racial identity development offer valuable tools in understanding the needs of individuals and groups as well as the dynamics of conflict and coalition building within and across racial communities.

The first edition of this book, *New Perspectives on Racial Identity Development: A Theoretical and Practical Anthology* (Wijeyesinghe and Jackson 2001) presented updated and emerging models of racial identity development across six racial groups (Black, White, Latino/a, Native American, Asian, and Multiracial). The text also illustrated the relevance and application of these models to the teaching, counseling, and conflict resolution professions. The goal of the first edition was to illustrate various *racial* identity processes and the use of these models and theories in several areas of practice.

In this second edition, we continue to examine how various groups in the United States experience race and racial identity. Such ongoing exploration is needed because approaches and perspectives on race and identity are constantly evolving in light of social, political, and cultural changes. Racism is a major aspect that affects identity and understanding of oneself, race, and intergroup dynamics, and the way racism is manifested, named, and understood also changes over time. Since 2000, the population of the United States has become increasingly diverse. In a summary of select data from the 2010 Census, Humes, Jones, and Ramirez (2011) indicate that between 2000 and 2010:

- The Hispanic population increased by 43 percent and represented half of the total increase in population between 2000 and 2010.
- People who indicated that they were Asian only (checking only the Asian box to indicate race) increased at a rate of 43 percent, the largest percentage change of all the racial groups, and ranked second in terms of greatest numerical increase.
- Blacks experienced the third largest numerical increase. However, the percentage increase of the Black community rose by only 1 percent, from 12 percent in 2000 to 13 percent in 2010.
- The White-alone population was the only major racial group to experience a decrease in its proportion of the total population, moving from 75 percent to 72 percent of the entire population between 2000 to 2010.
- The Native Hawaiian and Other Pacific Islander-alone population grew by a third, and from 0.1 percent to 0.2 percent of the total population in one decade. Individuals indicating they were American Indian and Alaska Native alone grew by 18 percent, but remained at about 0.9 percent of the total population.
- The number of people checking two or more races on the Census increased to over 9 million between 2000 and 2010. While representing just under 3 percent of the total population, this group grew by one-third in the ten years between the two national population surveys.

In addition to reporting and analyzing the results of the 2010 Census, Hume, Jones, and Ramirez indicated that "The race categories included in the census questionnaire generally reflect a social definition of race recognized in this country and are not an attempt to define race biologically, anthropologically, or genetically. In addition, it is recognized that the categories of the race question include race and national origin or sociocultural groups" (2011, 2). These statements reflect the growing understanding that the environment in which identity is formed is in constant flux in response to shifting demographic, social, and geopolitical dynamics.

Given the changing face of America, models of racial identity development must evolve if they are to remain relevant and effective tools. However, the evolution of frameworks is not driven solely by shifts in the racial composition of the country. A greater understanding of how race is lived within a specific context at a particular time, the dynamic nature of the social, cultural, and political climate, and new insights about the nature of racial and social identity are additional forces to be considered.

The path ahead necessitates that we honor the roots of racial identity development, grow its various branches, and expand the areas from which we draw insight and knowledge. As we move forward foundational models of identity provide needed information, reference points, and direction. New research and analysis, and collaborations across disciplines contribute cutting-edge knowledge and perspectives on how we understand, study, and experience race and other aspects of social identity. At this time, the framework of *Intersectionality* is perhaps the most significant new perspective being considered in social identity literature and research. Intersectionality emphasizes that identity development in one area (race in the case of *New Perspectives*) cannot be viewed as occurring outside of, or separate from, the developmental processes of other social identities (such as gender, class, sexual orientation, and religious/faith tradition) within individuals (Dill and Zambrana 2009; Dill, McLaughlin, and Nieves 2007; Weber 1998, 2010a, and 2010b). Intersectionality calls for models of social identity to take a more holistic and integrated approach in describing and representing the lived experience of individuals, and to link individual experiences to larger social, cultural, and institutional systems.

Viewed from an intersectional perspective, racial identity is seen as complex and holistic, influenced by specific historical and social contexts, and framed by the dynamics of social power and privilege. Intersectionality receives considerable attention in the chapters of this book, and readers are encouraged to consider how Intersectionality enhances our understanding of race and racial identity development. At the same time, racial identity models offer history, perspectives, and content that can be beneficial to scholars of Intersectionality. Therefore, we see analyzing racial identity development and Intersectionality together as yielding reciprocal benefits that each discipline can build upon in the future.

This book is one tool for understanding racial identity in a modern context. It offers updated and expanded models of racial identity development that incorporate cultural and institutional changes related to race in the United States. We recognize, however, that although we live in a time when our social perspective is increasingly global in nature, national norms, values, and approaches to race, identity, and racism have not been transcended, and may never be. In describing how systemic power and privilege underlie hierarchical relationships between social groups, Weber (2010b) notes that these social relationships are

> never static and fixed and are constantly changing as part of new economic, political, and ideological processes, trends, and events. Their meaning varies not only across historical time periods but also across nations and regions within nations during the same period. Because these systems must always be understood within a specific historical and geographical context, race, class, gender, and sexuality analysis tend to avoid the search for common meanings of the systems that would apply in all times and places. (93–94)

Although some chapters in this book discuss race and identity from a more global and transnational perspective, the primary focus and scope of the volume is racial identity within the context of the United States. In addition, the contributors provide cutting-edge perspectives on how race and social identity are understood by, and represented in, frameworks of identity development. Chapters use emerging research and paradigms from other disciplines that offer innovative approaches that have yet to be fully discussed in the literature on racial identity. Contributing authors discuss the impact of these perspectives on how we understand and study racial identity in a culture where race and other social identities are socially constructed and carry significant societal, political, and group meaning.

The models and perspectives in this book encourage and feed the exploration of critical questions related to race and identity today, including:

- What promises do evolving social dynamics and emerging paradigms from other disciplines hold for the exploration of racial identity, and what challenges do they present to the ways race and racial identity have been viewed up to this point?
- In what circumstances is it beneficial to view race and racial identity separately from the developmental processes of other social identities (such as

gender, class, sexual orientation, and religion/faith) within an individual? Does adopting an intersectional perspective require that new frameworks and research methodologies treat racial identity as inextricably linked and related to other processes of social identity?

- If a more holistic and inclusive perspective on identity is warranted, or even required as existing theories are revised and new ones developed, how does this affect how race and racial identity are researched, taught, and applied in classrooms, counseling settings, or educator training programs?

- How do the increasingly global nature of the human experience, the easier and more rapid exchange of information, and the integration of the practices and imagery of other countries and cultures influence how we see or define race and racial group membership in the United States? How do these forces affect the discussion of national issues related to race and ethnicity, such as citizenship and immigration?

- What is the impact of changes in the way racial groups are configured and named in the United States on racial identity and racial group membership? How will ascribed and chosen identities affect membership in different racial groups and between racial groups in the future?

In addressing these and other related questions, the chapters in this book contribute to an ongoing dialogue that has within it as many questions as it does answers. This conversation requires many voices, diverse perspectives, and varying approaches to race and identity. The authors in this volume in fact reflect a range of orientations toward race and racial identity. This broad scope of perspectives is the result of a number of factors. The chapters discuss racial identity in six different groups, each of which has unique histories and issues related to their experience in the United States. The authors represent various approaches to identity, including psychological and psychosocial, ecological, postmodern, and postfeminist perspectives. Each chapter contains the research, analysis, and perspective of its particular author or authors. Some chapters reflect a personal, introspective presentation. In others, the material finds greater grounding in a review or analysis of the literature.

While representing diverse perspectives on racial identity, the contributors are bound together by a common goal—to offer information, models, and insights on how racial identity is understood and represented in a modern context and, in some chapters, to explore how models based on race can inform the experience of other social groups (such as gender, sexual orientation, and class). All the chapters connect racial identity to the larger cultural norms, social practices, and institutional systems related to race in the United States. Each chapter provides examples of how models and perspectives on racial identity are relevant to the day-to-day lives of individuals. One of the primary goals of this volume is the integration of emerging theoretical frameworks, such as Intersectionality, with perspectives on racial identity. Therefore, the chapters are more focused on the consideration and reconsideration of models of identity, and less on the application of theory to specific situations such as counseling, mediation, and teacher training. However, the models presented in the book can be used to guide approaches to education, teaching, curriculum development, and counseling. This book is not only about *what* we teach, research, or use to understand racial identity, but also about *how* we teach, study, counsel, and understand each other and ourselves.

The book begins with a chapter that provides an overview of theoretical perspectives on racial identity. This piece is followed by chapters that focus on racial identity development in Black, White, Asian, Latino, Native American, and Multiracial populations. The chapters in the second section of the book discuss how social identities occur simultaneously and examine the implications of this orientation for racial identity; how identity is enacted in day-to-day interactions; and specific pedagogical approaches, techniques, and activities related to incorporating Intersectionality into teaching about racial identity.

In chapter 1, Kristen Renn illustrates how the concepts of race and racial identity reflect the social and political systems of the United States at varying historical periods. This chapter provides an important distinction between the concept of race as a larger social construct, and racial identity that has meaning at the individual and group level. Renn then highlights how various disciplines frame racial identity and contribute to our understanding of racial identity development. Concluding with a discussion of modern influences that will continue to affect orientations toward racial identity, this chapter provides a firm foundation for the key concepts that appear in subsequent chapters of the book.

In chapter 2, Bailey Jackson updates his Black Identity Development (BID) model in light of some of the events that have had a profound effect on the evolution of race, racism, and racial identity at the national and global level. Whereas previously Black identity development models, including BID, overemphasized the role that racism played in Black identity development, the main focus of this chapter is the expansion of the BID model to more explicitly address the influence of Black culture in the Black identity development process. In his revision of the BID model, Jackson enhances the description of each of his identity development stages to include the ways in which emphasizing Black culture, along with racism, can increase our understanding of the Black identity development process at each stage. The chapter also integrates the concept of Intersectionality in the final stage of the BID model, and discusses how this additional perspective complicates the challenges associated with the last phase of the Black identity development process.

In chapter 3, Plácida Gallegos and Bernardo Ferdman provide an analysis of the impact of the growing Latino and Latina population on U.S. politics, public policy, and economics, as well as how these changes influence the response to Latinos by other groups. The challenges of viewing the Latino/a experience through the lens of U.S. configurations of, and approaches to, race are also discussed. In presenting their expanded model of Latina and Latino ethnoracial identity orientations, Gallegos and Ferdman add several layers to their previous work, including the challenges, adaptive strategies, behavioral manifestations, and limitations of each of the six orientations in the model. The authors make recommendations for organizations wishing to integrate and utilize Latinos and Latino perspectives in the workplace and for programs related to fostering cross-cultural competencies.

Chapter 4 of the book represents an integration of the fields of Multiracial theory and Intersectionality by Charmaine L. Wijeyesinghe. The author identifies and discusses several core characteristics evident in both disciplines. Select models of Multiracial identity are reviewed and analyzed for their inclusion of key aspects of Intersectionality, including framing identity as fluid, connected to larger social and historical contexts, and influenced by multiple, intersecting factors. In presenting a new model of Multiracial identity that incorporates these themes and expands on the number of factors from the author's previous work, the chapter offers a unique image and representation of racial identity. Implications of the content and representation of this model for future research and theory development related to Multiracial racial identity are also discussed.

A twenty-first century Native American consciousness is the central focus of chapter 5 by Perry Horse. This chapter examines Native Americans' relationship with the concept of race and identity over several historical eras, and how these eras influenced the context and situations in which Native Americans develop individual and group consciousness. Drawing upon the historical record, as well as research, knowledge of tribal issues, and personal narrative, Horse frames the discussion of Native American identity around the larger theme of *orientations*. The chapter highlights these orientations as they relate to race consciousness, political consciousness, linguistic consciousness, and cultural consciousness. The chapter offers directions for framing Indian consciousness in the twenty-first century, based on Native Americans' response to, and recovery from, the many challenges they faced during the periods of colonization.

In chapter 6 Rita Hardiman and Molly Keehn distinguish between early theories of White identity development and the more recent perspectives of White people's view of race and racial privilege. Using data gained from their research study of White college students, Hardiman and Keehn identify several key themes that highlight how a select group of Whites understand race, racism, and their racial identity today. Topics discussed include how Whites relate to other Whites, research participants' perspective on Whites who adopted aspects of Black culture, and what these White youth understood to be the advantages and disadvantages of belonging to their racial group. The authors evaluate the data in light of foundational models of White identity and also reflect on their findings given contemporary perspectives on the experience of Whites in the context of the evolving meaning of race and racism. The chapter concludes by posing research questions that explore racial identity as a fluid process, and one that varies when other social identities (such as religion and economic class) are taken into account.

Jean Kim updates her foundational Asian American Racial Identity Development Theory in chapter 7. Distinguishing between Asian Americans' relationship to race and ethnicity, the author offers a more sophisticated perspective of how Asian American identity is affected by factors such as the salience of particular social identities, situational differences, immigration and generation, and stereotypes and American cultural myths. After reviewing the components of the Asian American Racial Identity Development theory, Kim reflects upon the structure and content of the model in light of research related to stage-based paradigms and emerging perspectives that place attention to multiple identities in the forefront of social identity frameworks. The chapter includes discussion of several current issues facing Asian Americans, including the increase in interracial marriages, the impact of generation since immigrating to the United States, and changes in the political climate related to race.

In chapter 8, Evangelina Holvino discusses the impact of the forces of globalization, postmodernism, and transnational feminism on the construction and meaning of identity—demonstrating that how we think and frame social differences influences how we construct models of social identity. The chapter includes an analysis of several models that illustrate the relationship between various social identities. Holvino then introduces a model of *simultaneity* that integrates many themes evident in transnational feminist conceptions of identity: positing identity as complex, socially constructed, and subjective, for example. The chapter includes discussion of the application of the model, the skills and assumptions that support it, and the challenges in applying the model to the lives of individuals in various situations.

In chapter 9, William Cross presents a model of identity enactment based on the African American experience, and then uses the core features of this model to construct a second, more generic framework that can be applied to a range of social groups. Positing identity as stable but flexible in the manner in which it is expressed in different situations and contexts, Cross discusses the enactment of Black racial and cultural identity under conditions of racism, within mainstream institutions, across racial groups, and in interactions within the Black community. These modes of enacting identity in different contexts are then demonstrated within the experience of Native Americans, Lesbian, Gay, Bisexual, and Transgendered people, and people with disabilities.

Diane Goodman and Bailey Jackson provide insights on integrating an intersectional perspective into both the pedagogy and practice of teaching about racial identity in chapter 10. Their analysis identifies core areas related to racial identity and how these can be addressed through an approach that integrates intersectional assumptions, content, and approaches in an incremental manner. The authors present a framework of four pedagogical approaches that move from teaching racial identity within a single-identity focus to incorporating the influence of numerous axes of social identity simultaneously with race. Description of each approach includes core assumptions, criteria, and rationale for use, learning objectives, and specific instructional techniques and activities. In addition, the chapter provides direction for addressing challenges and issues that may arise from the use of each approach.

The models, perspectives, and tools offered in this book are meant to further our understanding of how individuals experience race and identity in a country where the population, cultural and political forces, and intragroup and intergroup dynamics are evolving. In addition, we hope the volume contributes to the building of bridges between the field of racial identity and disciplines related to other social groups and the experience and development of identity within these groups.

REFERENCES

Dill, Bonnie, T., Amy E. McLaughlin, and Angel D. Nieves. 2007. "Future Directions of Feminist Research: Intersectionality." In *Handbook of Feminist Research,* edited by S. N. Hesse-Biber, 629–637. Thousand Oaks, Calif.: Sage.

Dill, Bonnie, T., and Ruth E. Zambrana. 2009. "Critical Thinking about Inequality: An Emerging Lens." In *Emerging Intersections: Race, Class, and Gender in Theory, Policy, and*

*Practice*, edited by Bonnie T. Dill and Ruth E. Zambrana, 1–21. New Brunswick, N.J.: Rutgers University Press.

Humes, Karen, A., Nicholas A. Jones, and Roberto R. Ramirez. 2011. "Overview of Race and Hispanic Origin: 2010." *2010 Census Briefs*. Accessed June 23, 2011. http://www.census. gov/prod/cen2010/briefs/c2010br-02.pdf

Weber, Lynn. 1998. "A Conceptual Framework for Understanding Race, Class, Gender, and Sexuality." *Psychology of Women Quarterly*, 22: 13–32.

———. 2010a. "Introduction." In *Understanding Race, Class, Gender, and Sexuality: A Conceptual Framework,* 2nd ed., 1–19. New York: Oxford University Press.

———. 2010b. "Themes: Historically and Geographically Contextual, Socially Constructed Power Relations." In *Understanding Race, Class, Gender, and Sexuality: A Conceptual Framework,* 2nd ed., 93–114. New York: Oxford University Press.

Wijeyesinghe, Charmaine L., and Bailey W. Jackson, III, eds. 2001. *New Perspectives on Racial Identity Development: A Theoretical and Practical Anthology.* New York: NYU Press.

1

Creating and Re-Creating Race

*The Emergence of Racial Identity*
*as a Critical Element in Psychological, Sociological,*
*and Ecological Perspectives on Human Development*

KRISTEN A. RENN

*[handwritten marginalia: only differs on physical appearance? based on appearance]*

In the United States, race is a highly salient organizing social category. Race is a social construction based on physical appearance (skin color, hair color and texture, facial features), ancestry, nationality, and culture. It is used for *identification*—for example, to place individuals into demographic groups for various purposes—and as *identity*—the meaning individuals and groups ascribe to membership in racial categories. Identification results from external assignment or categorization, whereas identity results from internal processes as individuals encounter external influences. The history of racial identification and racial identity in the United States began with the European colonization of North America and continues into the twenty-first century. Public policies related to affirmative action, school desegregation, immigration, and population demographics (for example, the decennial Census) rely on the maintenance of a system of racial categorization—identification—that reinforces the existence of the categories themselves. An emphasis on individual identity and identity politics within U.S. culture renders racial identity and racial group membership critical components of psychosocial identity.

What connects the macro level of public policy to the micro level of individual identity is the experience of living as a racialized human being in the United States, or the daily experience of seeing and being seen through the lens of race. Racial identification and identities form this lens for people of color and White people.

In this chapter, I elaborate on the connection of race at the macro and micro levels, illuminating the concepts of race and racial identity in the United States. I provide a foundation for understanding the context in which individuals and groups develop and maintain a sense of self in a society that keeps race, culture, and nationality in the foreground of identity, identity politics, and public policy. I then discuss theoretical perspectives on race and suggest contemporary influences on racial identity and identity development.

## Racial Identification in the United States

Europeans brought with them to the North American continent the roots of the word race (for example, the Spanish and Castilian "raza" and the Portuguese "raça") and a concept of racial hierarchy based on the preservation of generations of nobility untainted by undesirable heritage (Smedley 2001; Sollors 2002; Takaki 1993). Sollors (1999) argued that in the nascent United States, whiteness stood in for European nobility and became the category to be protected from the threat of racial dilution by mixing with African Americans (free, enslaved, or emancipated, and their descendents) and American Indians. Colonial and early U.S. Census efforts to count the population by race emphasized these distinctions by, at various times, not counting Indians and fractionally counting slaves (in 1783 Congress voted to count a state's slave population as three-fifths of its free population) (Anderson 2002). Language differences and physical appearance marked Asian immigrants as non-White, making them and their descendents an easy target for racial categorization. Similarly, Latinos and Latinas[1] were marked by language and in some (but not all) cases physical appearance as not belonging to the dominant White majority. From colonization to today, racial categorization has been a feature of public and private life.

The codification—and subsequent modification—of racial categories results from the interplay between public policy and the denial or provision of various human and civil rights. For example, tax policy and congressional representation in the new nation were at the root of the non-counting of American Indians (who were not taxed or represented in the government) and fractional counting of slaves (counted in taxation and representation, though not allowed to hold property or vote). The decennial Census emerged as a way for the United States to manage the population count, and the delineation of racial categories was a practical and political necessity. But as Anderson (2002) pointed out,

> Counting the population is a deceptively simple idea, which on further examination is much more complex. Who actually are "the people"? . . . Slaves were both "people" and a "species of property" expressly excluded from the possibility of political action. If sovereignty derives from the people, what about other "people" who exercise no political power and had no political authority: women, children, criminals, aliens, and the poor? (271)

Nevertheless, in 1790 Congress mandated collecting population data on the sexes, ages, and colors of every household member in the nascent United States (for a history of what was counted in each decennial Census, see Bryan 2004). The Census evolved over time, with questions related to racial categories frequently mired in controversies related to slavery and abolition, women's suffrage, and immigration trends (for example, would Irish, Italians, and Jews count as White?). Throughout history, the "one-drop rule," so-called because "one drop" of non-White blood rendered an individual non-White, persisted. As late as 1970, Black and White ancestry were parsed to one part in thirty-two, or one Black great-great-grandparent in one's otherwise White family tree, to designate an individual Black (see Omi 1997; Zack 1993).

The decennial Census represents the federal government's interest in counting people in different racial categories,[2] yet state-sponsored discrimination based on race is as old as the history of White people in North America. Black slaves and Native Americans were, of course, denied citizenship, freedom, and human rights. The same was true of Chinese laborers brought to work laying railroad tracks, Tejanos who lived in Mexico until the border changed across their ancestral homes, Japanese Americans interned during World War II, and countless other non-White peoples who immigrated voluntarily or involuntarily to the United States (see Takaki 1993). The immigration of Latinos, Asians, and Blacks remains a deeply fraught political issue, and race-based policies (for example, affirmative action in college admissions) attempting to provide redress for decades of state-supported racial discrimination are being challenged and removed, state by state.

Yet in the face of so much state-sponsored race-based policy, anthropological, sociological, philosophical, and popular perceptions of race have evolved from a belief in the permanence and rigidity of racial categories to a concept of race as socially constructed, fluid, and impermanent (Omi and Winant 1994; Smedley and Smedley 2005; Zack 1993). As Smedley and Smedley (2005) wrote,

> The consensus among most scholars in fields such as evolutionary biology, anthropology, and other disciplines is that racial distinctions fail on all three counts-—that is, they are not genetically discrete, are not reliably measured, and are not scientifically meaningful. (16)

The early twenty-first century is marked by the paradox of a society increasingly believing that race is not a biological reality—yet the social meanings, both positive and negative, ascribed to racial categories and the people who belong to them, are as powerful as ever. For example, individuals who understand that "race as biology is fiction" (Smedley and Smedley 2005, 1) may still participate in and perpetuate norms, traditions, and communication styles that have their roots in racially based cultural patterns, because this participation is a source of individual and group identity expression, development, and pride (see Jackson 2001). And people who understand race as "an unstable and 'decentered' complex of social meanings constantly being transformed by political struggle" (Omi and Winant 1994, 55) must also deal with the daily reality of that struggle, as experienced in racial micro-aggressions (see, for example, Solórzano, Ceja, and Yosso 2000) and overt acts of racism.

If, as authors from different disciplines (for example, Côté and Levine 2002; Omi and Winant 1994; Smedley and Smedley 2005; Zack 1993) and popular media (for example, Adler 2009 in *Newsweek*) believe, race is now widely seen as a social rather than scientific concept, what is the collective and individual interest in maintaining racial categories that continue to be used to oppress some groups? Why does public policy—from the Census to school desegregation to affirmative action—concern itself with these categories? Why do people locate themselves, sometimes with ease and pride, sometimes with struggle and ambivalence, within or outside certain racial identities? For that matter, why is it important to publish this volume about racial identity development? In short, the very fact that race is a *social* construction renders it a centrally important social concept for individual, interpersonal, group, and intergroup identities, understandings, and communication. At the individual and collective level, race matters. Race is a meaningful personal identity for many people, and racial categories may be used to understand the philosophical, epistemological, and social structures of different groups (see Ladson-Billings 2000, 2006; Solórzano, Ceja, and Yosso 2000). Racial identification—official processes of putting people into racial categories, for example for civil rights enforcement or tracking trends in health, education, and employment—is likely to remain a prominent factor in public life that has far-reaching effects in private lives as well.

## Racial Identity and Identity Development

In a social context in which racial identification is so salient, racial identity itself becomes a critical element of individual and group identities. From the psychological, sociological, social psychological, and human ecological standpoints, racial identities matter in the study of human development. Taken together, these disciplines contribute to a nuanced understanding of the concept of racial identity and the way that racial identity operates at the individual and group levels. In this section of the chapter I review the historical and contemporary contributions of these disciplines to the study and understanding of racial identity development. I point to the ways in which different perspectives on identity and identity development complement and reinforce one another and, sometimes, how they challenge or contradict one another. Understanding complementary and competing theories provides a rich background for considering the perspectives presented in later chapters in this volume.

### Psychology

Psychologist Erik Erikson (1959/1994) was a central figure in the movement to define, describe, and elaborate on Freud's concept of "ego identity." Erikson proposed a series of eight stages, each marked by a crisis, leading to healthy ego identity. He saw identity as "both a persistent sameness within oneself (selfsameness) and a persistent sharing of some kind of essential character with others" (Erikson 1959/1994, 109). As racialized beings, then, people develop both self-sameness in terms of racial identity and a shared racial identity with others of the same group. Erikson's theory was stage-based, with the resolution of more advanced crises at each of eight stages relying on the successful resolution of the crisis or question from earlier stages. Identity becomes stronger as one resolves each crisis and becomes more committed to one's identity.

Building on Erikson's work, James Marcia (1966) posited four "ego identity statuses." The statuses result from a balance of two conditions: crisis and commitment. In order to develop identity, one must experience crisis or conflict and then make a commitment to a resolution. The four statuses are *foreclosure* (no crisis, but commitment to existing choices, values, and goals), *moratorium* (crisis or exploration/questioning of choices, values, and goals, but no commitment yet to them), *diffusion* (no crisis/exploration, no commitment), and *identity achievement* (crisis experienced and commitments made). Achieved racial identity results from exploration or crisis related to racial identity and commitments made to having and expressing racial identity in particular ways. Marcia's model and subsequent studies by others based on it have been criticized for implying a developmentally ordered continuum and for not accurately reflecting Erikson's concept of identity formation (see Côté and Levine 1983).[3] The widespread use of this model has also been criticized for not being adequately inclusive of ethnically diverse populations (Sneed, Schwartz, and Cross 2006). Yet Marcia's foundational work set the stage for important research on ethnic identity (for example, Phinney 1990). Marcia's central concepts of identity exploration and commitment appear throughout the psychological literature on racial identity development.

The majority of psychological models of racial identity development follow a more or less sequential approach (as did Erikson)—sometimes called stages, phases, or statuses—and incorporate identity exploration and commitment (as did Marcia) within the stages/statuses and the transitions from one level to the next. Building on the Black identity development models of William Cross (1971, see also Cross and Fhagen-Smith 2001) and Bailey Jackson (1976, see also Jackson 2001), Atkinson, Morten, and Sue (1979) introduced a minority identity development (MID) model, which was followed by a series of revisions leading to a racial and cultural identity development (RCID) model (Sue and Sue, 2003). The MID and RCID[4] rely on a stage-based model with five stages:

1. Conformity, in which individuals of color identify with White culture and internalize negative stereotypes about their own culture;
2. Dissonance, in which their experiences contradict their White worldview and they begin to question the dominant culture and explore their own;
3. Resistance and Immersion, in which individuals reject White culture and immerse themselves in their own culture;
4. Introspection, in which they struggle to find a balance between the dominant culture and their own culture; and
5. Synergistic Articulation and Awareness, in which they integrate their own cultural heritage and knowledge to form an identity based on self-acceptance that balances racial/cultural identity with other aspects of self.

The contribution of the MID/RCID approach to including multiple racial groups might also be considered its limitation: the lack of specificity to the particular experiences of Latino/as, Native Americans, and Asian Americans.

The predominance of this stage approach—if not exactly the language of these stages themselves—in psychological models of racial identity formation is unmistakable. Building on the Cross (1971) and Jackson (1976) models, a family of theories following similar stages emerged and evolved (for example, Cross and Fhagen-Smith 2001; Hardiman 1982, 1994; Helms 1990, 1994, 1995; Jackson 2001; Kim 1981, 2001). These stage models provide useful frameworks for examining racial identity development in a variety of contexts. They are widely taught and have been used extensively in counseling and education for individual intervention, conflict mediation, and pedagogical design (see Hardiman and Jackson 1992; Reynolds and Baluch 2001; Tatum 2003; Wing and Rifkin 2001).

*Sociology*

Whereas psychologists focus more attention on the individual and his or her racial identity development, sociologists focus on an individual's identification with and roles in a social group, as well as on interactions among groups. These investigations might include studies of identity politics, social or group-on-group interactions, and social movements. Sociologists may concentrate less on a pattern of identity development (that is, how an individual moves from one stage of racial identity to another) and more on the forces acting on individuals as they come to understand themselves as racialized people. Although counselors and educators have based their work more often on psychological models of racial identity development, sociologists have much to offer in terms of theory and practice. For example, researchers interested in examining the influences of racial identity on college access, choice, and success have found sociological perspectives useful (see Carter 2001), and sociologists have contributed substantively to the study of biracial identity (see Rockquemore and Brunsma 2002).

Among the sociological approaches commonly used to examine the formation of racial identity is symbolic interactionism. Symbolic interactionism holds that individuals make meaning through microscale interactions with others (see Mead 1967). In terms of racial identity, these meanings are formed about the self in relation to others who are perceived to belong to the same and other groups (Stryker 1980). Meaning—or symbols—are attached to race, racial categories, and racial identity. Over time, these meanings may evolve or change, as when an individual moves from a racially homogeneous setting to one that is diverse, or vice versa. Sociologists posit that the composition of social networks in which an individual is located may have a substantial influence on racial and ethnic identity and related constructs (for example, see Porter and Washington 1993).

Sociological studies of identity provide an important context for understanding the identity development of individuals, even though they do not typically provide descriptive/predictive models of identity development typical of psychological models. A particular contribution is their attention to relationships among racial groups, a factor in both sociological and psychological conceptions of identity and identity development. Intergroup relations point to the ways that stereotypes, racism, and privilege shape individual identities.

*Social Psychology*

Social psychology is more than a simple combination of psychological and sociological theories; it is a field of study that has its own way of considering racial identity and racial identity development. Social psychologists who study identity focus on the intersection of self and society. Côté and Levine (2002) proposed that identity formation was a function of processes of culture and individual agency, thus combining social context and individual characteristics.

A concept from social psychology that shows promise for understanding racial identity development but that appears rarely in existing theories is what Markus and Nurius (1986) termed *possible selves*. In brief, possible selves represent an individual's hoped for or feared future self. Aspiring toward the desired possible self—or avoiding the unwanted one—links motivation, behavior, and cognition (Markus and Nurius 1986). In terms of racial identity development, a person's hoped for and feared possible selves may lead him or her into groups that encourage exploration and commitment to a particular racial identity. For example, a Latino college student who aspires to be a physician (the hoped for possible self) might take part in a service-learning project at a health center that serves migrant agricultural workers. Although motivated to participate on the basis of a professional possible self, while working with a Latino doctor who staffs the center the student is exposed to a career role model and new ways of thinking about Latino identity in the context of work. Conversely, ideas about possible selves may lead someone into a group that discourages developing a certain identity. The student might have chosen a service-learning project in which Latino identity was downplayed, ignored, or discouraged through interactions that emphasized a message of assimilation into White cultural norms of medicine; in this case, exploration of a professional possible self could have a negative influence on the development of a positive racial identity.

Although a new concept to many scholars of racial identity, elements of possible selves theory can be seen in, for example, the RCID model (Sue and Sue 2003), as when an individual is drawn to explore racial/cultural identity. The explicit articulation of possible selves theory is an important addition to literature and practice. Elaboration of the concept (Schwartz, Côté, and Arnett 2005) and examples of its use (Kao 2000; Pizzolato 2006) further illuminate the utility of possible selves in examining identity development. For example, Kao (2000) used possible selves theory to explore how racial and ethnic stereotypes interact with adolescents' educational goals and achievements. She found that the images and stereotypes held by adolescents inform their academic goals and also "maintain racially and ethnically segregated extracurricular activities that reinforce segregated peer groups" (407). Through the lens of possible selves theory, adolescent racial and ethnic identity development is deeply influenced by the ways that young people are motivated to achieve academically and to participate in groups that share their racial/ethnic identity.

Social psychology brings integrated emphasis on the individual and group to the study of racial identity development. The intersection of self and society is a powerful location for studying identity development. Compared to psychology and sociology, the field of social psychology is newer, and research on identity formation has not yet fully emerged. It has not yet developed a strong enough foundation to guide educators and counselors seeking to use robust, empirically sound theories of identity development in their work. Yet social psychology provides an important perspective through which to analyze the stage and symbolic interactionist approaches of psychologists and sociologists.

## Human or Developmental Ecology

Like social psychology, human ecology situates individual development within the social context and attends to mutual influences of self and context. Based in part on biological concepts such as the ways that organisms adapt to environments, human ecology models explain the *processes*, not the specific *outcomes*, of development. An ecological approach to racial identity development, then, examines how the individual interacts in the human ecosystem of family, school, and society (see Evans, Forney, Guido, Patton, and Renn 2010).

Psychologist Urie Bronfenbrenner was a pioneer in the field, introducing a model in the early 1970s that he refined throughout his career (for example, Bronfenbrenner 1977, 1993, 2005).[5] The core components of the model stayed the same: Process, Person, Context, and Time (PPCT). *Process* represents the interactions between the developing individual and the proximal environment (for example, people and symbols). Optimum development resulted from increasingly complex interactions over time, buffered by appropriate supports so as not to overwhelm the individual. *Person* represents the individual, with personal characteristics including race and gender and personality characteristics that lead him or her to interact with the world in ways that enhance or inhibit development. For example, some people are inclined to explore their environments, while others hold back. Some people are highly skilled at planning and others react better to spontaneous opportunities. These developmentally instigative characteristics (Bronfenbrenner 1993) operate to shape developmental processes.

*Context* represents levels of interactions an individual has in the immediate setting (microsystem), among/between microsystems (mesosystem), with settings at a distance (exosystem), and within the broader social-historical culture (macrosystem). As an ecosystem, these levels influence—and are influenced by—the developing individual. Finally, *Time* is as it sounds: The influence of both the timing of events in one's life (for example, birth of a sibling, parents' divorce) and timebound events (for example, the terrorist attacks of September 11, 2001). The PPCT model provides a rich, multidimensional approach to examining how development occurs and how, for example, two mixed-race individuals of the same racial heritage might develop different racial identities.

Although not designed specifically to address racial identity development, elements of the PPCT concepts are evident in racial identity development models, including the RCID (Sue and Sue 2003), Nigrescence Theory (Cross and Fhagen-Smith 2001), and BID (Jackson 2001). The ways that individuals affiliate with racial reference groups (see Cross 1985)—and their experiences in those groups—can be considered ecological in nature, with person and ecosystem exerting mutual influences. Renn (2004) and Root (1999) employed explicit ecological approaches to describe the identity development of multiracial identities; Wijeyesinghe's (1992, 2001) Factor Model of Multiracial Identity may also be considered in part ecological. They included personal and environmental factors such as appearance, gender, family composition, interpersonal interactions, and public policy.

The strength of an ecological approach lies in its ability to describe how racial identity development occurs and how the person and environment influence one another. This strength may be especially relevant to understanding individuals and in creating educational or clinical interventions. A limitation is that the specificity of individual lives makes the use of an ecological approach challenging for research, policy development, or any other purpose for which one seeks a generalizable theory. Nevertheless, incorporating aspects of the ecological approach into research on racial identity goes far to explain processes, if not outcomes, of development.

## Theoretical Perspectives on Racial Identification and Identity

In addition to the different disciplinary approaches to understanding racial identities, a variety of cross-disciplinary theoretical perspectives inform contemporary scholarship and practice. For most of the twentieth century, a scientific-rational view of race prevailed (Smedley and Smedley 2005). This perspective held that racial categories were biologically defined. The social meanings attached to racial group membership were based on the modernist notion that human beings are governed by rationality in their efforts to reason through the challenges of everyday life (see Gergen 1991), which in the United States in the twentieth century included varying levels of racial discrimination, oppression, and violence. Beginning in about the 1980s critical, poststructuralist, and postmodern views challenged a fixed, biological, "scientific" approach to understanding racial categories and identities. Psychological, sociological, and ecological models featured in this chapter and throughout this volume provide examples. Critical Race Theory (CRT) and Intersectionality—approaches that incorporate intersections of identities such as race, class, and gender—are two of the most recent additions. Although some of these frameworks are epistemologically incompatible with one another, each has something to say about race, racial identification, and racial identity development. They are thus important to keep in mind when considering models of identity development. It is beyond the scope of this chapter to provide a detailed description of each of these rich, and richly contested, perspectives, but a brief introduction serves to ground theories of racial identity development in the context of broader intellectual and theoretical movements.

### Poststructuralism and Postmodernism

Developed in the humanities, particularly literary studies, and incorporated into the social sciences, poststructuralism and postmodernism are philosophical approaches founded on the premise that "there are no objective and universal truths, but that particular forms of knowledge, and the ways of being that they engender, become 'naturalised' in culturally and historically specific ways" (Sullivan 2003, 39). Poststructural and postmodern theorists destabilize the idea of fixed categories and question what counts as "normal." They hold that identities are social constructions, under constant deconstruction and reconstruction (see Gergen 1991).

Poststructural and postmodern perspectives provide a number of challenges to the study of racial identity development. First, they call into question the meaning of racial categories and personal identification with racial groups. Second, full subscription to a postmodern philosophy renders impossible research that attempts to measure or assess racial identity levels or stages or positions; the constant construction and reconstruction of racial identity implies that it cannot be fixed for the purpose of completing a racial identity assessment instrument, or if it can, it is meaningless outside that moment. Third, in a philosophy in which all knowledge and meaning are historically and culturally bound, it is impossible to make any generalizations, even tentative ones, from research on racial identities. Finally, in very distilled forms postmodernism takes no clear stand on social hierarchies and oppression, holding that even while some socially constructed categories are at the margins and others at the center, they are in the end constructions that rely on the participation of all social actors to uphold. Social and political privilege, viewed through this lens, depends on the existence of both those who have it and those who do not. Identities exist in relation to one another, constructing one another (see Holvino, this volume).

For these reasons, there is very little genuinely poststructural or postmodern research on racial identity development. Yet key aspects of these philosophies, such as questioning categorical identification and asserting multiple healthy endpoints to racial identity processes have entered research on, for example, mixed-race identities (see Root 1999; Wijeyesinghe 1992, 2001). In short, these philosophies have influenced the study of racial identities by amplifying the important idea that identities are socially constructed and culturally bound, an idea that has evolved with racial identity development theories from their earliest iterations (e.g., Cross 1971; Jackson 1976). It is important to note, however, that the tendency of poststructuralists to theorize about racial identities in the face of real social inequities renders this perspective suspect in the eyes of many scholars, educators, and social justice advocates.

*Critical Race Theory*

Critical Race Theory (CRT) emerged from critical legal studies and spread to other social sciences. CRT and a race-specific family of theories, including

Latino Critical Race Studies (LatCrit), Asian American Critical Race Studies (AsianCrit), and American Indian Critical Race Studies (TribalCrit) challenge the premise that a color-blind approach to law, education, and policy can create equity and social justice. Building on an earlier philosophy of critical theory, which centered on the experiences of members of groups targeted by racialized forms of oppression, CRT makes visible and vocal the lives and experiences of people of color in the United States (Delgado 1995).

Consistent with other theoretical and philosophical approaches, CRT considers racial identity to be socially constructed. Research using CRT places the influence of culture at the center of what is being studied, with an emphasis on race, ethnicity, and the unavoidable influence of racism in the United States (Delgado and Stefancic 2001). Instead of advocating a color-blind approach to research, CRT embraces an epistemology that values individual knowledge based on the experiences of people of color in the United States. CRT has been criticized for being overly subjective, a criticism deflected by one prominent education researcher who responded, "CRT never makes claims of objectivity or rationality. Rather, it sees itself as an approach to scholarship that integrates lived experience with racial realism" (Ladson-Billings 2006, vii). Another criticism is that CRT's focus on race and racism appears to reify racial categories, an outcome that many CRT scholars seek to avoid.

CRT and related theories provide a rich theoretical foundation for studies of racial identity construction, but inherently limit the generalizability of findings. Attending to context and lived experience, CRT is ideally suited to qualitative explorations of racial identity development. Phenomenological, ethnographic, narrative, and grounded theory designs have the potential to maximize the utility of CRT. Longitudinal designs in particular are well suited to understanding how race, racism, and racial identities influence lived experience and how lived experience influences personal experiences of race, racism, and identity. CRT's reliance on the existence of categories of race and ethnicity provides potential traction for quantitative studies that examine racial identities and experiences, though there are no examples to date.

## Intersectionality

As a theoretical perspective on identity, Intersectionality brings together "both the parts and the whole of the self as well as the individual in context" (Torres, Jones, and Renn 2009, 585). Research on identities and identity development in the 1980s and 1990s typically focused on one domain (e.g., race, gender, sexual orientation, ability) at a time, with occasional acknowl-edgment that these identities might have some influence on one another. An African American man, then, might experience racial identity differently from the way an African American woman might. A White gay man's sexual orientation identity development might differ from an Asian American les-bian's. Bowleg (2008) contended that before attention was paid to Intersec-tionality, these approaches might be additive but they were not integrative in a way that reflected the complexity of lived experience. Rather than take a parallel or additive approach to identities and identity development across domains, Intersectionality holds domains as both separate and inextricably fused. One's racial identity development, therefore, cannot be truly under-stood apart from one's gender, sexuality, social class, or other significant social identities.

Intersectionality honors the social construction standpoint on identities. Race cannot be isolated from other identity domains, nor can gender, ability, or sexuality be understood without race as a coinfluence (Dill and Zambrana 2009). Each one influences and is influenced by the other in constant recon-struction through interactions with others and the world.

As a foundation for research on identity development, Intersectionality is still a young perspective.[6] Although simple categorization of sex variables is not uncommon in studies of racial identity, few studies to date have inte-grated an intersectional heuristic fully into their design and analysis. An example of an area already benefitting from an intersectional approach is the study of Black masculinity, which merges constructions of race, gender, and sexuality (for example, Cooper 2005–2006; Ferber 2007; McCready 2010). In this work, what it means to be a Black man is different—more than the sum of its parts—from an additive approach to the development of racial, gender, and sexual identities.

## Summary

Theoretical perspectives on race and racial identities have evolved from a positivist, clinical approach to a more fluid conception of racial identity as an individual experience of a socially constructed phenomenon. Postmod-ern, CRT, and intersectional approaches provide new ways of considering race, racial categories, and racial identity development. These approaches are adopted differently within and across the disciplinary traditions (e.g., psy-chology, sociology) and provide a common language—if not a common phi-losophy—for understanding emerging research on identity development and lived experience.

## Contemporary Influences on Racial Identities and Identity Development

No matter what perspective they take, theories of racial identity development are bounded in cultural and historical meanings attached to racial categories and identities. These meanings have changed and continue to change over time. Factors operating at the larger sociohistorical level influence how individuals and groups understand and develop racial identities (Dill and Zambrana 2009; Root 1999; Wijeyesinghe 1992, 2001). Four such factors of importance in the United States in the early twenty-first century are globalization, technology, immigration, and the increasingly multiracial population.

Globalization provides a perspective for understanding one's racial identity in a multinational, cross-historical context. In this global context, the meanings of race and racial group membership change over time and place. For example, understanding African American identity in relation to the African diaspora and ongoing tribal and political conflict in Africa is different from understanding it solely from the perspective of life in the United States in the twenty-first century. American Indian identity can be understood in the context of indigenous peoples around the world, a perspective that does not negate the very real and often tragic consequences of White settlement in North America, but which enhances that perspective by joining the struggles of native people on several continents. Economic, political, educational, and media globalization complicate and amplify meanings attached to race and racial identity.

Since the steamship, railroads, automobiles, and radio communication began to close distances between communities of people like and unlike one another, technology has influenced identities. The ability to instantly access images, sounds, and text from someone in the next room or around the world provides radically changed opportunities for identity development. A mixed-race middle-school student growing up in an ostensibly monoracial community can read about and connect with people who share her background. A cross-racial or international adoptee can explore his heritage and learn about his native culture. Race-based political movements can summon a virtual or in-person action to advance their cause. Compelling sounds and video from around the world link people who feel a common bond based on, among other factors, racial identity. The ways in which individuals interact online (in social networking sites, for example) represent further opportunities that technology provides for identity exploration, construction, and representation (see Martínez Alemán and Wartman 2009).

Immigration to the United States is another factor that will continue to influence racial identities and identity development. What it means to be, for example, "Asian American," "Latino American," or "White American" is shaped in part by how one views oneself in the context of a nation that has shifted its population demographics over time as a result of its newest arrivals and the ways that they and their children contribute to the United States. Many White Americans are reminded that their families were not always in the United States and that they may, in fact, have not been considered "White" when they arrived (Takaki 1993). Asian Americans of Japanese, Chinese, and Filipino descent whose families have been in the United States for several generations may consider what it means to be in a "racial" category with more recent immigrants from Southeast Asia (Espiritu 1992). Likewise, "Latino Americans" come from multiple cultural and national backgrounds, and may share with one another little more than roots in now Spanish-speaking countries (Ferdman and Gallegos 2001). Yet the racial identification imposed by society creates opportunities for personal racial identities as White, Asian, or Latino no matter when one's family came to the United States and what one has in common with others from similar regions. Immigration—and the fierce, vocal, and sometimes violent debates it stirs—draws attention to these categories and identities.

The increasing population of mixed-race people also draws attention to categories and identities. Without question, the number and proportion of mixed-race individuals in the United States will continue to grow during this century. Of the 6.8 million respondents to the 2000 U.S. Census who chose two or more races, 2.9 million (42%) were under age 18 (Jones and Smith 2001). Overall, 6.3 percent of the U.S. population identifying with Hispanic/Latino ethnicity marked two or more races, and 7.7 percent of the population under age 18 with Hispanic/Latino ethnicity did so. As these mixed-race youth grow up and as more monoracial adults partner with members of other racial groups, the overall proportion of the population that is multiracial will increase. Mixed-race people themselves undergo a racial identification process (see Renn 2004; Wijeyesinghe 2001), and the increasing visibility of individuals who do not fit neatly into existing monoracial categories calls attention to the way that those categories are socially constructed and maintained. The extent to which this attention influences the identity development of monoracial individuals is not yet known, but is potentially interesting.

Conclusion

The study of racial identities and identity development has evolved in the century since pseudo-scientific eugenicists attempted to plot the physical and mental profiles of so-called superior and inferior races. Demographic studies of health, living conditions, employment, income, and education still use racial categories as meaningful indicators of differences across social groups. These studies provide evidence that although race may be socially constructed, membership in different racial groups is related to sometimes radically different life circumstances, experiences, and expectations. From the arrival of White colonists to the present, race has mattered in the United States. And in such a highly racialized society, racial identities matter in individuals' understanding of self.

The perspectives of psychology, sociology, social psychology, and human ecology highlight the interaction of person and environment in a way that illuminates the connection of racial categorization (or identification by society) with racial self-identification as a critical element in personal, political, and social contexts in the twenty-first century. Postmodernism, Critical Race Theory, and Intersectionality have created new ways of thinking about race, racial categories, and individual racial identity development. As globalization, technology, immigration, and an increasingly multiracial population influence ideas about race and racial identity in the twenty-first century, these newer theoretical perspectives may be especially useful ways to use disciplinary approaches to understanding individuals, groups, and intergroup relations. New ways of thinking about racial identity may emerge as generations of young people assert their unique selves in contexts previously unimaginable.

NOTES

1. Although the U.S. government considers Hispanic or Latino *ethnicity*, not race, evidence suggests that the lived experience of Latino Americans supports a racial categorization as defined in this volume (see Brown, Hitlin, and Elder 2006; Ferdman and Gallegos 2001).

2. Since 1997, the official racial categories have been: Black or African American, Asian, American Indian and Alaska Native, Native Hawaiian and Other Pacific Islander, and White. Ethnicity is "Hispanic/Latino" or "Not Hispanic/Latino" (Office of Management and Budget 1997).

3. Specifically, Côté and Levine (1983) tested the validity of the assumption that Marcia's ego identity statuses were aligned on a continuum from diffusion to achieved identity. They concluded that "not one instance of the postulated ordering of Marcia's four statuses is observed" and "that Marcia's measure is not an adequate operationalization of Erikson's perspective on identity formation" (43).

4. The MID and RCID are reviewed in detail in this chapter. Jackson and Cross contribute chapters in this book, including revised versions of their respective Black identity models. Hence these are not outlined in detail in this chapter.

5. Interestingly, William Cross and Urie Bronfenbrenner were colleagues at Cornell University. In a chapter on Personal Identity and Reference Group Orientation (Cross 1985), Cross acknowledges a 1977–1980 Administration on Children, Youth

and Families research grant ("Black families and the socialization of Black children: An ecological approach") he shared with Bronfenbrenner and Moncrieff Cochran.

6. Other areas of scholarship, notably law and women's studies, have employed the concept of intersecting social categories for some time (for example, see Williams 1994) and a number of identity theorists have gestured toward the importance of considering multiple identity categories (for example, Ferdman and Gallegos 2001; Wijeyesinghe 2001). Intersectionality builds from these ideas and employs poststructuralism to challenge established categories (man/woman, straight/gay, Black/White/Asian/Latino/American Indian). The use of Intersectionality as a key theoretical framework in research on identity development is relatively recent (see Abes 2009).

## REFERENCES

Abes, Elisa S. 2009. "Theoretical Borderlands: Using Multiple Theoretical Perspectives to Challenge Inequitable Power Structures in Student Development Theory." *Journal of College Student Development* 50: 141–156.

Adler, Jerry. 2009, January 12. "What's Race Got to Do with It?" *Newsweek.* http://www.newsweek.com/id/177737 (accessed February 12, 2010).

Anderson, Margo J. 2002. "Counting by Race: The Antebellum Legacy." In *The New Race Question: How the Census Counts Multiracial Individuals*, edited by Joel Perlmann and Mary C. Waters. New York: Russell Sage Foundation.

Atkinson, Donald R., George Morten, and Derald W. Sue. 1979. *Counseling American Minorities: A Cross-Cultural Perspective.* Dubuque, Iowa: W. C. Brown.

Bowleg, Lisa. 2008. "When Black + Lesbian + Woman ≠ Black Lesbian Woman: The Methodological Challenges of Qualitative and Quantitative Intersectionality Research." *Sex Roles* 59: 312–325.

Bronfenbrenner, Urie. 1977. "Toward an Experimental Ecology of Human Development." *American Psychologist* 32: 513–531.

———. 1993. "The Ecology of Human Development: Research Models and Fugitive Findings." In *Development in Context: Acting and Thinking in Specific Environments*, edited by Robert H. Wozniak and Kurt W. Fischer. Mahwah, N.J.: Lawrence Erlbaum.

Bronfenbrenner, Urie, ed. 2005. *Making Human Beings Human: Bioecological Perspectives on Human Development.* Thousand Oaks, Calif.: Sage.

Brown, J. Scott, Steven Hitlin, and Glen H. Elder, Jr. 2006. "The Greater Complexity of Lived Race: An Extension of Harris and Sim." *Social Science Quarterly* 87: 411–431.

Bryan, Thomas. 2004. "Basic Sources of Statistics." In *The Methods and Materials of Demography,* 2nd ed., edited by David Swanson, Jacob S. Siegel, and Henry S. Shryock. San Diego: Elsevier Academic Press.

Carter, Deborah Faye. 2001. "College Students' Degree Aspirations: A Theoretical Model and Literature Review with a Focus on African American and Latino Students." In *Higher Education: Handbook of Theory and Research, Volume XVII,* edited by John C. Smart. Dordrecht, The Netherlands: Kluwer Academic Press.

Cooper, Frank Rudy. 2005–2006. "Against Bipolar Black Masculinity: Intersectionality, Assimilation, Identity Performance, and Hierarchy." *UC Davis Law Review* 39: 855–906.

Côté, James E., and Charles G. Levine. 1983. "Marcia and Erikson: The Relationships among Ego Identity Status, Neuroticism, Dogmatism, and Purpose in Life." *Journal of Youth and Adolescence* 12 (1): 43–83.

———. 2002. *Identity Formation, Agency, and Culture: A Social Psychological Synthesis*. Mahwah, N.J.: Lawrence Erlbaum Associates.

Cross, William E., Jr. 1971. "The Negro-to-Black Conversion Experience: Towards a Psychology of Black Liberation." *Black World* 20 (9): 13–27.

———. 1985. "Black Identity: Rediscovering the Distinction between Personal Identity and Reference Group Orientation." In *Beginnings: The Social and Affective Development of Black Children*, edited by Margaret B. Spencer, Geraldine K. Brookins, and Walter R. Allen. Hillsdale, N.J.: Lawrence Erlbaum.

Cross, William E., Jr., and Peony Fhagen-Smith. 2001. "Patterns of African American Identity Development: A Life Span Perspective." In *New Perspectives on Racial Identity Development: A Theoretical and Practical Anthology*, eds. Charmaine L. Wijeyesinghe and Bailey W. Jackson III. New York: NYU Press.

Delgado, Richard, ed. 1995. *Critical Race Theory: The Cutting Edge*. Philadelphia: Temple University Press.

Delgado, Richard, and Jean Stefancic. 2001. *Critical Race Theory: An Introduction*. New York: NYU Press.

Dill, Bonnie Thornton, and Ruth Enid Zambrana. 2009. *Emerging Intersections: Race, Class, and Gender in Theory, Policy, and Practice*. New Brunswick, N.J.: Rutgers University Press.

Erikson, Erik H. 1959/1994. *Identity and the Life Cycle*. New York: W. W. Norton.

Espiritu, Yen Le. 1992. *Asian American Panethnicity: Bridging Institutions and Identities*. Philadelphia: Temple University Press.

Evans, Nancy J., Deanna S. Forney, Florence M. Guido, Lori D. Patton, and Kristen A. Renn. 2010. *Student Development in College: Theory, Research, and Practice*, 2nd ed. San Francisco: Jossey-Bass.

Ferber, Abby L. 2007. "The Construction of Black Masculinity: White Supremacy Now and Then." *Journal of Sport and Society* 31 (1): 11–24.

Ferdman, Bernardo M., and Plácida I. Gallegos. 2001. "Racial Identity Development and Latinos in the United States." In *New Perspectives on Racial Identity Development: A Theoretical and Practical Anthology*, eds. Charmaine L. Wijeyesinghe and Bailey W. Jackson III. New York: NYU Press.

Gergen, Kenneth J. 1991. *The Saturated Self: Dilemmas of Identity in Contemporary Life*. New York: Basic Books.

Hardiman, Rita. 1982. "White Identity Development: A Process Oriented Model for Describing the Racial Consciousness of White Americans." Ed.D. dissertation. *Electronic Doctoral Dissertations for UMass Amherst*. Paper AAI8210330. http://scholarworks.umass.edu/dissertations/AAI8210330

———. 1994. *White Racial Identity Development in the United States*. Washington, D.C.: National Multicultural Institute.

Hardiman, Rita, and Bailey W. Jackson III. 1992. "Racial Identity Development: Understanding Racial Dynamics in College Classrooms and on Campus." In *Promoting Diversity in College Classrooms: Innovative Responses for the Curriculum, Faculty, and Institutions*, edited by Maurianne Adams. San Francisco: Jossey-Bass.

Helms, Janet E. 1990. *Black and White Racial Identity: Theory, Research, and Practice*. New York: Greenwood Press.

———. 1994. "The Conceptualization of Racial Identity and Other 'Racial' Constructs." In *Human Diversity: Perspectives on People in Context*, edited by E. J. Trickett, R. J. Watts, and D. Birman. San Francisco: Jossey-Bass.

———. 1995. "An Update of Helms's White and People of Color Racial Identity Models." In *Handbook of Multicultural Counseling,* edited by J. G. Ponterotto, J. M. Casas, L. A. Suzuki, and C. M. Alexander. Thousand Oaks, Calif.: Sage.

Jackson, Bailey W., III. 1976. "Black Identity Development." In *Urban, Social, and Educational Issues,* edited by Leonard H. Golubchick and Barry Persky. Dubuque, Iowa: Kendall/Hunt.

———. 2001. "Black Identity Development: Further Analysis and Elaboration." In *New Perspectives on Racial Identity Development: A Theoretical and Practical Anthology,* edited by Charmaine L. Wijeyesinghe and Bailey W. Jackson III. New York: NYU Press.

Jones, Nicholas A., and Amy Symens Smith. 2001. *The Two or More Races Population: 2000.* A Census Brief. Washington, D.C.: U.S. Department of Commerce, Economics and Statistics Administration, U.S. Census Bureau.

Kao, Grace. 2000. "Group Images and Possible Selves among Adolescents: Linking Stereotypes to Expectations by Race and Ethnicity." *Sociological Forum* 15 (3): 407–430.

Kim, Jean. 1981. "Processes of Asian American Identity Development: A Study of Japanese American Women's Perceptions of Their Struggle to Achieve Positive Identities as Americans of Asian Ancestry." Ed.D. dissertation. *Electronic Doctoral Dissertations for UMass Amherst.* Paper AAI8118010. http://scholarworks.umass.edu/dissertations/AAI8118010.

———. 2001. "Asian American Identity Development Theory." In *New Perspectives on Racial Identity Development: A Theoretical and Practical Anthology,* edited by Charmaine L. Wijeyesinghe and Bailey W. Jackson III. New York: NYU Press.

Ladson-Billings, Gloria J. 2000. "Racialized Discourses and Ethnic Epistemologies." In *Handbook of Qualitative Research,* 2nd ed., edited by Norman K. Denzin and Yvonna S. Lincoln. Thousand Oaks, Calif.: Sage.

———. 2006. "Foreword." In *Critical Race Theory in Education: All God's Children Got a Song,* edited by Adrienne D. Dixson and Celia K. Rousseau. New York: Routledge.

Marcia, James E. 1966. "Development and Validation of Ego-Identity Statuses." *Journal of Personality and Social Psychology* 3: 551–558.

Markus, Hazel, and Paula Nurius. 1986. "Possible Selves." *American Psychologist* 41: 954–969.

Martínez Alemán, Ana M., and Katharine L. Wartman. 2009. *Online Social Networking on Campus: Understanding What Matters in Student Culture.* New York: Routledge.

McCready, Lance T. 2010. *Making Space for Diverse Masculinities: Difference, Intersectionality, and Engagement in an Urban High School.* New York: Peter Lang.

Mead, George H. 1967. *Mind, Self, and Society.* Chicago: University of Chicago Press.

Office of Management and Budget. 1997. *Revisions to the Standards for the Classification of Federal Data on Race and Ethnicity,* Federal Register Notice, October 30, 1997, Volume 62, Number 210. Available at http://www.census.gov/population/www/socdemo/race/Ombdir15.html

Omi, Michael. 1997. "Racial Identity and the State: The Dilemmas of Classification." *Law and Inequality* 15: 7–23.

Omi, Michael, and Howard Winant. 1994. *Racial Formation in the United States: From the 1960s to the 1990s,* 2nd ed. New York: Routledge.

Phinney, Jean S. 1990. "Ethnic Identity in Adolescents and Adults: Review of Research." *Psychological Bulletin* 108: 499–514.

Pizzolato, Jane Elizabeth. 2006. "Achieving College Student Possible Selves: Navigating the Space between Commitment and Achievement of Long-Term Identity Goals." *Cultural Diversity and Ethnic Minority Psychology* 12 (1): 57–69.

Porter, Judith, and Robert Washington. 1993. "Minority Identity and Self-Esteem." *Annual Review of Sociology* 19: 139–161.

Renn, Kristen A. 2004. *Mixed Race Students in College: The Ecology of Race, Identity, and Community*. Albany: SUNY Press.

Reynolds, Amy L., and Suraiya Baluch. 2001. "Racial Identity Theories in Counseling: A Literature Review and Evaluation." In *New Perspectives on Racial Identity Development: A Theoretical and Practical Anthology,* edited by Charmaine L. Wijeyesinghe and Bailey W. Jackson III. New York: NYU Press.

Rockquemore, Kerry Ann, and David L. Brunsma. 2002. *Beyond Black: Biracial Identity in America*. Thousand Oaks, Calif.: Sage.

Root, Maria P. P. 1999. "The Biracial Baby Boom: Understanding Ecological Constructions of Racial Identity in the 21st Century." In *Racial and Ethnic Identity in School Practices: Aspects of Human Development,* edited by Rosa Hernández Sheets and Etta R. Hollins. New York: Routledge.

Schwartz, Seth J., James E. Côté, and Jeffrey Jensen Arnett. 2005. "Identity and Agency in Emerging Adulthood: Two Developmental Routes in the Individuation Process." *Youth & Society* 37: 201–209.

Smedley, Audrey. 2001. "Social Origins of the Idea of Race." In *Race in 21st Century America,* edited by Curtis Stokes, Theresa Meléndez, and Genice Rhodes-Reed. East Lansing: Michigan State University Press.

Smedley, Audrey, and Brian D. Smedley. 2005. "Race as Biology Is Fiction, Racism as Social Problem Is Real: Anthropological and Historical Perspectives on the Social Construction of Race." *American Psychologist* 60: 16–26.

Sneed, Joel R., Seth J. Schwartz, and William E. Cross, Jr. 2006. "A Multicultural Critique of Identity Status Theory and Research: A Call for Integration." *Identity: An International Journal of Theory and Research* 6 (1): 61–84.

Sollors, Werner. 1999. *Neither Black Nor White Yet Both: Thematic Explorations of Interracial Literature*. Cambridge: Harvard University Press.

———. 2002. "What Race Are You?" In *The New Race Question: How the Census Counts Multiracial Individuals,* edited by Joel Perlmann and Mary C. Waters. New York: Russell Sage Foundation.

Solórzano, Daniel, Miguel Ceja, and Tara Yosso. 2000. "Critical Race Theory, Racial Microaggressions, and Campus Racial Climate: The Experiences of African American Students." *Journal of Negro Education* 69 (1/2): 60–73.

Stryker, Sheldon. 1980. *Symbolic Interactionism: A Social Structural Version*. Menlo Park, Calif.: Benjamin Cummings.

Sue, Derald W., and David Sue. 2003. *Counseling the Culturally Diverse: Theory and Practice,* 4th ed. Hoboken, N.J.: Wiley.

Sullivan, Nikki. 2003. *A Critical Introduction to Queer Theory*. New York: NYU Press.

Takaki, Ronald. 1993. *A Different Mirror: A History of Multicultural America*. Boston: Little, Brown.

Tatum, Beverly Daniel. 1992. "Talking about Race, Learning about Racism: The Application of Racial Identity Theory in the Classroom." *Harvard Educational Review* 62 (1): 1–24.

————. 2003. *"Why Are All the Black Kids Sitting Together in the Cafeteria?" and Other Conversations about Race,* 3rd ed. New York: Basic Books.

Torres, Vasti, Susan R. Jones, and Kristen A. Renn. 2009. "Identity Development Theories in Student Affairs: Origins, Current Status, and New Approaches." *Journal of College Student Development* 50: 577–596.

Wijeyesinghe, Charmaine 1992. "Towards an Understanding of the Racial Identity of Bi-Racial People: The Experience of Racial Self-Identification of African-American/Euro-American Adults and the Factors Affecting Their Choices of Racial Identity." Ed.D. dissertation. *Electronic Doctoral Dissertations for UMass Amherst.* Paper AAI9305915.

————. 2001. "Racial Identity in Multiracial People: An Alternative Paradigm." In *New Perspectives on Racial Identity Development: A Theoretical and Practical Anthology,* edited by Charmaine L. Wijeyesinghe and Bailey W. Jackson III. New York: NYU Press.

Williams, Kimberlé Crenshaw. 1994. "Mapping the Margins: Intersectionality, Identity Politics, and Violence against Women of Color." In *The Public Nature of Private Violence,* edited by Martha Albertson Fineman and Rixanne Mykitiuk. New York: Routledge.

Wing, Leah, and Janet Rifkin. 2001. "Racial Identity Development and the Mediation of Conflicts." In *New Perspectives on Racial Identity Development: A Theoretical and Practical Anthology,* edited by Charmaine L. Wijeyesinghe and Bailey W. Jackson III. New York: NYU Press.

Zack, Naomi. 1993. *Race and Mixed Race.* Philadelphia, Pa.: Temple University Press.

2

# Black Identity Development

*Influences of Culture and Social Oppression*

BAILEY W. JACKSON III

## Introduction

It has been a little over ten years since the Black Identity Development (BID) model as a theoretical framework (Jackson 2001) was presented in the first volume of *New Perspectives on Racial Identity Development: A Theoretical and Practical Anthology* (Wijeyesinghe and Jackson 2001). Since then, there have been a number of national, global, and environmental events and changes in thinking about social issues and constructions that must be considered when approaching an update on BID as a theoretical framework for understanding Black identity development. In this chapter there will not only be a consideration of some of the more significant events of the past decade, there will also be an updated discussion of the role of Black/African American culture and its impact on the stages of Black identity development . The consideration of the events, changes in thinking about social identities, and the updating of the consideration of culture on BID will culminate in the presentation of the BID developmental stages.

Black Identity Theory: A Decade of Changes

Since 2000, there have been natural disasters, such as the aftermath of the Katrina Hurricane, that highlighted the nature of class- and race-based discrimination and unequal treatment affecting hundreds of thousands of lives; there were wars in part resulting from reactions to the "9/11" attack on the United States, after which time a new manifestation of social oppression, "Islamophobia," gained prominence; there were two presidential elections including the reelection of George W. Bush and an administration that was to continue a politically, fiscally, and socially conservative set of policies within the United States carried over from President Bush's first term in office, and the following presidential election, that of current President Barack Obama, which was for many one of the most significant events in this country's history. The idea of considering a person who was not a White man for this exalted position caused considerable consternation and anticipation throughout the country and around the world. The notion that in one election, unlike in all previous elections in the United States, instead of there being four White men running for president and vice-president in the most wealthy and powerful country in the world, there were two White women, two White men, and one Biracial man as finalists for these positions in and of itself made this a turning point for the United States. Both race and gender were now front and center in the country's consciousness in ways that they had never been before. One of the consequences of this election was the open dialogue that took place about where the country was in relation to issues of race and racism. What might have been fairly straightforward questions such as, "What is he? Black, African American, or Biracial?" became a point of seemingly endless discussion. And, after the election, the question was, "Is the United States now in a *post-racial* era?" Was race now a nonissue? Had we eliminated racism? Obama's election was a significant event for the whole world. These are but a few of the many events in the first decade of this century that have had an impact on the way we think of race, racism, and racial identity, and which perhaps foretell of a future period in which reconceptualizations of race and racial identity will rapidly shift and expand again.

A Decade of Changing Perspectives on Race and Social Identity

In addition to world events such as the ones mentioned above, there are new and different concepts and perspectives on social groups, issues, and identity that have been introduced or that in some cases gained more notoriety in the past ten years. Examples, including the recent conflicts in the Middle East and northern Africa, the recent world financial crisis, and earthquakes and other natural disasters have caused a higher level of global awareness of the many ways that we are connected. This expanded and intensified focus on the *global community* (Jandt 2007; Marsella 1998) has taken our understanding of social identity and intergroup interaction to another level. Our heightened global awareness means we can no longer assume that the way social groups and social issues are defined in a U.S. context is in fact the way that the rest of the world understands them. We also cannot assume that the salience that we give to any individual social identity in the United States will be consistent with how others in this global community view salience. For example, we cannot assume that because race and class are highly salient in the United States that they are equally salient in other countries. This is not to say that race and class do not have some level of salience in other countries: but there may be countries, for example, where religion and ethnicity are more determinate of what affects one's social identity than race and class. This notion of contextual salience of social identities needs further study and definition as it relates to racial identity globally. And we may well find that modifications need to be made to existing racial identity development models in order to assist in the understanding of individual and social group dynamics, as well as the dynamics between social identity groups, to accommodate increasingly global perspectives and experiences.

*Intersectionality and Impact on Racial Identity Theory*

Another theoretical framework that has a significant impact on the way social identity is viewed is termed *Intersectionality*. Rooted in feminist sociological theory (Crenshaw 1991), Intersectionality supports methodologies of studying "the relationships among multiple dimensions and modalities of social relationships and subject formations" (McCall 2008, 49). Theories of Intersectionality suggest that to gain a full understanding of any aspect of our social identity we must examine how each identity interacts with every other social identity. The figure 2.1 is a representation of how some of the social identities intersect.

In this figure, there is emphasis on race, sex, and class to reflect the focus on these social identities and the types of oppression that these groups experience (racism, sexism, and classism), as discussed in the literature on Intersectionality.

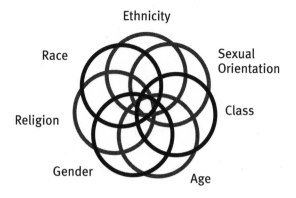

Figure 2.1 Representation of Intersectionality

Likewise, Intersectionality theory suggests that we must also understand how each manifestation of social oppression (i.e., racism, sexism, classism, etc.) interacts with every other manifestation of social oppression and the ways that social oppression in all its manifestations sustains itself through these intersectional relationships (see figure 2.2).

While Intersectionality challenges us to think about our social identity from a multi-identity perspective rather than simply from a racial/monoidentity perspective, it also challenges us to review the ways that the many forms of social oppression operate as well. Intersectionality is currently being influenced by theorists such as Crenshaw (1991) and Collins (1998, 2005) who focus on the intersection of social identities rather than a singular focus on one dimension. As a Black Identity Development theorist, I am offering perspectives on the implications of Intersectionality on BID theory. Some of those perspectives are shared as part of this chapter. I suggest that Intersectionality is an especially important perspective to consider when examining the fifth stage in the BID model, namely, Internalization.

The BID model, not unlike Cross's (1971) and Helms's models (1990), was heavily influenced by the civil rights movement of the 1960s and its renewed focus on racism and the many forms of discrimination that Blacks/African Americans experienced in the United States. In an effort to understand the various ways that Black people made sense of and responded to the sixties, Jackson, Cross, Helms, and others developed different versions of Black Identity Development theoretical frameworks. The driving forces behind the interest in developing these frameworks/models were to understand the different ways

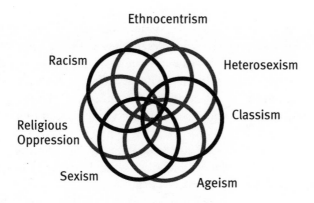

Fig. 2.2 Intersection of Manifestations of Social Oppression

that Black people were responding to this era of civil rights; to understand how this change was influencing the thinking and behavior of Black people; and to examine the way that Black identity was evolving or developing as a result.

Because the sixties were such a dynamic era, and because the battle against racism was the dominant influence in the way that social scientists approached questions about Black people and the Black community, the effect of racism and the process of reacting to racism became the predominant lens though which BID was conceived and examined. Although there was acknowledgment that experiences not directly connected to racism also had an impact on Black Identity Development, it was never very clear where and how those cultural or racial influences impacted each stage in the developmental process.

In this essay the suggestion is that both the experience of growing up in and living in a racist society, as well as growing up in and living in a society as a member of an ethnic and racial group with its own culture, influences our racial identity. As noted above, virtually none of the current BID models, while heavily grounded in the notion that racism has had a significant impact on Black Identity Development, fully explore or acknowledge the impact of the culture of the Black community on Black Identity Development. To better understand the BID process, there must be a fuller appreciation and examination of the culture of race and the ethnic cultures that contribute to the culture of race.

The essence of culture as used in this context suggests that it is a *meaning-making system* (Matarasso 2001; Hatch and Schultz 1997; Malik 1996; Lederach 1995) comprised of five elements: (1) philosophy/theology; (2) customs/

traditions; (3) collective history; (4) communication/language; and (5) family structure. Race is made up of a group's culture, usually drawn from ethnic groups who share similar cultural attributes and similar physical features. While there are many variations and descriptions of the elements that make up a culture, the ones used in this model are frequently noted elements that provide a perspective on group culture most useful for the BID model. The working definitions for the elements used to understand race-based culture are therefore drawn from numerous definitions of culture, and are as follows:

> *Philosophy*: beliefs about existence, knowledge, values, and reason; and *The-ology*: the study of religious faith, practice, and experience, *especially* the study of God and of God's relation to the world.
>
> *Customs/Traditions*: a habitual practice; the usual way of acting in given circumstances. A *tradition* is a *ritual, belief* or object passed down within a *society*, still maintained in the present, with origins in the past.
>
> *Collective History*: shared experiences of a social/racial group over time, historical experience shared by a group that has an effect on the worldview over generations.
>
> *Communication/Language*: body of words and the systems for their use common to a people who are of the same community or nation, the same geographical area, or the same cultural tradition.
>
> *Family Structure*: the composition and membership of the *family* and the organization and patterning of relationships among individual *family* members.

## Black Identity Development

Black Identity theories have undergone a number of transformations since their introduction in the 1970s (Jackson 1976, 2001; Cross 1971, 1991; Cross and Fhagen-Smith 1996, 2001). The BID introduced a theoretical framework that emerged from research conducted by Jackson and was designed to establish the existence and nature of stages of Black Identity Development. The BID framework introduced the levels/stages of consciousness that Black people tend to follow in the development of their Racial/Black Identity. There are several others who followed Cross's Nigrescence and Jackson's BID models with similar models or frameworks, including those of Milliones 1973; Toldson and Pasteur 1975; and Sue and Sue 1990. Cross's stages and Jackson's BID stages almost mirror each other in their descriptions of this developmental sequence. Cross and Fhagen-Smith present Cross's Nigrescence model in five stages:

Stage One—*Pre-Encounter,* outlines the ongoing and stable identity that will eventually be the object of the metamorphosis;

Stage Two—*Encounter,* depicts the event or series of events that challenge and destabilize the ongoing identity;

Stage Three—*Immersion-Emersion,* frames the simultaneous struggle to bring to the surface and destroy the moorings of the old identity, while decoding the nature and demands of the new identity; and given that regression or stagnation are avoided,

Stage Four—*Internalization,* signals the habituation, stabilization, and finalization of the new sense of self.

Stage Five—*Internalization Commitment,* describes a person who, after having achieved a strong Black Identity at the personal level, joins with others in the community for long-term struggles to solve Black problems and to research, protect, and propagate Black history and Black culture. (Cross and Fhagen-Smith 2001, 244–245)

The BID model was researched and developed independently of the Nigresence model. It shares many of the same perspectives as Cross's model. However, the snapshots of the process, aka stages, are taken at slightly different points and therefore describe slightly different junctures in the development process.

The primary modification to my previous BID model presented here is seen in a more significant focus on the importance of *Black culture* as a major influence in four of the five stages, thus promoting an understanding of racial identity development that is construed not solely as a consequence of racism, but rather as an interweaving of both the effects of racism and elements that are part of a heritage of Black culture that exists independently, to varying degrees, of the primary influence of racism. The five BID stages— *naïve; acceptance; resistance; redefinition;* and *internalization*—are therefore reviewed with added descriptions of modifications that reflect an emphasis that a race/culture perspective brings to each stage.

*Black Identity Development Stages*

STAGE ONE—NAÏVE

The Naive stage of BID was not in the original conceptualization of BID (Jackson 1976). Initially, the influence of Erikson's model (1968), which suggests that social identity issues do not occur until adolescence, had resulted in my giving little consideration to preadolescent identity development. Somewhat later, as a result of work with elementary and junior high school students, I began to notice that there were indeed instances in which children and youth were demonstrating a degree of awareness of racial identity. For the most part, it appeared that there was a mimicking or imitation of the racial identity issues that could be observed in those who were in their late teens and older. Other scholars, for example Tatum (1997), likewise hold that there are emergent signs of identity development among children. Importantly, Tatum suggests that the racist incidents that children experience in school, coupled with the positive experiences that their parents often provide at home, can shape the identity experience of Black children. This perspective is actually similar to what I am positing throughout the current version of the BID model.

In BID, the *Naïve* stage is that point in our development, very early childhood or from birth to age three, in which there is little or no conscious social awareness of race per se (Derman-Sparks, Higa, and Sparks 1980). During this period, children are vulnerable to the logic system and worldview of their socializing agents (such as parents, teachers, the media, and significant others). Children at this stage become aware of the physical difference and some of the cultural differences between themselves and others, and while they may not feel comfortable with people who are different, they generally do not feel fearful or hostile, inferior or superior. They may display a curiosity about or an interest in understanding the differences between people, but they have not yet learned to value some differences over others in the social world. While Clark and Clark's early studies suggested that very young children had already internalized positive attributes associated with being White and negative attributes associated with being Black (Clark and Clark 1939, 1947), later research, as reported by Swanson et al. (2009, 270), indicated that "neither racial preference nor attitude about one's membership in their racial group was a significant predictor of self-concept." This is significant in that it echoes Tatum's assertion that self-concept is not influenced solely by external manifestations of racism but simultaneously by positive influences of Black culture. With the influence of a multicultural education and antibias curriculum (Derman-Sparks 1989; Ramsey 1998) on young children, and more open, inquiry-based education in which children are encouraged to voice their questions and observations, there may well be earlier awareness of racial difference, but it remains likely that fully realized racial identity is only in its earliest stages among preschool children.

In the *transition* from the *Naïve* to the *Acceptance* stage of consciousness, two related changes take place. One is that children begin to learn and adopt an ideology about their own racial group as well as other racial groups. For most Blacks in the United States, this involves internalizing many covert and some overt messages that being Black means being less than, and that whiteness equals superiority, or *normalcy*, beauty, importance, and power. The second change is that children learn that formal and informal rules, institutions, and authority figures do not treat everyone the same way. They learn, for example, that people face negative consequences if they violate the rules regarding the way the races relate to one another.

When we adjust for an appreciation of the notion that Black children are in fact influenced by more than the racism in their midst and the collusion with racism that exists in their own community, we have to look to those experiences that introduce them to the five elements of culture embedded in their socializing agents and institutions, namely, the biological and extended family; the Black community; faith-based institutions; social clubs; schools; and other socializing institutions that carry the uniqueness of Black/African American culture. Depending on the salience of Black culture in their growing up experience, the Black cultural messages do have an effect on the BID process. The philosophical and theological messages and experiences, the exposure to the shared historical experiences and contributions to the Black community and the larger society made by other Black people, the implicit and explicit lessons taught about the nature and structure of the Black family and other intra-group interactions, are significant to the BID process. While the salience of these experiences can vary considerably depending on the messages and experiences in the socializing environment to which the Black child is exposed, thereby influencing their BID process, there is nonetheless an effect.

## STAGE TWO—ACCEPTANCE

The *Naïve* stage of consciousness is followed by a stage of *Acceptance*. This stage has been described to this point as representing the internalization, conscious or unconscious, of an ideology of racial dominance and subordination which touches all facets of one's private and public life. Again, like other models, the focus is primarily on the effect of racism on the experience at each stage. A person at this stage has internalized many of the messages about what it means to be Black in the United States. Those messages are rarely positive. Consider, for example, the barrage of negative information about educational outcomes for Blacks, or the statistics regarding the incarceration of Black males over and against the positive contributions and achievements of Blacks in the United States.

The core premise that undergirds the Acceptance stage has remained essentially unchanged since BID was developed. The Black person in the Acceptance stage of consciousness has been described as following the prevailing notion that "White is right." This person attempts to gain resources—such as approval, sense of worth, goods, power, and money—by accepting and conforming to White social, cultural, and institutional standards and values. His or her response to the dominant social mode is an unexamined rather than explicitly examined pattern of behavior consciously adopted for personal survival. The internal acceptance of these standards as a worldview requires the rejection and devaluation of all that is Black. A Black person who consciously (active acceptance) adopts the prevailing White view of the world weakens his or her positive self-concept or positive view of Black people. This consciousness typically causes a Black person to avoid interactions with other Blacks and to desire interactions with Whites, a behavioral pattern which may appear to conform to the dominant mode in most social situations.

It is at this stage in the BID process that Black youth, usually between their teenage years and their twenties, struggle with their developing understanding of racism and with decisions about how much they are doing to fight or collude with the expectations that a White racist society imposes on them. It is also at this point that exposure to and adoption of elements of Black culture can have a positive influence on the BID process. There is often a tension between the positive socializing messages a young person receives from the Black family and community and the negative messages he or she receives from the White racist society. Until now, the name of this BID stage, "acceptance," has referred to the degree and manner of acceptance of the requirements of the White racist society on Black people. In this current iteration, I am suggesting that there is also another set of decisions that the Black person is making at this point in the BID process. Those decisions are linked to considerations of how one will continue to cling to, value, and develop the Black cultural influences that are not racism-based. For example, a young Black person might have to consider whether a conception such as "afrocentrism" (Asante 1968, 1998), which for some is viewed as an overt challenge to a Eurocentric view of the world, represents a more viable perspective that allows for the study of a view of the world through the eyes of Black people and their culture.

The transition from the stage of Acceptance to Resistance can be confusing and often painful. This transition generally occurs over time and is usually stimulated by a number of events that have cumulative effects. Black people in an Acceptance consciousness begin to be aware of experiences that contradict the Acceptance worldview, experiences they had earlier ignored or passed off as isolated exceptional events. But gradually, as a person begins to encounter greater dissonance, the isolated incidents form a discernible pattern. The contradictions that initiate the transition period can occur in the form of interactions with people, social events, the media, or as a result of so-called "racial incidents." Many who saw racism as a "sixties issue" often reevaluate their thinking in light of events such as the numerous acts of open hostility and unconscionable violence against Black people in the workplace, on the college campus, and in the community. Black Americans have had to ask difficult questions, for example, about the government response to the victims of Hurricane Katrina or about the seemingly unending birth conspiracy theory about Barack Obama's legitimacy as a presidential candidate.

The recognition that racism is embedded in the implicit and often explicit socialization of Black people in the United States, coupled with the frustration of finding little support for efforts to learn about and live in Black culture, can serve as a strong motivator for the transition to the next stage.

STAGE THREE—RESISTANCE

The initial questioning that begins during the exit phase of Acceptance continues with greater intensity during the third stage, Resistance. The worldview that people adopt during Resistance is dramatically different from that of the Acceptance stage. At this third stage, one begins to understand and recognize racism in its complex and multiple manifestations—at the individual and institutional, conscious and unconscious, intentional and unintentional, attitudinal, behavioral, and policy levels. Individuals in Resistance become painfully aware of the numerous ways in which covert as well as overt racism impacts them daily as Black people.

The values, moral codes, and codes of personal and professional development handed down by the majority White culture and those who collude with it are the first things to be scrutinized through the lens of this new and more critical consciousness. These values and codes are reexamined for their role in the perpetuation of racism. Gradually, the Black person becomes more skilled at identifying racist premises that have been woven into the fabric of all aspects of social experience. This person experiences a growing hostility toward White people, as well as toward fellow Blacks or other people of color, who collude with manifestations of White racism.

The often overt expression of hostility to the existence and effects of racism marks the transition from the entry phase to the adoption phase of the Resistance stage. It is at this point of the Resistance stage that the Black individual fully internalizes the antithesis of the Acceptance stage of development. The person experiences anger, pain, hurt, and rage. The effects of racism may appear to be all-consuming. In extreme cases, some people may become so consumed by these emotions that they remain at this stage of consciousness for some time. In other instances, individual Blacks may find that by fully embracing the Resistance stage they stand to lose the "benefits" they enjoyed when they were in Acceptance. They may choose the path of passive Resistance, in the hope that they will be able to stay in favor with White society while rejecting racism. This strategy usually proves too frustrating and contradictory to be sustained. For most Blacks at this stage the primary task is to stop colluding in their own victimization. It is time to cleanse their consciousness of those internalized racist notions that have served to stifle their own personal development and to stop passively accepting the racism of their environment.

At this stage, it may be difficult to see an explicit focus on Black culture. The person can become so consumed with the expression of anger, and with overtly challenging the various ways in which racism is manifested in individuals and institutions, that attention to Black culture is not often sought out or sustained. So much of the person's energy is focused on a kind of internal cleansing of the toxic residue of the effects of being socialized from a White racist perspective that often Black culture is embraced simply because it isn't White. The appreciation of Black culture for its own sake is often lost or stalled in the process.

### REDEFINITION STAGE

The Redefinition stage is that point in the development process in which the Black person is concerned with defining her- or himself in terms that are independent of the perceived strengths and/or weaknesses of White people and the dominant White culture. At this juncture the Black person focuses attention and energy on developing primary contact and interacting with other Blacks at the same stage of consciousness. Unlike the Black person at the Acceptance and Resistance stages, the Black person with a Redefinition consciousness is not concerned either with emulating or rejecting Whites and White culture. The Redefining person does not see interaction with Whites as necessary and useful in the quest for a positive or nurturing sense of self and racial identity. Because renaming and in some cases reclaiming is the primary concern in this person's life, he or she begins a search for paradigms that will facilitate the accomplishment of this task.

This is the point where the Black cultural perspective is strongest and most salient in one's life. All the cultural elements previously mentioned are fully engaged. Here the individual is proactive and focused on claiming and/ or reclaiming key elements of the Black culture. During this stage reacting to White people, institutions, and culture is not particularly important. Unlike the Acceptance stage, where the approval of White people, institutions, and culture is very important, and unlike the Resistance stage, where the rejection of all that is White is the focus, in this stage the only thing that matters is to fully embrace Black culture.

### INTERNALIZATION STAGE

The transition from Redefinition to Internalization occurs when an individual begins to apply or to integrate some of the newly defined aspects of Black culture. This transition is somewhat different from the transition processes between the earlier stages. The transition to Internalization brings the cumulative growth and development from all previous stages forward into this final stage. The learning and awareness derived from living in the Acceptance, Resistance, and Redefinition stages of consciousness, as well as some of the pain and frustration experienced during that developmental process, is critical to the realization of this stage. To demonstrate this point, I will highlight some of the experiences that are typically carried forward into the Internalization stage.

Black people at the Internalization stage no longer feel a need to explain, defend, or protect their Black identity, although they may recognize that it is important to nurture this sense of self. Nurturing is seen as particularly important when the environment continues to ignore, degrade, or attack all that is Black. For example, Blacks who have decided to organize their lives and sense of blackness around an Afrocentric perspective and the lifestyle that goes with it may find that it takes some special attention to keep the focus healthy and alive as long as they are living in a society dominated by a Eurocentric culture and worldview.

Some Blacks have or will adopt a multicultural perspective, which brings together worldviews from as many compatible cultural perspectives as possible. This might mean integrating two or more racial/panethnic cultural perspectives (such as Asian, Asian American, Pacific Islander, Native American, Latino, or White/Euro-American). And there are those who follow the thinking of W.E.B. DuBois ([1903] 1961), who prescribed a bicultural perspective for Black people in America, one that integrates the cultures of people of African and European heritage. Some have suggested that Dr. Martin Luther King manifests this stage, while others add Maya Angelou or Malcom X to the list of those who should be considered. Clearly, the BID stages of development are evident in their autobiographies (Carson 2001; Haley 1965), in the case of King and Malcolm X; and in the works of Angelou herself (1969). Although there do not appear to be many Black people who can be held up as role models or exemplars of the Internalized stage of consciousness or identity, these individuals notwithstanding, we can point to specific attitudes and behaviors in specific situations as evidence that many of us can and do operate from this stage of consciousness to varying degrees.

A significant change in this last stage comes as a result of the consideration of *Intersectionality,* or the recognition that all salient social identities within a given context such as the United States have an influence on each other. For example, considering that the following social identities are currently most salient in the United States: race, ethnicity, gender, class, sexual orientation, physical/developmental ability, age, religion, nationality, for the Black person at the Internalization stage, the challenge is to consider how his or her racial/Black identity is influenced by each of the individual's other identities. In other words, he or she may ask what it means to think of him or herself as a Black man or woman, with a particular sexual orientation, within a particular social class, and religion, and so on. Clearly this complicates and expands their view of themselves as Black and ultimately as a member of all the other social groups. The figure below represents the view of the person at the Internalization stage. There is still a focus on the person's race and racial identity. What is new is the consideration of all other social identities in her or his identity development process.

It is not clear what might follow an Internalization stage. In all previous iterations of BID, Internalization represents the final stage, the assumption being that when one reached this stage, the process of developing a full and healthy Black identity was complete. The way of describing the arrival at this stage was presented by focusing on the ways in which the person had

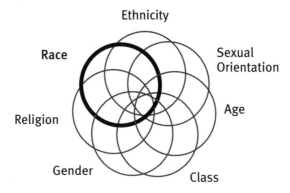

Fig. 2.3 Internalization through the Lens of Intersectionality

internalized her or his new sense of blackness into all the roles that she or he played in life, for example; as parent, spouse, worker and coworker, citizen, friend, and the like. And while those role-based connections are important, the contribution to understanding this stage with the added lens of Intersectionality is in recognizing the interconnections among other social identities. Now the Black person at this stage is attending to that part of her or his identity development that asks what it means to be a Black person who is of a particular ethnic group, has a specific gender expression, is of a particular social class, is of a particular age, has a physical or developmental disability, and so on. This is the contribution of Intersectionality.

Clearly many of the notions advanced in this chapter will require the scrutiny of research that uses various methodologies to establish the validity of these changes in BID. The notions of particular import presented in this chapter have to do with a recognition that many events in the first decade of this century have had a significant impact on the way that race, racism, and racial identity are thought about. While the events cited in this chapter seemed extremely significant to this author, it could be important to study which events of varying types have had an impact on the way race, racism, and racial identity development is evolving among a broad range of Black people and to begin to explore how new generations of Black Americans are or are not moving through these or other stages in similar or new ways. For example, how will Black Americans experience their identity development when there are no living representatives of the civil rights era to share first-person narratives of the struggle? Will there be another civil rights-type struggle that will cause the next new racial awakening? The introduction of Intersectionality as a way of thinking about the internalization stage of BID should provide a solid way of considering more of what is transpiring for a Black person at that stage. Intersectionality may also begin to provide some sense of what could be a next stage leading from BID to a stage of social identity development.

*[handwritten margin note: black perspective in gay rights movement.]*

## Conclusion

The introduction of or increased emphasis on Black culture in BID is the main purpose of this chapter. It was important to make it clear that the Black Identity Development process is guided by elements of Black culture and influenced by racism. This perspective on BID may be contradicted by those who hold to the proposition that race is a social construct that was invented to support racism. When starting from this position it is easy to see how any model that attempts to describe Black Identity Development could be drawn to overemphasize the dynamic of racism. In this chapter, I stand on the other side of this debate. I suggest that a race is a collection of ethnic groups with similar cultural and physical characteristics and that there were groups of this type before the term race, as it is referred to currently, was popularized. Following this perspective, I have offered the notion that Black Identity Development must be essentially grounded in a Black heritage/culture. While the many manifestations of racism are also part of the collective history of Black people, especially that of African Americans, and must be considered a part of the Black Identity Development process, focusing solely on the influence of racism in that process borders on a significant misrepresentation of the process. Because I expect that this debate will continue as thinking about race and racism evolves, I will leave the larger ongoing debate about what race is and where it comes from to scholars in fields such as history, anthropology, and sociology.

Finally, I have woven in important considerations of Intersectionality to add to our understanding about various stages of BID, particularly at the Internalization stage. Intersectionality has clearly expanded the way Black Identity Development is being conceptualized and will likely continue to have an increasingly significant place in discussions about BID and its evolution.

REFERENCES

Angelou, Maya. 1969. *I Know Why the Caged Bird Sings*. New York: Random House.
Asante, Molefi Kete. 1968. *Afrocentricity*. Trenton, N.J.: Africa World Press.
———. 1998. *The Afrocentric Idea*. Philadelphia: Temple University Press.
Carson, Clayborne, ed. 2001. *The Autobiography of Martin Luther King, Jr.* New York: Grand Central Publishing.
Clark, Kenneth B., and Mamie K. Clark. 1939. "The Development of Consciousness of Self and the Emergence of Racial Identity in Negro Preschool Children." *Journal of Social Psychology* 10: 591–599.
———. 1947. "Racial Identification and Preferences in Negro Children." In *Readings in Social Psychology*, edited by Theodore Newcomb and Eugene L. Hartley, 602–611. New York: Holt.
Collins, Patricia Hill. 1998. "Intersections of Race, Class, Gender and Nation: Some Implications for Black Family Studies." *Journal of Comparative Family Studies* 29 (1): 27–36.
———. 2005. "An Entirely Different World: Rethinking the Sociology of Race and Ethnicity." In *Handbook of Sociology*, edited by Craig Calhoun, Bryan Turner, and Chris Rojek, 208–222. London: Sage.
Crenshaw, Kimberle W. 1991. "Mapping the Margins: Intersectionality, Identity Politics, and Violence against Women of Color." *Stanford Law Review* 43 (6): 1241–1299.
Cross, W. E. 1971. "The Negro-to-Black Conversion Experience: Towards a Psychology of Black Liberation." *Black World* 20 (9): 13–27.

————. 1991. *Shades of Black: Diversity in African-American Identity.* Philadelphia: Temple University Press.

Cross, William E., Jr., and Peony Fhagen-Smith. 1996. "Nigrescence and Ego Identity Development: Accounting for Different Black Identity Patterns." In *Counseling across Cultures,* edited by P. B. Pederson, J. G. Draguns, W. J. Lonner, and J. E. Trimble, 108–123. Thousand Oaks, Calif.: Sage.

————. 2001. "Patterns of African American Identity Development: A Life Span Perspective." In *New Perspectives on Racial Identity Development: A Theoretical and Practical Anthology,* edited by Charmaine L. Wijeyesinghe and Bailey W. Jackson III, 243–270. New York: NYU Press.

Derman-Sparks, Louise. 1989. *Anti-Bias Curriculum: Tools for Empowering Young Children.* National Association for the Education of Youth, No. 242, January. Accessed April 28, 2011. http://teachingforchange.org/files/025-A.pdf.

Derman-Sparks, Louise, Carol T. Higa, and Bill Sparks. 1980. "Children, Race and Racism: How Race Awareness Develops." *Interracial Books for Children Bulletin* 11 (3–4): 3–9.

DuBois, William E. B. [1903] 1961. *The Souls of Black Folk: Essays and Sketches.* Greenwich, Conn.: Fawcett.

Erikson, Erik H. 1968. *Identity: Youth and Crisis.* New York: W. W. Norton.

Haley, Alex. 1965. *The Autobiography of Malcom X, as Told by Alex Haley.* New York: Grove Press.

Hatch, Mary Jo, and Majken Schultz. 1997. "Relations between Organizational Culture, Identity and Image." *European Journal of Marketing* 31 (5/6): 356–365.

Helms, Janet E. 1990. *Black and White Racial Identity: Theory, Research and Practice.* New York: Greenwood Press.

Jackson, Bailey W. 1976. "Black Identity Development." In *Urban, Social, and Educational Issues,* edited by L. H. Golubchick and B. Persky, 158–164. Dubuque, Iowa: Kendall-Hung.

————. 2001. "Black Identity Development: Further Analysis and Elaboration." In *New Perspectives on Racial Identity Development: A Theoretical and Practical Anthology,* edited by Charmaine L. Wijeyesinghe and Bailey W. Jackson III, 8–31. New York: NYU Press.

Jandt, Fred E. 2007. *An Introduction to Intercultural Communication: Identities in a Global Community.* Thousand Oaks, Calif.: Sage.

Lederach, John Paul. 1995. *Preparing for Peace–Conflict Transformation across Cultures.* Syracuse: Syracuse University Press.

Malik, Kenan. 1996. *The Meaning of Race: Race, History and Culture in Western Society.* New York: NYU Press.

Marsella, Anthony. 1998. "Toward a 'Global Community Psychology': Meeting the Needs of a Changing World." *American Psychologist* 53 (12): 1282–1291.

Matarasso, Francois. 2001. "Culture, Economics and Development." In *Recognizing Culture: A Series of Briefing Papers on Culture and Development,* edited by Francois Matarasso, 3–9. London: Comedia/Canadian Heritage/UNESCO. Accessed April 28, 2011. http://unesdoc.unesco.org/images/0015/001592/159227e.pdf.

McCall, Linda. 2008. "The Complexity of Intersectionality." In *Intersectionality and Beyond: Law, Power and the Politics of Location,* edited by Emily Grabham, Davina Cooper, Jane Krishnadas, and Didi Herman, 49–75. New York: Routledge-Cavendish.

Milliones, Jake. 1973. "Construction of a Developmental Inventory of Black Consciousness." Ph.D. dissertation, University of Pittsburgh.

Ramsey, Patricia G. 1998. *Teaching and Learning in a Diverse World: Multicultural Education for Young Children*. New York: Teachers College Press.

Sue, Derald Wing, and David Sue. 1990. *Counseling the Culturally Different: Theory and Practice*. New York: John Wiley and Sons.

Swanson Dena P., Michael Cunningham, Joseph Youngblood, and Margaret Beale Spencer. 2009. "Racial Identity Development during Childhood." In *Handbook of African American Psychology*, edited by Helen A. Neville, Brendesha M. Tynes, and Shawn O. Utsey, 269–281. Thousand Oaks, Calif.: Sage.

Tatum, Beverly Daniel. 1997. *"Why Are All the Black Kids Sitting Together in the Cafeteria?" and Other Conversations about Race*. New York: Basic Books.

Toldson, Ivory L., and Alfred E. Pasteur. 1975. "Developmental Stages of Black Self-Discovery." *Journal of Negro Education* 44: 130–138.

Wijeyesinghe, Charmaine L., and Jackson Bailey W. III, eds. 2001. *New Perspectives on Racial Identity Development: A Theoretical and Practical Anthology*. New York: NYU Press.

3

# Latina and Latino Ethnoracial Identity Orientations

*A Dynamic and Developmental Perspective*

PLÁCIDA V. GALLEGOS AND BERNARDO M. FERDMAN

Since 2000, the visibility of Latinas and Latinos in the United States has increased dramatically.[1] Yet, in our experience, in spite of a great increase in the amount of scholarly and popular literature addressing Latino issues, this growth both in numbers and in the national consciousness has not been accompanied by a deeper, more nuanced, and shared understanding of the complexities of Latino[2] identity and experience.

In 2000, just before we first published our model of Latina and Latino racial identity orientations (Ferdman and Gallegos 2001), Latinos constituted 13.7 percent of the U.S. population (including Puerto Rico), and there was a growing awareness of the notable increase and spread of this group throughout the country. Since then, Latinos have become an even larger proportion of the population—15.4 percent in 2008, over 16 percent in 2010, and projected to be 30 percent in 2050—and are present more visibly and in greater numbers in communities where previously "diversity" implicitly meant the presence of Blacks. These proportions will continue to increase, largely because of the relative youth of the Latino population. Indeed, in

2008 Latinos constituted 21.2 percent of the U.S. population younger than 18 (and 24.0 percent of those younger than 5). Also, in spite of common rhetoric and media portrayals of Latinos as being primarily immigrants, the U.S. Census reported that in 2008 the proportion of Hispanics who were U.S. native-born stood at 61.2 percent.

In reflecting on the period between 2001 and 2010, many issues discussed in our prior chapter (Ferdman and Gallegos 2001) have become amplified and even more complex. As a whole, the Latino population has grown even more rapidly than predicted and has consequently moved into greater prominence in the public eye. Electoral politics, marketing efforts, and media representations are only some of the manifestations of this growing influence. This heightened visibility has had both positive and negative repercussions.

On the positive side, Latinos are increasingly viewed as significant players in the political realm,[3] where Latino votes are actively courted by both parties; some would argue, for example, that Latino support of Barack Obama made the critical difference in the outcome of the 2008 presidential election (see, e.g., Kettle 2008; Lopez 2008; National Association of Latino Elected Officials 2008). More recently, the midterm elections in November 2010 showed that the influence of Latino voters continues to grow, along with projections about how Latinos will impact the next presidential election in 2012 and subsequent major elections (e.g., Barreto, Collingwood, and Manzano 2010; Higuera 2010). Efforts to market to Latino consumers have heated up and have led to intense competition in most sectors to gain access to their earning power. Latinos continue to be overrepresented in the ranks of the military, including among casualties in various international fronts (see, e.g., Gifford 2005). On televisions and movie theaters across the country and the world, Latino images are becoming more commonplace and perhaps even less stereotyped.[4]

On the negative side, the growing population of Latinos has increased hostility and fear, especially in regions such as Arizona in 2010 that have seen rapid growth—whether real or imagined—in the number of undocumented workers. Harsh legislation has been passed, leading to stiffer enforcement of immigration laws and decreased public services available to this segment of the Latino population. At the time of this writing, many other states are discussing the enactment of similar legislation. A recent report published by the National Council of La Raza describes the dangers of ethnic and racial profiling by law enforcement which "has created a threatening and insecure environment for all Latinos" (Lacayo 2010, 2). In a similar report, the Pew Hispanic Center documented the negative impact of these laws on U.S.-born Hispanic citizens and families, in spite of claims to the contrary by proponents of such legislation (Lopez and Minushkin 2008).

Some politicians have not hesitated to fuel anti-immigrant sentiment, and their statements can be seen to incorporate thinly veiled racial or ethnic referents. In a recent interview with Univision's Jorge Ramos, Arizona Governor Jan Brewer attempted to defend herself from accusations of racism by asserting that: "I've lived in the Southwest my whole life. I've got many friends, of many cultures and certainly a great deal of them are Hispanics, and I love them from the bottom of my heart." She was unable to explain how the law would address the root causes of the issue or to understand why many Latinos saw the legislation as punitive (CBS Business Network 2010; Wing 2010). The debate over Arizona's SB1070, which requires officials to ask those reasonably suspected of illegally being in the country to produce their papers, suggests that those who are Brown and fit the stereotype of an undocumented immigrant are more likely to be stopped and questioned than those who are White and do not fit that stereotype (see, e.g., Kradenpoth and Deane 2010).

Another negative trend is that Latinos continue to have the highest dropout rates in high school and the lowest graduation rates in college, compared to other groups, including African Americans and Asian Americans (Kao and Thompson 2003).[5] Current economic crises are having a disproportionate impact on lower-income families, resulting in lower rates of home ownership and foreclosure as well as increased unemployment in many sectors (Cooper 2011). Though largely unjustified, there is a stereotype among many in the general population that Latinos are taking employment away from White Americans desperate for jobs (Markert 2010). In that sense, even when Latinos are seen as having a strong work ethic, negative stereotypes about them persist (Weaver 2005). In other words, because many Latinos are willing to work hard without complaining, they can be more easily exploited, and this, rather than being seen as a positive quality, adds to the negative perception of Latinos.[6]

## Latinos, Race, and Identity

Since 2000, we have seen much attention to race and racial identity, and the degree to which Latinos are viewed as a distinct racial category seems to have increased in spite of the U.S. Census instruction that people of "Hispanic origins are not races" (U.S. Census Bureau 2010). Some authors go further to advocate the use of "ethnoracial" identification as a more inclusive descriptor of Latinos; this is how Torres-Saillant (2003) makes the case:

> Using race and ethnicity synonymously may lead us out of the epistemological and political *cul-de-sac*. When it comes to oppressed minorities of

color, we do not need to know the difference if they both translate into a common exclusion and disempowerment. Ultimately ethnicity is no less a construct than race. Both are fictitious. Both come from a similar effort to imagine a collective internally or externally. Their reality occurs only as they translate into social, political, and economic advancement or retardation. I would venture to say that we have little to gain from subverting the pentagonal paradigm bequeathed by the Civil Rights movement. Our mental energies could best be invested in efforts aimed at fashioning a Latino ethnoracial identity space devoid of white supremacist assumptions. (147)

Similarly, Grosfoguel (2004) argues for using a notion of "racial/ethnic identity" instead of trying to separate these into distinct categories. Based on an analysis of historical and contemporary relations of power among various groups, he shows how the concepts of ethnicity and race are often conflated, and can result in "racialized ethnicities"—such as Puerto Ricans in New York—and "ethnicized races"—such as Blacks in the United States. In a related analysis, Aranda and Rebollo-Gil (2004) discuss the experience of Puerto Ricans in particular and conclude that, given the multiple factors that are involved in the social construction of race, it makes more sense to talk about *ethnoracism*. As they put it:

> How do we account for the experiences of racism toward multiracial minority groups in a context in which much of the dominant racial discourse is color-coded? We argue that the racialization of ethnicity has resulted in ethnoracism. Race in 20th-century America is not limited to phenotype; the social construction of race involves ethnic and global dimensions such as national origin, culture, language, religion, the historical relationship between colonial powers and their political subjects, and race. (193)

Although we do see important distinctions between the concepts of *race* and *ethnicity* (see, e.g., Ferdman 1999; Ferdman and Gallegos 2001), we are influenced by Torres-Saillant's and Grosfoguel's arguments and see the value of utilizing the hybrid term *ethnoracial* in the context of our discussion of Latino and Latina identity, especially given the persistence and apparent intractability of race consciousness and racialized language in current U.S. society. If anything, there has been more rather than less emphasis on race in recent years, as well as continued confusion regarding where Latinas and Latinos fit in the predominant Black-White racial paradigm.

Since 2000, the world has become more complex and our understanding of Latinos needs to become even broader and deeper. In our earlier work (Ferdman and Gallegos 2001; Gallegos and Ferdman 2007), we cautioned against overgeneralizations about Latino identity and the stereotyping of Latinos as a group. At the same time we sought to provide a framework for meaning-making that would be useful to Latinos and non-Latinos alike. We begin the present chapter with the same caveat, which we believe is more important than ever. Here, we attempt to demonstrate why "complicating" perspectives on Latina and Latino ethnoracial identity is more valid than providing simplistic definitions or categorizations, and how it is possible to consider race and ethnicity in conjunction with other aspects of identity such as gender and class (Holvino 2010). Scholars of social identity development are increasingly influenced by concepts related to *Intersectionality* (e.g., Jones and Wijeyesinghe 2011; McEwen 2003; Torres, Jones, and Renn 2009), an analytic lens that allows for the integration of multiple identities. By more explicitly incorporating this framework, we hope to avoid some of the pitfalls of essentialism, which is the tendency to define individuals or groups based solely on narrow aspects of their identity, as if that aspect fully defined the person or group, and to inappropriately generalize across individuals and groups (see Holvino, this volume). In particular, we expand on our prior model, considering the adaptive functions of the various Latina and Latino identity orientations, and conceptualizing identity as fluid, situational, and affected by a wide range of variables.

In her work on multiracial identity development, Wijeyesinghe (2001; this volume) discusses some of these factors, including racial ancestry, early socialization experiences, cultural attachment, physical appearance, social and historical context, political awareness and orientation, and spirituality. Our goal in this chapter is to broaden this already complex picture by providing greater consideration of the contextual factors that influence the Latino orientations we introduced in our earlier work (Ferdman and Gallegos 2001; Gallegos and Ferdman 2007), as well as to consider the adaptive potential of the various orientations and the possible triggers that could shift individuals from one identity orientation to another.

The emphasis in our previous work was on how Latinos saw themselves and made meaning of their groupness, and the diversity in these views. In this chapter we extend our analysis to consider the social location of Latinos in terms of institutional, cultural, and societal power, paying attention to how these external forces may shape and influence the identity orientation of Latinas and Latinos. By considering issues of power distribution, oppression, dominance, and subordination, one can develop a fuller understanding of the adaptive value and creativity of the various identity orientations in responding to powerful societal pressures.

Multiple identities such as gender, class, and sexual orientation intersect in complex ways that simultaneously influence behavior and perceptions (Dill, McLaughlin, and Nieves 2007). While considering these influences, we make a concerted effort to avoid the common trap of essentializing the Latino experience by narrowly focusing on a few aspects while excluding a wide array of other dimensions; for example, statements such as "Latinos have big families and are family oriented"—while true in a generalized statistical sense—can obscure important variations within the group and fail to consider the structural impact of economic, religious, and cultural systems. Jones and Wijeyesinghe (2011) challenge educators and advisors to incorporate intersectional perspectives into their classroom practices and pedagogy. They also challenge researchers and theorists to integrate consideration of power and interconnected structures of inequality into their analyses and interventions. We have developed our model to take into fuller account these external shaping forces and to highlight the dynamic aspects and adaptive utility of each identity orientation.

## Intersectionality and Latina and Latino Identity Orientations

Models of identity development are attempts to describe and deepen understanding of highly complex phenomena. Our model focuses on the ways Latinos come to think about themselves in a diverse and ever-changing society against the backdrop of a wide range of historical and cultural influences. Rather than occurring in a vacuum, these identity formations occur in the context of multiple identities that are interrelated and simultaneous (Holvino, this volume). These various identifications do not occur in isolation but in the context of organizational and cultural systems that tend to favor certain groups and disadvantage others. For example, Latinas also identify themselves as women, as straight or gay, as educated or privileged, as having children or not, as light-skinned or dark-skinned, as being able-bodied or as having disabilities, and so on. These various identities all connect to and interact with each other, to create unique individual identities tied to multiple social categories (Ferdman 1995). Attention to how these interrelationships are experienced relates to the framework of *Intersectionality*, which argues for the integrated study of various systems of inequality based on race, class, gender, sexuality, ability, and nationality (Kirk and Okazawa-Rey 2007). This perspective or analytic lens shifts from a focus on a single dimension of identity—which neglects the richness and complexity provided by the intersections of race, gender, sexual, and other identities—to a focus on the connections and mutual influences among multiple identities (see, e.g., Ferdman 1995; Ferdman 1999). From this perspective, particular dimensions of identity are not seen as separate and distinct but rather as interrelated with all other facets of one's identity and as dependent on contextual influences, including those related to unequal power distribution and structural inequities. This approach leads to a progression from an *either/or* perspective of categorizing people to a more integrated *both/and* approach. Various facets of identity are seen as so vitally linked that they become multiplicative or interactive rather than additive, creating a complex matrix that integrates the individual facets of identity to construct a total identity (Jones and Wijeyesinghe 2011).

Relating this idea to our model of Latino and Latina identity orientations, we encourage users of the model to avoid oversimplification, acknowledging the interrelated aspects of various and simultaneous social identities. Rather than providing a one-size-fits-all approach to identity, our model invites curiosity, humility, and exploration. The central premise in our research and practice continues to be openness to the great variety of ways Latinas and Latinos make meaning of who they are and where they fit in the U.S. social order.[7] Instead of giving the reader answers to understanding the complexity of Latino identity, our intent is to suggest deeper and better questions to guide ongoing learning and inquiry.

## Latinos and U.S. Racial Categories

We have previously described many of the complexities involved in thinking about Latino identity in the context of race, particularly as it is constructed in the United States (Ferdman and Gallegos 2001). Various other authors (e.g., Campbell and Rogalin 2006; Cobas, Duany, and Feagin 2009; Frank, Akresh, and Lu 2010; Golash-Boza and Darity 2008; Grosfoguel 2004; Jiménez 2004; Logan 2004; Lopez 2005; López 2008; Montalvo and Codina 2001; Tafoya 2004; Torres-Saillant 2003; Uhlmann, Dasgupta, Elgueta, Greenwald, and Swanson 2002; Vaquera and Kao 2006) also provide details about the current and historical relationship of U.S. Latinos to racial categories as applied in the United States. Because of the Black/White or White/non-White paradigm, as well as the "one-drop rule" dominating racial discourse in the United States, Latinos have not fit easily into the U.S. racial framework. In Latin America, Central America, Mexico, and the Caribbean, while race and color certainly play a role, the racial paradigm is somewhat different and more fluid and polychromatic than in the United States (Massey and Sanchez 2007). The encounter between the North American and Latin American racial orders has often resulted in a particularly complex view of race among U.S. Latinos that can be challenging and even quite confusing to the surrounding society.

According to the U.S. Census, Latinos "can be of any race" and hence are not simply categorized in the U.S. system of racial classification. Indeed, Latinos vary greatly in their responses to the race question on the Census, and these responses depend on a number of factors. In 2000, across the country as a whole (not including Puerto Rico), 47.9 percent of Hispanics indicated they were White, 2.0 percent said they were Black, 1.2 percent said they were American Indian, 0.3 percent said they were Asian, and 42.2 percent indicated they were of "some other race."[8] Approximately 6 percent of Latinos (or 2.2 million people) identified with two or more racial categories (with 81 percent of these marking "some other race" and one more). Nevertheless, within these responses there is great diversity, depending on national origin, state of residence, and a variety of other demographic characteristics (see, e.g., Logan 2004; Tafoya 2004). Thus, many Latinos experience their identity as incorporating racial elements, but for many others, race is a different type of identity that is not addressed by their identification as Latino or Hispanic. In either case, Latinos tend to see race in a more continuous and less dichotomous or either/or manner than what has been typical in the surrounding society in the United States. As Denton and Massey point out, many Puerto Ricans and other Latinos of Caribbean origin perceive "race . . . as a spectrum running from White to Black, with many people falling in between" (1989, 791). Similarly, Mexicans and Mexican Americans perceive a spectrum ranging from White to Indian.

One could argue that between 2000 and 2010 there have been some shifts in the United States, such that there is more awareness of multiplicity and complexity with regard to race. For example, both in 2000 and in 2010 the U.S. Census permitted respondents to check more than one race category, and based its racial coding of individuals solely on self-identification. Yet in much of the country the press and popular discourse refer to Latinos as a distinct racial category. Indeed, in 2000 Hispanics constituted 98 percent of those who responded "Some Other Race" to the race question on the U.S. Census. In fact, the proportion of Hispanics claiming to be of "some other race" has increased over the years. In 1980, 64 percent of Hispanics said they were White on the U.S. Census, but less than 50 percent did so in 2000. On this basis, it could be argued that in many ways Latinos now constitute a distinct racial category in the United States, and in many parts of the country they see themselves and are seen by others as such. Yet, as mentioned above, this varies greatly by region and state, as well as by geographic origin.

For example, of the 1.2 million Latinos reporting Cuban ancestry in 2000, 85 percent said they are White, 3.6 percent indicated they are Black, and only 7.1 percent said that they are of "some other race." In contrast, only 23 percent of the 796,000 Dominicans said they are White, 8.9 percent said they are Black, and 58.4 percent claimed "some other race" (Tafoya 2004).

Montalvo and Codina (2001), in their review of the historical, social, and psychological role of skin color and physical appearance among Latinos— including the Spanish colonial system of *castas*, or castes, in Mexico—find that phenotype relates to Mexican Americans' psychological well-being, to their acculturation, and to their opportunities in life, although these effects depend on gender and whether the individuals were immigrants or native-born. Among Puerto Ricans, the effect of the Black/White dichotomy on the mainland resulted in separation into three phenotype-based groups. Tafoya (2004), in an analysis of the sociodemographic differences among Latinos based on their responses to the race question on the 2000 Census, found that there are systematic differences in both social variables and attitudes between those Latinos who indicate that they are White and those who identify with "some other race." Specifically, those who self-identify as being of "some other race" (rather than White, Black, or Asian), compared to those who self-label as White, tended to have less formal education, to have lower incomes and wealth, to be less likely to be monolingual in English, and to have a lower rate of intermarriage with non-Hispanic Whites. Tafoya summarized her findings in this way:

> Consistently across a broad range of variables, Hispanics who identified themselves as white have higher levels of education and income and greater degrees of civic enfranchisement than those who pick the some other race category. The findings of this report suggest that Hispanics see race as a measure of belonging, and as a measure of inclusion, or of perceived inclusion. (2004, 1)

Hayes-Bautista (2004) summarizes the complex history of Mexicans and Mexican Americans in the U.S. Southwest with regard to racial categorization. In particular, after 1848, when the United States took half of Mexico's territory, many of the residents, as well as later arrivals, were denied citizenship because they were thought to be Indian, and most Mexicans in any case were seen as non-White. Yet in 1940 the U.S. Census reclassified Latinos as White.

As pointed out by Cobas, Duany, and Feagin (2009) as well as the various contributors to their edited volume, processes of racialization in the United

States have generally served to portray Mexicans and other Latin Americans as racially inferior and Latinos as "a color-coded category" (2009, 8). It is in this context that Latinos develop ways of orienting themselves with regard to the racial order.[9]

## Key Questions

The primary focus of our original model (Ferdman and Gallegos 2001) was to provide a lens for understanding the different approaches that can be and are manifested by Latinas and Latinos in the context of environmental events and challenges. The idea is that the worldview of Latinas and Latinos is closely related to how they interpret and respond to situations, and that worldview both influences and is influenced by their ethnoracial identity. For example, to the extent that essentialism informs Latinos' thinking and outlook, this can affect the extent to which they see themselves as similar to or different from other Latinos. Someone who considers all Latinos to belong to a single racial category may see herself as more similar to other Latinos than someone who focuses primarily on national origins and is also sensitive to within-group racial variation. In terms of our model of identity orientations, for example, someone who is subgroup-identified may operate from a narrow view of their group as essentially distinct from and not connected in any way to Latinos from other subgroups. This can manifest in political behavior, such as when Latinos who are U.S.-born have hostile attitudes toward Latin American immigrants (National Institute for Latino Policy 2010).

Thus, we ask the question: How does identity orientation affect Latinos' interactions with each other and with non-Latinos as well as the ways in which Latinos sees themselves as similar to or different from other Latinos? For example, how likely are we—one a White Argentine middle-class immigrant who grew up in Puerto Rico, and the other a brown-skinned New Mexican Chicana with roots predating the formation of the United States—to feel a sense of connection and kinship with each other? Certainly, many variables can affect this experience; a key factor, we believe, is our understanding of race and culture and their connections to our identity. In our particular case, we feel quite connected; notwithstanding our many differences, we share an important identity as Latinos. But we know many others with similar backgrounds to our own who would not have the same sense of kinship across parallel differences. We also acknowledge that the ability to incorporate our differences in service of our shared goals and values has been achieved as a result of concerted effort and investment in building a relationship through shared experience and relational learning (see, e.g., Wasserman, Gallegos, and Ferdman 2008).

There is a great deal of work focusing on the acculturation process and experience among Latinos (e.g., Cabassa 2003; Gonzales, Fabrett, and Knight 2009; Holleran 2003; Schwartz, Zamboanga, and Jarvis 2007; Umaña-Taylor and Alfaro 2009), as well as others. This body of work seeks to describe the psychological and social processes that accompany intercultural contact. Although we do not review that literature here, acculturation is certainly relevant to the process of forming and shifting identity. A key question then is: How are acculturation and enculturation filtered through a racially tinted lens? In this sense, identity orientations can both influence and be influenced by the acculturation process. For example, Bernardo's family arrived from Argentina to the Upper West Side of Manhattan (briefly) in the mid-1960s, and quickly learned that the outside world saw them as, in many ways, part of the same group as the Puerto Ricans living in that neighborhood. Yet, at least initially, they had no sense of sharing an identity with that group. Their acculturation experience involved learning how they were seen and then adapting to that external view. This is similar in some ways to the experience of many newcomers to the United States from Latin America, who in a sense only become Latinos at the moment of arrival, and then must learn to adapt to U.S. notions of who Latinos are. Plácida's experiences represent the other end of the spectrum. Having been born into a family that has been in this country for generations, her initial assumptions were that Latinos were primarily Mexican Americans born in the southwestern United States. Expanding her definition of Latinos to include Latin American immigrants from a wide range of nations and regions greatly influenced and broadened her ethnoracial identification.[10]

Such experiences inevitably combine not only elements of race and racial thinking (both on the part of the acculturating individual and the surrounding society), but also culture, social class, and other identities, in a mix that is difficult if not impossible to sort out. A key question in this regard has to do with the ethnic versus racial aspects of Latino identity. The degree to which a particular individual focuses on being Latino as a racial versus an ethnic identity, varies, of course, from person to person and subgroup to subgroup (Logan 2004; Tafoya 2004). For example, on the U.S. Census in 2000, individuals who indicated they were of Dominican origin or ancestry were much more likely to indicate that they were Black or African American on the race question—12.7 percent did so—than individuals who were Mexican or of Mexican origin (1.1 percent), South American (1.6 percent), or Central American (4.1 percent) (Logan 2004). At the same time, Dominicans were also the most likely (63.1 percent), compared to other Latino subgroups (e.g., 49.7 percent of those of Mexican or Mexican American origin, 42.8 percent of Puerto Ricans, 37.4 percent of South Americans, and only 9.8 percent of Cubans), to indicate that they were "Some Other Race" (other than White, Black, Asian, etc.). Related to this, there were systematic variations—connected not only to national origin, but also to other indicators such as educational level, employment situation, nativity—in the likelihood of seeing Hispanic as a racial identity or not. Further complicating this is the process described by Grosfoguel (2004), who distinguishes between "racialized ethnicities"—as in the example of Puerto Ricans in New York—and "ethnicized races"—as in the example of using "Black" as an ethnic category. Ultimately, ethnic concepts continue to interact with racial identities. López (2008), for example, in a study of Puerto Rican women in a northeastern city, found that skin color interacted with ethnic identity in predicting self-esteem. Although for any given skin color, self-esteem tended to be higher with a stronger ethnic identity, this was particularly the case for light-skinned women.

Another focal question has to do with the conditions under which Latinos will see themselves as linked to the larger community around them. When will they make the effort, for example, to bridge their neighborhoods and relatively homogeneous communities with the larger world? For Latinos embedded in a highly Latina/o community: when will they venture out, and for what purposes? For those Latinos embedded in a mostly non-Latino context, what will trigger or lead them to reconnect (or connect) to the Latino world? And how do they feel about such connections? One example we have encountered repeatedly in our leadership development workshops for Latina and Latino leaders relates to those who have been separated from Latino culture and suddenly find themselves immersed in the company of other Latino professionals. While cautious or resistant at first, many of these managers undergo what they describe as epiphanies about the value of claiming their Latino identity and sadness at having been separated from their Hispanic roots for too long.

Another paradox of advancement in a multicultural society is that it requires, at the same time, seemingly contradictory demands. On the one hand, at times we may need to submerge our differences to some extent, or at the very least learn to interact effectively across cultural and other identity boundaries with people who are different from us. On the other hand, we also need to be more willing to identify as a member of and even a representative of our group depending on the circumstances and our intentions (see, e.g., Ferdman 1997). When one is embedded in one's own group, the identity issues and tasks are different than in a multiethnic and multicultural context.

In this regard, then, another question our model seeks to address is the following: When and how do Latinos see (and experience) their differences from others as an advantage and value, rather than as a hindrance? How do they make attributions about differences?

Souto-Manning (2007) describes the poignant case of a mother from Mexico who changed the name of her third son from Idelbrando to Tommy when he entered kindergarten "so that no one would know he is Mexican. So that he would have a better chance to be successful in school than his brothers" (402). We contend that choices in such situations often reflect particular identity orientations. This mother apparently believed that success required a certain degree of assimilation, rather than contesting dominant values, for example. This is also a clear example of class and gender distinctions related to power and of the way in which subordinate status can limit one's range of response to different individuals and situations. We believe that if the mother had been a father instead, had come from the upper class, had been highly educated, or had other educational options open to her, she might have been more likely to challenge negative behaviors and to assert her rights and those of her son, without necessarily trying to change his name.

Another related question we raise is: How do Latinos understand and explain discrimination (Ferdman 2008)? This will also depend on their identity orientation, and in turn affect their identity development. Major, Gramzow, McCoy, Levin, Schmader, and Sidanius (2002), for example, found that Latinos who were rejected or experienced a negative outcome from Anglos[11] were less likely to interpret the event as discrimination to the degree that they believed in an individual mobility ideology (i.e., that it is possible for individuals to move upwards in the social hierarchy). In other words, those Latinos who believed strongly in the legitimacy of the intergroup status system were less likely to view rejection as associated with systematic discrimination. Thus it is likely that those individuals with more activist or systemic perspectives will more readily identify external barriers as contributing to incidents of discrimination. Absent such a broad view, other Latinos may internalize negative experiences and blame themselves for the poor treatment they are receiving. This kind of internalized oppression may be quite common among members of subordinated groups, especially when positive models from their group are scarce or absent.

Torres (2009), in a paper in part grounded in our 2001 model, argues that dealing with racism is a central developmental task for Latinos. The ability to recognize discrimination when it is present and to have multiple strategies to address these barriers is one important challenge for Latinos. The other challenge is to avoid claiming to be experiencing prejudice when it is not present.

Unfortunately, it is not always clear or possible to easily identify the difference based on the subtle nuances of organization dynamics.[12]

## Latino/a Identity Orientations as Adaptive Strategies

We have expanded our model of Latino and Latina ethnoracial identity orientations to take into fuller account these external shaping forces and to highlight the dynamic and adaptive utility of each orientation. This allows us to avoid the perception that any orientation is better or worse than another. We also reinforce the idea that identity is in a constant state of flux and is continuously shifting, depending on the circumstances of people's lives and how they are meeting the challenges they encounter. Our expanded model allows a deeper analysis of additional issues that are emerging. These issues include the following:

- The usefulness of each identity orientation in assisting individuals to adapt to and address issues in their environment.
- The societal and organizational demands that Latinos are encountering in various geographical and situational contexts in the United States, and the ways in which their current identity may lead to outcomes that are more versus less functional. For example, considering the current anti-immigrant sentiment sweeping much of the country, Latinos living in states adjacent to the Mexican borderlands may be faced with more blatant and negative encounters, policies, and legislation than those residing in areas with fewer Latinos and a lower perceived threat.
- Given the fluidity of the orientations we describe, the ways in which these orientations may form in the first place and the triggers of movement between them.

In this section we present our current thinking about how the Latino identity orientations we described in our earlier work (Ferdman and Gallegos 2001; Gallegos and Ferdman 2007) have shifted and developed based on our ongoing practice, expanded perspective, and further inquiry. In particular, the issue of "choice" as it relates to social group identification has continued to interest us over the years (Ferdman 1990; Ferdman 1995; Ferdman 1997; Ferdman and Gallegos 2001; Garza and Gallegos 1995). Although we maintain that individuals do ultimately determine their own relationship to their racial and ethnic group memberships, it is also true that these choices are not made in a vacuum. There are forces at play in our families, organizations, and institutions that exert considerable pressure on individuals and strongly influence the range of likely choices available. The stronger these forces, the more difficult it becomes to make independent choices about how one thinks and feels about one's group identifications. To further complicate matters, these forces are not static but rather are in constant motion and interact with each other in a wide range of permutations. As a result, our identities morph and change depending on how we respond and react to the changing contexts of our lives. We are interested in how external and internal forces interact to create certain typical patterns of identity among Latinos.[13] Consistent with our earlier admonitions, we are challenged to honor and validate each of the orientations without ranking some over others. We find it helpful to recognize the adaptive value of each and how they are able to support Latinos in meeting the complexity of their social worlds with integrity and coherence.

In thinking about what is adaptive, we draw from the writing of Ronald Heifetz (e.g., Heifetz 1994; Heifetz, Grashow, and Linsky 2009) who contrasts technical and adaptive work. In Heifetz's conceptualization, related to Complex Adaptive Systems (Holland 1995), he acknowledges that most situations require a combination of technical and adaptive solutions. For example, a monolingual Spanish-speaking child may enter the U.S. school system with a sense of clear identification with her Mexican culture, having spent the majority of her life surrounded primarily by Mexican family and friends. At that point, she is most likely to have a Subgroup-Identified orientation, seeing herself as Mexican (American), and having little awareness of or contact with Latinos from other backgrounds or cultures. As she begins to become acclimated to the school system, she may become increasingly aware that her teacher and many of the other students are not like her in significant ways, and she may begin to question her previously taken-for-granted worldview. Before that, adjusting to her environment could be described primarily as a technical adaptation, one that "can be resolved through the application of authoritative expertise and through the organization's current structures, procedures and ways of doing things" (Heifetz, Grashow, and Linsky 2009, 19). She was able to rely on developing skills and knowledge based on what worked for her in the past, rather than needing to create new understandings or mental models.

As she comes in contact with teachers and students who distinctly are not Mexican and who do not even speak Spanish, her world becomes more complex and her previous models are challenged. It is at this point that she may find her identity unsettling and perhaps even upsetting. In Kegan's (1994) language, this person is distinctly "in over her head," with a growing awareness that what has helped her perform and succeed in the past is no longer enough to support her through current challenges. But at the same time, she has not yet developed the necessary competencies or perspectives to navigate in the new environment. This experience of encountering a "disorienting dilemma" is consistent with transformative learning theory, which posits these moments as learning opportunities that serve to further expand individuals' definition of their personal and collective identities (Wasserman and Gallegos 2009, 156).

Here, we argue that each Latino identity orientation has value and is useful at meeting particular environmental demands. As outlined in Table 3.1, we see the challenges and limitations together with the value in each orientation, and these depend on the context and the individual's particular situation. Four of the orientations are best suited for relatively homogeneous situations in which technical solutions can guide behavior. The other two orientations are better suited for more complex and unpredictable environments, in which adaptive solutions are particularly required.

In revisiting the orientations, we discuss the key challenges and dilemmas that must be managed by individuals who maintain those perspectives. To maximize the value of each orientation, one should be aware of and have strategies for managing the dilemmas that are associated with it. We also highlight those situations for which each orientation is ideally suited as well as how the particular orientation might manifest behaviorally. In other words, what might a person who holds that worldview be likely to think and do in response to environmental challenges and opportunities? We then discuss the limitations of each perspective and how it may constrain an individual's ability to effectively manage in certain contexts and situations. Far from representing a predetermined set of outcomes, we argue that individuals are quite adaptive and creative in their ways of solving life's problems and maintaining an equilibrium through an empowered sense of themselves in the world. This sense of agency allows Latinos to cope and thrive in a wide range of circumstances and creatively meet the world every day in unique ways.

### WHITE-IDENTIFIED

White-Identified individuals tend to be assimilated into the dominant American ideology and culture, and to view the environment from the White perspective and in the context of White, European American culture. They see themselves as different from and perhaps superior to people of color and in some cases may not self-identify as Latino or Hispanic. The person who maintains a White-Identified orientation has often survived through the challenges of environments in which positive images of Latinos were absent and in which negative images were often typical. Under these circumstances,

*Table 3.1: Latina and Latino Identity Orientations as Adaptive Strategies*

| Orientation | Lens | Identify as/prefer | Latinos are seen | Whites are seen | Framing of Race | Key Challenges | Most Adaptive for | Behavioral Manifestations | Limitations |
|---|---|---|---|---|---|---|---|---|---|
| Latino-Integrated | Wide | Individuals in a group context | Positively | Complex | Dynamic, contextual, socially constructed | Retain identity while remaining open to differences | Highly diverse and changing environments | Hold multiple perspectives & adaptability | When need to advocate for own group |
| Latino Identified | Broad | Latinos | Very positively | Distinct; could be barriers or allies | Latino/not Latino | Maintaining positive view of group yet not diminishing others | Called upon to develop strategies to support Latinos | Capacity to maximize differences constructively | Might miss complexity within or between Latino groups/Over-identification |
| Subgroup Identified | Narrow | Own sub-group | My group OK, others maybe | Not central (could be barriers or blockers) | Not clear or central; secondary to nationality, ethnicity, culture | Maintaining balanced view of subgroup/Avoiding gaps in vision | Relatively homogenous environments with minimal interaction | Maintaining close ties to culture of origin | Where coalitions or allies needed, or interactions with diverse groups or changing environments |
| Latino as Other | External | Not White | Generically, fuzzily | Negatively | White/not White | Making strategic choices; avoiding superficial solutions | Where dominant groups are "others" & accentuating differences not supported | Risk aversion; Minimal attention to variations, patterns | Encapsulated marginality; confusion or disorientation in the face of complexity |
| Undifferentiated/Denial | Closed | People | "Who are Latinos?" | Supposedly color-blind (accept dominant norms) | Denial, irrelevant, invisible | Recognizing benefits and costs; Missing out on richness of diversity | Where differences aren't central or don't matter & homogeneity is valued | Maintain harmony especially in relation to dominant groups | Situations where do not or cannot see that differences = disadvantage |
| White-Identified | Tinted | Whites | Negatively | Very positively | White/Black, either/or, one-drop or "mejorar la raza" (i.e., improve the race) | Seeing limitations and positive aspects of Latinos & Whites | Oppressive environment; where need to achieve outcomes depends on fitting in | Avoidance of multi-ethnic environments where differences emphasized | Impact on group identification and individual or collective esteem |

it may be very difficult to develop a sense of Latino identity that includes seeing one's group as having favorable assets and valuable cultural character-istics. Either passively or actively, these individuals have been encouraged to see dominant groups (i.e., European Americans) more favorably, and as hav-ing qualities and cultural capital that is better than that of Latinos. In these situations, there is sometimes a "disidentification" with one's own cultural group and an elevated perception of Whites. It is challenging for Latinos with this perspective to develop a balanced view of either Whites or Latinos that includes both positive and negative aspects.

White-Identified Latinos may have developed a tendency to avoid situ-ations where ethnoracial differences are highlighted, finding them uncom-fortable and awkward. This way of relating to the world can be functional when conformity to the dominant culture is required and when the inability to fit in has serious negative consequences. For example, some organizations may be homogeneous with minimal social diversity, or if they contain indi-viduals from diverse backgrounds, may continue to operate in a primarily monocultural manner. Senior leaders in such organizations may emphasize similarity and see those who challenge the status quo as threatening the sta-bility of the operation. In these situations—whether maintained intention-ally or unintentionally—it may be quite difficult or even harmful for Latinos to view or amplify their difference from the dominant majority. Consistent with the intersectional approach, consideration of the larger forces of power and privilege allows us to better understand and interpret the White-Identi-fied perspective beyond simply an individual level of analysis (Collins 2009).

### UNDIFFERENTIATED/DENIAL

Latinos with an Undifferentiated or Denial orientation tend either to deny or not to see cultural and ethnic differences. They generally tend not to con-nect with other Latinos based on lack of contact or awareness about their group. The Undifferentiated orientation can be distinguished from other ori-entations by the absence of negative or positive attitudes toward Latino iden-tity. This may develop in individuals who have not been exposed to Latino culture, or among those for whom there was an overall absence of overt cul-tural influences. The challenge for those with this orientation is first to rec-ognize their own cultural and ethnic influences, and then to recognize the assets or limitations of their culture.

The Undifferentiated orientation can be functional in circumstances where it is normative not to notice or comment on color, race, or cultural identity, and where performance is seen as unrelated to personal or interper-sonal dimensions. This includes highly regimented production environments or those in which individual contributions are valued over team or group collaboration. The costs of the Undifferentiated orientation can be felt in situations in which having an attachment to and/or knowledge of one's culture would be beneficial, for example during times of transition when having shared cultural experiences can provide support. An Undifferentiated orientation can also result in a sense of cultural confusion or disorientation when individuals find themselves in multicultural situations in which having a cultural identification is expected or valued, such as when an undergraduate attends a college where Latino students have formed student groups for support and advocacy. Encountering overt or covert discrimination may also be confusing for people with this orientation, because they have a limited understanding of systemic or structural analyses of societal phenomena. A potential advantage to the Undifferentiated orientation can be the maintenance of harmony at all costs and confluence where differences are ignored and conflict is avoided.

### LATINO AS OTHER

Individuals with this orientation generally see themselves as "not White" but without much differentiation among Latinos. Those with this orientation generally see themselves as "minorities" or "people of color" (in contrast to Whites). Thus, the Latino as Other orientation represents those who do have a general association with and consciousness of being Latino, but who do not have an in-depth sense of the history, traditions, or cultural markers associated with the collective and with their particular heritage. They are not identified closely with any Latino subgroup in particular, and yet are aware of their connection to the group as a whole. This orientation can develop in those who live in a highly diverse community where Latinos are from a wide range of countries, classes, and backgrounds, or whose parents come from multiple backgrounds. Those with this orientation see themselves as "not White," but have not gone beyond that awareness to have a more nuanced perspective of the cultural complexities of their group. Given that many Latinos who are raised in the United States were not taught world history, and particularly Latin American and Latino history, and so remain largely oblivious to the wide range of backgrounds and histories represented under the large umbrella of "Latino," this may be a differentiating factor from Latin American immigrants whose education and exposure was broader in this sense.

This orientation may be especially adaptive in heterogeneous situations where many groups and subgroups are involved and where recognizing subtle patterns and variations is not a priority. Particularly among urban and young populations, the common identification with many groups may be organized around other dimensions, such as popular culture, world music, or the urban lifestyle (Kao and Joyner 2006). Indeed, Latino music has shown a great deal of convergence and a blurring of boundaries (see, e.g., Padilla 1989). In some contexts, those with the Latino as Other orientation may not attend to or discuss cultural differences between Latinos and other groups or among Latinos from different subgroups in any depth or may not see them as being particularly relevant to their day-to-day interactions. A challenge for those with this orientation is the necessity to make strategic choices about when their differences might be valuable and when the ability to attend to within-group variation would further their purpose (for example, political outreach to various subgroups requiring a nuanced understanding of how best to interface with each group in a distinct way).

### SUBGROUP IDENTIFIED

Latinos who are Subgroup Identified see themselves primarily in the context of their own separate and distinct national-origin group (e.g., Puerto Rican, Cuban, Colombian, etc.), often seeing their own group more positively than other Latino subgroups. This orientation involves a strong attachment to one's country of origin and the culture of one's particular group.[14]

The challenge here is when there is a need to interact and/or ally with those from other subgroups. Latinos who are Subgroup Identified may have had minimal lived experiences with other Latinos and may be ill-prepared to deal with those from other backgrounds. They need to balance their awareness and positive attachment to their own group with the recognition that other groups also have positive traditions and values that are equally valid. As long as these Latinos remain in circumstances where they have limited need to engage across these boundaries, being Subgroup Identified can be a functional choice. There is value in maintaining one's sense of subgroup membership, as this can provide a strong and secure foundation for meeting the world. On the other hand, in situations where having clear alliances across groups is important, this orientation might be challenging. This orientation also has political ramifications, as the emphasis on the differences between Latino subgroups could lead to negative judgments of other Latinos and unwillingness to form coalitions to address societal issues affecting Latinos as a whole, such as immigration, educational disparities, and adequate representation on the local and national levels.

### LATINO IDENTIFIED

Individuals who are Latino Identified generally see Latinos in a unitary and unified way, tending to advocate for Latinos as a whole, and to be aware of but not to emphasize subgroup differences, some of which they may gloss over. They view Latinos overall as constituting a distinct ethnoracial category across all national origin subgroups, while maintaining a distinctly Latino and dynamic view of race.[15] The Latino Identified orientation is relatively broad, and those with this perspective feel a sense of connection to all who may fit into the category of Latino, essentially transcending particular cultural markers. Those with this orientation tend to emphasize the unity and connections among all Latinos, and often have a good deal of knowledge and awareness of Latino culture and history, particularly the shared values, histories, and traditions that cut across subgroups. Given the expansiveness of this perspective, those with this orientation are best suited for developing strategies and policies with a wide reach. They are able to distinguish those situations where maximizing differences is ideal as well as those times where strategically minimizing them would serve their interests. Clearly, for political organizing and mobilizing resources, they can build bridges and bring people together from many distinct groups in service of collective objectives.[16]

## LATINO INTEGRATED

Those individuals with a Latino Integrated orientation see being Latino as important in the context of all their other identities, which are also seen as vital. Latinos with this orientation are aware of the ways in which race is dynamic, contextual, and socially constructed, and they understand how their own experience and that of others integrates aspects not only of their particular Latino story, but also of their gender, class, religion, profession, and so on. Thus, the Latino Integrated orientation is the most complex of all the orientations. Latino Integrated individuals can tolerate ambiguity and live in a world of paradox and contradiction. They are able to maintain a clear but fluid sense of their own multiple identifications, while continuing to be able to empathize with others and to view the world from many, and sometimes contradictory, perspectives. They are best adapted for rapidly changing environments where there is little predictability or routine and where constant adaptation is needed. Their orientation may develop and emerge from lived experiences that allowed their view of their Latino identity to expand and broaden with minimal constraint. They were exposed to many different geographical regions, classes, generations, and lifestyles, which taught them to avoid stereotyping others or forming narrow opinions. Latino Integrated individuals can often be misunderstood by Latinos who locate themselves in the other orientations and may perceive this group as having lost their subgroup identification or as too willing to tolerate societal injustice due to their equanimity in the face of contradictions. Here again we see the simultaneous intersection of race, class, gender, and education with Latina and Latino ethnoracial identity. Access to a wide range of cultures different from one's own is heavily influenced by socioeconomic status, gender roles, and mobility. Absent contact with these other environments and cultures, it becomes difficult for an individual to experience cultural variations and to develop the broader perspective of this particular orientation.

## Closing Reflections and Practical Applications

Other authors (e.g., Adams 2001; Atkinson, Morten, and Sue 1998; Phinney, DuPont, Espinosa, Revill, and Sanders 1994) have made strong and convincing arguments in favor of collapsing various racial identity models into overarching models that take into account the similarities among subordinated groups in the United States. While appreciating the validity of those theoretical directions for certain purposes, we also see the emphasis on distinctions among racial and ethnic groups as having value. Given the unique aspects of the Latino experience in the United States, we think it is particularly important that the nuances of Latino identity be understood and more deeply explored. As the Latino presence continues to expand and issues related to the inclusion of Latinos into mainstream society become increasingly urgent, we see it as critical to attend to the adaptive challenges facing Latinos and the requisite cross-cultural competencies required of non-Latinos.

Key elements of intercultural competence that have been identified by a wide range of researchers include the capacity to amplify rather than minimize the differences among various identity groups (Bennett and Bennett 2004). Although sometimes well-intended, the tendency to focus only on similarities and to avoid differences can lead to negative outcomes. In other words, we contend that the myth of the melting pot was never a useful metaphor for guiding us through the paradoxical terrain of social identities. In spite of the idealization of the melting pot by many as the paramount goal of a democratic society, we believe that it is only by identifying, appreciating, and using our differences that the true competitive advantages of diversity can be achieved. The full utilization and inclusion of the Latino community demands more sophisticated analysis and more complex analytical tools and models that do not simplistically equate them with all other subordinated groups or that gloss over important within-group diversity.

We are hopeful that ongoing exploration of the questions and issues we have raised in this chapter will lead to greater dialogue with, about, and among Latinos. We are especially interested in the implications of our work for organizational leaders as they consider what to make of the burgeoning Latino workforce, population, and market. Once Latinos have proven themselves as committed workers, organizations must turn to the more difficult challenge of integrating them into all functions and levels. In our consulting practice, savvy organizations are investing in developing their own leadership from within by identifying high potential employees and providing them with the right developmental experiences and coaching them to successfully navigate through the political and cultural labyrinths of each organization. Finding ways to tap into Latino talent is a strategic issue that requires foresight and upfront investment of time and resources but will eventually pay huge dividends when Latinos are able to bring all aspects of their identities to bear on creating competitive advantage. Realizing this goal will require recognizing the great diversity among Latinos and its implications, some of which we have tried to describe in this chapter.

A related area that is ripe for further research and reflection has to do with the challenges and opportunities of developing effective partnerships between Latinos and other ethnoracial groups, such as African Americans, Native Americans, Jews, and Asians. Given the complexity of and diversity within each of these and other groups, finding points of alignment and creative approaches to deal with cultural, social, and historical conflicts requires focused scholarly and practical attention. In our future work, we hope to provide further examples and case studies of organizational efforts that have been successful as well as those that have failed to accomplish their desired outcomes. Significant examples derived from educational, political, and business situations help elucidate the role that environmental factors play in determining which of the identity orientations is best suited for each particular context.

We have described the imperative to take into account the multiple dimensions of social identity that occur simultaneously and how the analytic framework of Intersectionality allows us to do so. There is also an ongoing challenge for researchers and practitioners to utilize this approach. Given that the shifting nature of identity depends on specific circumstances and social locations, it becomes a daunting task to identify which aspects are most salient at any particular time and how other aspects are interrelated. The scholars represented in this volume and others are making progress in developing methods of addressing the challenges of the intersectional approach. As it relates to Latinas/os and our model, we encourage further exploration and testing of our perspective so as to support greater clarity about and insight into Latino/a identity, and we hope that it is done in ways that can effectively inform ethical practice in organizations such that it is inclusive and that it recognizes and honors the rich diversity among Latinos.

As we have highlighted in this chapter and in our previous work, acknowledging the vast range of diversity present within the Latino community is essential if we are to succeed in maximizing their contribution. We are hopeful that our expanded perspectives on Latino ethnoracial identity orientations will lead to deeper engagement and greater tolerance for ambiguity and the inherent contradictions of carving out an identity in our increasingly diverse society.

## NOTES

1. This chapter was written in full collaboration. Authorship is listed in reverse alphabetical order.

2. We generally use the term *Latinos* to refer both to women and men, to avoid using the cumbersome *Latina/o* or the phrase *Latinas and Latinos* in every case, although we often use the longer terms to highlight our discomfort with the exclusive use of the male-gendered noun or adjective, *Latino*. We have also reversed the order in many cases by placing Latinas before Latinos in our attempt to further rectify the problematic language issue.

3. In government, we have seen appointments of Latinos across the political spectrum, including Alberto Gonzales as Attorney General by President George W. Bush and Ken Salazar as Secretary of the Interior by President Obama. Richard Carmona served as Surgeon General of the United States from 2002 to 2006, and Bob Menendez (D-NJ) and Marco Rubio (R-FL) serve in the U.S. Senate. Also, twenty-four Latinos and Latinas serve in the current (2011) House of Representatives, constituting 5.5 percent of that body.

4. We see Latinos on various TV shows including *American Idol*, *CSI*, and even *Lost*, in many cases without much note of their ethnicity. Other notable Latinas and Latinos on television include Jimmy Smits, Lauren Velez, David Zayas, Valerie Cruz, Jason Manuel Olazabal, Ana Ortiz, Tony Plana, Freddy Rodriguez, Salma Hayek, and Demi Lovato on Disney's "Camp Rock."

5. According to the National Center for Educational Statistics (http://nces.ed.gov/fast-facts/display.asp?id=16), in 2008 the dropout rate for Hispanic youths ages 16 to 24 was 18.3 percent, compared to 14.6 percent among Alaskan Native/American Indian youth, 9.9 percent among Black youth, 4.8 percent among White youth, and 4.4 percent among Asian/Pacific Islander youth.

6. Hayes-Bautista (2004) describes the reactions of non-Hispanic White focus groups to a television commercial created by the Mexican American Legal Defense Fund (MALDEF) in 1998 to portray positive and more realistic images of Latinos. These focus group participants tended to reject the images in the commercial as inconsistent with their assumptions about Latinos; the participants did not believe that Latinos could be part of the middle class or that they had aspirations to obtain an education or to achieve some of the outcomes portrayed in the commercial.

7. Juan Flores (2000), in his book, *From Bomba to Hip-Hop: Puerto Rican Culture and Latino Identity*, quotes Martha Giménez to point out a great danger in using the

generic, overarching "Hispanic" category: "'these labels are racist,' Giménez says, 'in that . . . they reduce people to interchangeable entities, negating the qualitative differences between, for example, persons of Puerto Rican descent who have lived for generations in New York City and newly arrived immigrants from Chile or some other South or Central American country'" (Giménez, cited in Flores 2000, 153). We do not go as far as Giménez in advocating elimination of the concept of *Latino* or *Hispanic*, but we do share the view that it should not be used as a way of glossing over the great diversity that exists within this group.

8. Interestingly, 97 percent of the people who indicated that they were of "some other race" alone were Latinos.

9. For example, Uhlmann, Dasgupta, Elgueta, Greenwald, and Swanson (2002) found preferences in implicit attitudes among both U.S. Latinos and Chileans for "Blancos" (i.e., those with lighter complexions) over "Morenos" (those with darker complexions), and this was true regardless of the respondent's own identification with regard to skin color. Interestingly, Chileans showed an implicit bias in favor of Whites ("Gringos") relative to "Hispanos," but U.S. Hispanics did not.

10. Jiménez (2004) studied individuals in California who had one Mexican American and one White non-Hispanic parent. In an interview study with twenty such participants, he found that even though they tended to prefer a Mexican American ethnic identity, there was some variation in this regard, and factors such as skin color or last name played an important role. The interviewees' choices were complicated by their experience of what Jiménez refers to as "sharp boundaries between ethnic categories" (2004, 84), or the requirement in some situations to make mutually exclusive choices. In some cases, for example around Mexican American relatives, or in Mexican American cultural events or groups, the respondents did not feel sufficiently Mexican American. In other case, for example when confronted with White racism, their sense of connection with Mexican Americans was heightened. Ultimately, Jiménez describes a range of approaches adopted by his interviewees, including adopting symbolic identity—connections based largely on symbols such as food or some holidays, taking on a strong Mexican American identity, and a multiethnic approach.

11. We and others use this term to refer to non-Hispanic Whites. This was the term used by Major et al. (2002) in their paper.

12. Interestingly, the experience of racial discrimination can be affected by other identities in addition to race. Ibañez, Van Oss Marin, Flores, Millett, and Diaz (2009), for example, in their study of racism as experienced by Latino gay men, found that those men who were darker or had more Indian features, as well as those who had been in the United States longer, reported more experiences of racism, both in general and in gay environments.

13. One example of the variation in how Latinos think about their group membership comes from a study by Charmaraman and Grossman (2010). Using questionnaires asking for ratings of the importance of race/ethnicity in respondents' self-concept together with a grounded theory approach to analyze explanations for these responses, these researchers found great diversity among Latino adolescents in how they thought about their racial/ethnic identity and its importance. While the largest proportion (40%) of Latino responses focused on internal pride, these responses also included uncertainty (5%), awareness of both stereotypes (8%) and discrimination (4%), color-blindness (8%), and external pride (24%).

14. Ek (2009), for example, presents an ethnographic and longitudinal case study of a Pentecostal Guatemalan American young woman, daughter of immigrants, and shows how the combination of her religious identity and practice with frequent visits to Guatemala allowed her to maintain an identity distinct from the Mexican and Chicano culture surrounding her.

15. Masuoka (2006) found that Latinos were more likely to have a panethnic view of Latinos to the extent that they had more education, were foreign-born, were involved in politics, and perceived more discrimination. Women tended to have more of a sense of Latino group consciousness than men.

16. Interestingly, Sanchez (2008), using data from the 1999 National Survey of Latinos, found that Latinos were more likely to perceive commonalities with African Americans as a function of their own sense of group consciousness or of having something in common with other Latinos, as well as their perceptions of discrimination against Latinos. Sanchez concludes that a strong sense of Latino panethnicity can be an important contributor to developing political alliances with African Americans.

REFERENCES

Adams, Maurianne. 2001. "Core Processes in Racial Identity Development." In *New Perspectives on Racial Identity Development: A Theoretical and Practical Anthology*, edited by Charmaine L. Wijeyesinghe and Bailey W. Jackson III, 209–242. New York: NYU Press.

Aranda, Elizabeth, and Guillermo Rebollo-Gil. 2004. "Ethnoracism and the 'Sandwiched' Minorities." *American Behavioral Scientist* 47: 910–927.

Atkinson, Donald R., George Morten, and Derald Wing Sue. 1998. *Counseling American Minorities: A Cross-Cultural Perspective*, 5th ed. New York: McGraw-Hill.

Barreto, Matt A., Loren Collingwood, and Sylvia Manzano. 2010. "A New Measure of Group Influence in Presidential Elections: Assessing Latino Influence in 2008." *Political Research Quarterly* 6: 908–921. doi:10.1177/1065912910367493.

Bennett, Janet M., and Milton J. Bennett. 2004. "Developing Intercultural Sensitivity: An Integrative Approach to Global and Domestic Diversity." In *Handbook of Intercultural Training*, 3rd ed., edited by Dan Landis, Janet M. Bennett, and Milton J. Bennett, 147–165. Thousand Oaks, Calif.: Sage.

Cabassa, Leopoldo J. 2003. "Measuring Acculturation: Where We Are and Where We Need to Go." *Hispanic Journal of Behavioral Sciences* 25: 127–147.

Campbell, Mary E., and Christabel L. Rogalin. 2006. "Categorical Imperatives: The Interaction of Latino and Racial Identification." *Social Science Quarterly* 87: 1030–1052.

CBS Business Network. 2010, September 17. "Univision Anchor Jorge Ramos Sits Down with Arizona Governor Jan Brewer for First Exclusive Spanish-Language Interview." http://findarticles.com/p/articles/mi_m0EIN/is_20100917/ai_n55271158.

Charmaraman, Linda, and Jennifer M. Grossman. 2010. "Importance of Race and Ethnicity: An Exploration of Asian, Black, Latino, and Multiracial Adolescent Identity." *Cultural Diversity and Ethnic Minority Psychology* 16: 144–151. doi:10.1037/a0018668.

Cobas, José A, Jorge Duany, and Joe R. Feagin, eds. 2009. *How the U.S. Racializes Latinos: White Hegemony and Its Consequences*. Boulder, Colo.: Paradigm Publishers.

Collins, Patricia Hill. 2009. "Foreword: Emerging Intersections—Building Knowledge and Transforming Institutions." In *Emerging Intersections: Race, Class, and Gender in Theory,*

*Policy and Practice*, edited by Bonnie Thornton Dill and Ruth Enid Zambrana, vii–xvii. New Brunswick, N.J.: Rutgers University Press.

Cooper, Kenneth J. 2011. "New Analysis: Home Mortgages to Minorities Plummet by 62 Percent." *Truth Out*, accessed February 13, 2011. http://www.truth-out.org/new-analysis-home-mortgages-minorities-plummet-62-percent67653.

Denton, Nancy A., and Douglas S. Massey. 1989. "Racial Identity among Caribbean Hispanics: The Effect of Double Minority Status on Residential Segregation." *American Sociological Review* 54: 790–808.

Dill, Bonnie Thornton, Amy E. McLaughlin, and Angel David Nieves. 2007. "Future Directions of Feminist Research: Intersectionality." In *Handbook of Feminist Research*, edited by Sharlene N. Hesse-Biber, 629–637. Thousand Oaks, Calif.: Sage.

Ek, Lucila D. 2009. "Allá en Guatemala": Transnationalism, Language, and Identity of a Pentecostal Guatemalan-American Young Woman." *The High School Journal* 92, no. 4: 67–82.

Ferdman, Bernardo M. 1990. "Literacy and Cultural Identity." *Harvard Educational Review* 60: 181–204.

———. 1995. "Cultural Identity and Diversity in Organizations: Bridging the Gap between Group Differences and Individual Uniqueness." In *Diversity in Organizations: New Perspectives for a Changing Workplace*, edited by Martin M. Chemers, Stuart Oskamp, and Mark Costanzo, 37–61. Thousand Oaks, Calif.: Sage.

———. 1997. "Values about Fairness in the Ethnically Diverse Workplace." Special Issue: Managing in a Global Context: Diversity and Cross-Cultural Challenges. *Business and the Contemporary World: An International Journal of Business, Economics, and Social Policy* 9: 191–208.

———. 1999. "The Color and Culture of Gender in Organizations: Attending to Race and Ethnicity." In *Handbook of Gender and Work*, edited by Gary N. Powell, 17–34. Thousand Oaks, Calif.: Sage.

———. 2008. "Who Perceives More Discrimination? Individual Difference Predictors among Latinos and Anglos." *Business Journal of Hispanic Research* 2: 71–75.

Ferdman, Bernardo M., and Plácida I. Gallegos. 2001. "Racial Identity Development and Latinos in the United States." In *New Perspectives on Racial Identity Development: A Theoretical and Practical Anthology*, edited by Charmaine L. Wijeyesinghe and Bailey W. Jackson III, 32–66. New York: NYU Press.

Flores, Juan. 2000. *From Bomba to Hip-Hop: Puerto Rican Culture and Latino Identity*. New York: Columbia University Press.

Frank, Reanne, Ilana Redstone Akresh, and Bo Lu. 2010. "Latino Immigrants and the U.S. Racial Order: How and Where Do They Fit In?" *American Sociological Review* 75: 378–401.

Gallegos, Plácida I., and Bernardo M. Ferdman. 2007. "Identity Orientations of Latinos in the United States: Implications for Leaders and Organizations." *Business Journal of Hispanic Research* 1: 27–41.

Garza, R. T., and Plácida I. Gallegos. 1995. "Environmental Influences and Personal Choice: A Humanistic Perspective on Acculturation." In *Hispanic Psychology: Critical Issues in Theory and Research*, edited by Amado M. Padilla, 3–14. Thousand Oaks, Calif.: Sage.

Gifford, Brian. 2005. "Combat Casualties and Race: What Can We Learn from the 2003–2004 Iraq Conflict?" *Armed Forces & Society* 31: 201–225.

Golash-Boza, Tanya, and William Darity, Jr. 2008. "Latino Racial Choices: The Effects of Skin Colour and Discrimination on Latinos' and Latinas' Racial Self-Identifications." *Ethnic and Racial Studies* 24: 1–36.

Gonzales, Nancy A., Fairlee C. Fabrett, and George P. Knight. 2009. "Acculturation, Enculturation, and the Psychological Adaptation of Latino Youth." In *Handbook of U.S. Latino Psychology: Developmental and Community-Based Perspectives*, edited by Francisco A. Villarruel, Gustavo Carlo, Josefina M. Grau, Margarita Azmitia, Natasha J. Cabrera, and T. Jaime Chahín, 115–134. Thousand Oaks, Calif.: Sage.

Grosfoguel, Ramán. 2004. "Race and Ethnicity or Racialized Ethnicities? Identities within Global Coloniality." *Ethnicities* 4: 315–336. doi: 10.1177/1468796804045237.

Hayes-Bautista, David E. 2004. *La Nueva California: Latinos in the Golden State*. Berkeley: University of California Press.

Heifetz, Ronald. 1994. *Leadership without Easy Answers*. Cambridge, Mass.: Belknap Press.

Heifetz, Ronald, Alexander Grashow, and Marty Linsky. 2009. *The Practice of Adaptive Leadership: Tools and Tactics for Changing Your Organization and the World*. Boston: Harvard Business Press.

Higuera, Jonathan. 2010, December. "The Sleeping Giant Is Waking Up." *Latino Perspectives*. http://latinopm.com/features/the-sleeping-giant-is-waking-up-5309.

Holland, John H. 1995. *Hidden Order: How Adaptation Builds Complexity*. New York: Perseus Books.

Holleran, Lori K. 2003. "Mexican American Youth of the Southwest Borderlands: Perceptions of Ethnicity, Acculturation, and Race." *Hispanic Journal of Behavioral Sciences* 25: 352–369.

Holvino, Evangelina. 2010. "Intersections: The Simultaneity of Race, Gender, and Class in Organization Studies." Special Issue: Gender and Ethnicity. *Gender, Work and Organization* 17: 248–277. doi: 10.1111/j.1468-0432.2008.00400.x.

Ibañez, Gladys E., Barbara Van Oss Marin, Stephen A. Flores, Gregorio Millett, and Rafael M. Diaz. 2009. "General and Gay-Related Racism Experienced by Latino Gay Men." *Cultural Diversity and Ethnic Minority Psychology* 15, no. 3 (July): 215–222.

Jiménez, Tomás R. 2004. "Negotiating Ethnic Boundaries: Multiethnic Mexican Americans and Ethnic Identity in the United States." *Ethnicities* 4: 75–97.

Jones, Susan R., and Charmaine L. Wijeyesinghe. 2011. "The Promises and Challenges of Teaching from an Intersectional Perspective: Core Components and Applied Strategies." In *New Directions for Teaching and Learning: An Integrative Analysis Approach to Diversity in the Classroom*, edited by Mathew L. Ouellett, 11–20. Wilmington, Del.: Wiley.

Kao, Grace, and Kara Joyner. 2006. "Do Hispanic and Asian Adolescents Practice Panethnicity in Friendship Choices?" *Social Science Quarterly* 87: 972–992.

Kao, Grace, and Jennifer S. Thompson. 2003. "Racial and Ethnic Stratification in Educational Achievement and Attainment." *Annual Review of Sociology* 29: 417–442.

Kegan, Robert. 1994. *In Over Our Heads: The Mental Demands of Modern Life*. Cambridge: Harvard University Press.

Kettle, Martin. 2008, November 7. "The Hispanic Vote Shaped the Contours of This Election." *The Guardian*.

Kirk, Gwyn, and Margo Okazawa-Rey, eds. 2007. *Women's Lives: Multicultural Perspectives*. New York: McGraw-Hill.

Kradenpoth, Jennifer, and Barbara Deane. 2010, September. "Diversity Practitioners Weigh in on Arizona's New Immigration Law." DiversityCentral.com.

Lacayo, A. Elena. 2010. "The Impact of Section 287(g) of the Immigration and Nationality Act on the Latino Community." Issue Brief no. 21, National Council of La Raza, Washington, D.C., http://www.nclr.org/images/uploads/publications/287gReportFinal.pdf.

Logan, John R. 2004. "How Race Counts for Hispanic Americans." *SAGE Race Relations Abstracts* 29: 7–19.

López, Ian Haney. 2005. "Race on the 2010 Census: Hispanics and the Shrinking White Majority." *Daedalus* 134: 42–52.

López, Irene R. 2008. "'But You Don't Look Puerto Rican': The Moderating Effect of Ethnic Identity on the Relation between Skin Color and Self-Esteem among Puerto Rican Women." *Cultural Diversity and Ethnic Minority Psychology* 14: 102–108.

Lopez, Mark H., and Susan Minushkin. 2008. *Hispanics See Their Situation in U.S. as Deteriorating: Oppose Key Immigration Enforcement Measures.* 2008 National Survey of Latinos. Washington, D.C.: Pew Hispanic Center. http://pewhispanic.org/reports/report.php? Report ID=93.

Major, Brenda, Richard H. Gramzow, Shannon K. McCoy, Shana Levin, Toni Schmader, and Jim Sidanius. 2002. "Perceiving Personal Discrimination: The Role of Group Status and Legitimizing Ideology." *Journal of Personality and Social Psychology* 82: 269–282.

Markert, John. 2010. "The Changing Face of Racial Discrimination: Hispanics as the Dominant Minority in the USA—A New Application of Power-Threat Theory." *Critical Sociology* 36: 307–327.

Massey, Douglas S., and Magaly Sanchez R. 2007. "Latino and American Identities as Perceived by Immigrants." *Qualitative Sociology* 30: 81–107.

Masuoka, Natalie. 2006. "Together They Become One: Examining the Predictors of Panethnic Group Consciousness among Asian Americans and Latinos." *Social Science Quarterly* 87, no. 1 (December): 993–1011. doi:10.1111/j.1540-6237.2006.00412.x.

McEwen, Marylu K. 2003. "New Perspectives on Identity Development." In *Student Services: A Handbook for the Profession,* edited by Susan R. Komives and Dudley B. Woodard, 203–233. San Francisco: Jossey-Bass.

Montalvo, Frank F., and G. Edward Codina. 2001. "Skin Color and Latinos in the United States." *Ethnicities* 1: 321–341. doi: 10.1177/146879680100100303.

National Association of Latino Elected Officials. 2008. *Latino Voters in the 2008 Presidential Election: Post-Election Survey of Latino Voters.* NALEO Educational Fund. http://www.naleo.org/downloads/Post-Election%20Survey.pdf.

National Institute for Latino Policy. 2010, September 20. *U.S.: Is There Racism among Hispanics?* http://myemail.constantcontact.com/NiLP-FYI—Racism-among-Latinos-.html?soid=1101040629095&aid=meM7ga1Oyio.

Padilla, Felix M. 1989. "Salsa Music as a Cultural Expression of Latino Consciousness and Unity." *Hispanic Journal of Behavioral Sciences* 11: 28–45. doi: 10.1177/07399863890111003.

Phinney, Jean S., Stephanie DuPont, Carolina Espinosa, Jessica Revill, and Kay Sanders. 1994. "Ethnic Identity and American Identification among Ethnic Minority Youths." In *Journeys into Cross-Cultural Psychology: Selected Papers from the Eleventh International Association for Cross-Cultural Psychology,* edited by A. Bouvy, Fons Van de Fijver, Pawel Boski, and P. Schmitz, 167–183. Berwyn, Pa.: Swets and Zeitlinger.

Sanchez, Gabriel R. 2008. "Latino Group Consciousness and Perceptions of Commonality with African Americans." *Social Science Quarterly* 89, no. 2: 428–444.

Schwartz, Seth J., Byron L. Zamboanga, and Lorna Hernandez Jarvis. 2007. "Ethnic Identity and Acculturation in Hispanic Early Adolescents: Mediated Relationships to Academic

Grades, Prosocial Behaviors, and Externalizing Symptoms." *Cultural Diversity and Ethnic Minority Psychology* 13: 364–373.

Souto-Manning, Mariana. 2007. "Immigrant Families and Children (Re-)Develop Identities in a New Context." *Early Childhood Education Journal* 34: 399–405.

Tafoya, Sonya. 2004. *Shades of Belonging*. Washington, D.C.: Pew Hispanic Center

Torres, Vasti. 2009. "The Developmental Dimensions of Recognizing Racist Thoughts." *Journal of College Student Development* 50: 504–520.

Torres, Vasti, Susan R. Jones, and Kristen A. Renn. 2009. "Identity Development Theories in Student Affairs: Origins, Current Status, and New Approaches." *Journal of College Student Development* 50: 577–596.

Torres-Saillant, Silvio. 2003. "Inventing the Race: Latinos and the Ethnoracial Pentagon." *Latino Studies* 1: 123–151.

Uhlmann, Eric, Nilanjana Dasgupta, Angelica Elgueta, Anthony **G.** Greenwald, and Jane Swanson. 2002. "Subgroup Prejudice Based on Skin Color among Hispanics in the United States and Latin America." *Social Cognition* 20: 198–226.

Umaña-Taylor, Adriana J., and Edna C. Alfaro. 2009. "Acculturative Stress and Adaptation." In *Handbook of U.S. Latino Psychology: Developmental and Community-Based Perspectives*, edited by Francisco A. Villarruel, Gustavo Carlo, Josefina M. Grau, Margarita Azmitia, Natasha J. Cabrera, and T. Jaime Chahín, 135–252. Thousand Oaks, Calif.: Sage.

U.S. Census Bureau. "Census 2000 Gateway." http://www.census.gov/main/www/cen2000. html. Accessed November 17, 2010.

———. "United States Census 2010: It's in Our Hands." http://2010.census.gov/2010census/ data. Accessed December 3, 2010.

Vaquera, Elizabeth, and Grace Kao. 2006. "The Implications of Choosing 'No Race' on the Salience of Hispanic Identity: How Racial and Ethnic Backgrounds Intersect among Hispanic Adolescents." *Sociological Quarterly* 47: 375–396.

Wasserman, Ilene, and Plácida V. Gallegos. 2009. "Engaging Diversity: Disorienting Dilemmas that Transform Relationships." In *Innovations in Transformative Learning: Space, Culture, and the Arts*, edited by Beth Fisher-Yoshida, Kathy Dee Geller, and Steven A. Schapiro, 155–175. New York: Peter Lang.

Wasserman, Ilene C., Plácida V. Gallegos, and Bernardo M. Ferdman. 2008. "Dancing with Resistance: Leadership Challenges in Fostering a Culture of Inclusion." In *Diversity Resistance in Organizations*, edited by Kecia M. Thomas, 175–200. New York: Taylor & Francis.

Weaver, Charles N. 2005. "The Changing Image of Hispanic Americans." *Hispanic Journal of Behavioral Sciences* 27: 337–354.

Wijeyesinghe, Charmaine L. 2001. "Racial Identity in Multiracial People: An Alternative Paradigm." In *New Perspectives on Racial Identity Development: A Theoretical and Practical Anthology*, edited by Charmaine L. Wijeyesinghe and Bailey W Jackson III, 32–66. New York: NYU Press.

Wing, Nick. 2010, September 20. "Jan Brewer: 'I Love' Hispanics and I'm 'Hurt' that They Would Think I'm Racist (VIDEO)." *Huffington Post*. http://www.huffingtonpost. com/2010/09/20/jan-brewer-i-love-hispani_n_731643.html

4

# The Intersectional Model of Multiracial Identity

*Integrating Multiracial Identity Theories and*
*Intersectional Perspectives on Social Identity*

CHARMAINE L. WIJEYESINGHE

## Introduction

Since 2000 research, literature, and commentary on Multiracial people has grown in both quantity and diversity.[1] From an initial focus on individuals of Black and White ancestry the literature on Multiracial people now includes the experiences of other Multiracial populations, such as Asian and Native American or Black and Latino individuals, as well as Multiracial people in other countries.[2] Results from research, advocacy, and social movements related to Multiracial people have advanced not only our understanding of Multiracial identity, but of identity development in other racial groups, and of the broader field of social identity development.

Other academic disciplines such as Women's Studies and Feminist Studies have identified innovative approaches to identity development that have yet to be fully discussed in the literature on racial identity development. In its next era of growth and refinement, Multiracial identity literature must consider the impact of these emerging perspectives on how we understand and depict the experience of Multiracial people. At this time, the framework of Intersectionality presents the most promise and urgency for attention and analysis. Intersectionality encourages, and some would contend requires, theorists to incorporate other social identities (gender, sexual orientation, and class, for example) in their description of how individuals develop and experience their racial identity.

This chapter explores the relationship between Multiracial identity and Intersectionality. The chapter begins with a brief overview of key terms that appear in the text, and then moves to a discussion of characteristics common to both Intersectionality and Multiracial identity literature. Next, the chapter reviews three Multiracial identity models, including the Factor Model of Multiracial Identity (Wijeyesinghe 1992; 2001), that highlight the impact of various influences on choice of racial identity. Additional factors not included in the FMMI but that appear in the new, intersectional model presented later are discussed next. The chapter then discusses the representation of intersectional models of identity, using a review of the Multiple Dimensions of Identity Model (Jones and McEwen 2000) as an example. The Intersectional Model of Multiracial Identity which integrates the analysis and content of the previous sections is presented next. The chapter concludes with a discussion of opportunities and challenges related to additional attempts to integrate Multiracial and racial identity theory with Intersectionality.

## Terminology

Many terms are used in the discussion of racial identity. However, the meaning of each is not always agreed upon. The following definitions indicate what key terms and concepts refer to in this chapter.

*Race* and *Ethnicity* are socially constructed concepts that divide the overall human population into subgroups based on aspects such as physical appearance, place of ancestral origin, historical and cultural experiences, language, and customs (Wijeyesinghe 1992; Wijeyesinghe, Griffin, and Love 1997). The definition of these concepts, and the name and number of groups used to indicate them evolve over time and in response to larger social and political changes. *Racial ancestry* and *ethnic ancestry* represent the race and ethnicity, respectively, claimed by a person's ancestors.

*Racial identity* refers to the racial category or categories that an individual uses to name him- or herself based on factors including racial ancestry, ethnicity, physical appearance, early socialization, recent or past personal experiences, and a sense of shared experience with members of a particular racial group. Reflecting a choice made by an individual at a given point in life, racial identity can change or remain the same throughout a person's lifetime.

*Ascribed racial group membership* is the racial group or groups that are assigned to an individual by other people and social institutions based on factors such as physical appearance, racial ancestry, and the social construction of race at a given social, cultural, and historical period. This ascribed racial group may or may not be consistent with the racial group that the individual actually identifies with, defined in this chapter as *chosen racial group membership*.

*Monoracial* and *multiracial* can refer to (1) a person's racial ancestry; (2) a person's chosen racial identity; (3) a racial group membership ascribed to a person; or (4) a person's chosen racial group membership. Monoracial represents any of these concepts when they reflect a single racial group. Multiracial refers to any of the concepts based on two or more racial groups.

## Core Characteristics Shared by Intersectionality and Multiracial Theory

The literature on Multiracial identity and Intersectionality share a number of characteristics and assumptions, including:

1. Emerging at the same time as more organized disciplines in order to address populations not represented in the existing literature or discussion of identity, social oppression, or social justice.
2. Framing identity at the individual level in a broader and more holistic manner, and the result of the interaction of multiple factors at particular moments in a person's life.
3. Acknowledging that individuals can simultaneously inhabit positions of social privilege and marginality, and that these social positions influence both the experience of a particular aspect of identity (such as race, class, or gender) and overall identity.
4. Viewing identity at the individual (or micro) level as complex and complicated, evolving and changing over the course of an one's life span; at the same time accounting for the impact of larger social and political contexts (at the macro level) on how identity is framed and experienced.
5. Placing at the forefront of discussion and study the voices of individuals who were previously excluded from research and movements for social justice, and promoting grounded research to investigate the lived experience of individuals within these groups.
6. Using the discipline to enact social change in order to address inequity and promote social justice.

Each of these areas is now discussed in more detail.

Emergence: When and Why

Focused research and writing on Multiracial identity and Intersectionality emerged in the late 1980s and early 1990s with studies, commentary, and papers in both disciplines highlighting the need to expand our understanding of how individuals experienced identity. In the case of Intersectionality, Kimberle Crenshaw (1989, 1991) noted that the social justice concerns of, and violence against, Black women were often overlooked in feminist analysis that reflected the experience of White women.[3] She indicated that "dominant conceptions of discrimination condition us to think about subordination as disadvantages occurring along a single categorical axis" (1989, 140), and that the prevailing view of identity did not consider how race, class, and gender interfaced in the lives of women of color.

In her foundational anthology *Racially Mixed People in America*, Maria Root (1992) noted that the monodimensional construction of race and identity at that time affected racial identity models, and "the theories, like our racial classification system, are characterized by dichotomous or bipolar classification schemes and as such can only marginalize the status of racially or ethnically mixed persons" (1992, 6). As part of her doctoral study of Black and White Multiracial adults, Wijeyesinghe (1992) analyzed theories of Black identity (Cross 1971; Thomas 1971; Jackson 1976) and White identity (Hardiman 1982; Helms 1984), and found that these models could not speak to the experience of Multiracial people. At the time in which these early Monoracial theories were developed, Multiracial people of Black and White ancestry were considered Black by social custom and institutional practice, and therefore their racial identity development was assumed to be covered by Monoracial models that did not account for, or include, their experiences.

In summary, early Intersectional and Multiracial scholarship gave voice to populations who had been part of the fabric of the United States for centuries, but whose experience had yet to be captured by existing research and theory. The models that emerged from these disciplines introduced new perspectives on both racial and social identity.

Identity: Holistic and Multiply Influenced

A core tenet of Intersectionality is that individuals do not experience identity and the world through various components of themselves, taken individually and separately. Dill and Zambrana noted that "both individual and group identity are complex—influenced and shaped not simply by a person's race, class, ethnicity, gender, physical ability, sexuality, religion, or nationality—but by a combination of all of those characteristics" (2009, 6). Early writing on Multiracial identity referenced the "either-or" experience reported by some Multiracial people, based on the social forces that individuals felt required them to choose identities based on only one of the groups in their backgrounds (Kich 1992; Wijeyesinghe 1992; Poston 1990). However, models by Wijeyesinghe (1992, 2001), Root (2001), and Renn (2003) indicated that naming oneself as Multiracial represented a new identity based on the integration and simultaneous expression of an individual's multiple racial ancestry.

Early Intersectional and Multiracial scholarship used some of the same images to describe complex identities that went beyond dichotomous or segmented approaches to identity. For example, Weber (2010, 6) referred to individuals who gained knowledge of privileged groups without having personal access to the social power of that group as engaging in "border crossing." Root used the same term to describe strategies that Multiracial people use to "subvert" the structure of a set number of monoracial categories proscribed by social and political contexts (1996a, xx). Her edited volume entitled *The Multiracial Experience: Racial Borders as the New Frontier* (1996) contained several chapters addressing the interplay of race, gender, and sexuality within the lives of Multiracial people.

## Individuals Encompass Identities of Both Power and Marginalization

Intersectionality and select models of Multiracial identity illustrate how individuals can simultaneously embody positions of power and marginality by attending to the multiple social positions that each individual inhabits. Dill, McLaughlin, and Nieves (2007) described Intersectionality as "grounded in feminist theory, asserting that people live multiple, layered identities and can simultaneously experience oppression and privilege" (2007, 629).

Multiracial literature on individuals with White ancestry is another vehicle for understanding how individuals live, negotiate, and understand identities that reflect both socially dominant groups (Whites) and socially marginalized racial groups (Black, Asians, and other people of color) within the same social category of race. Although phenotype may confound or limit access to social power based on race, Multiracial people with White ancestry may experience aspects of White culture, norms, and values during their socialization and continued interaction with White family members. The influence of White racial ancestry is not separated out, as in considering the effect of "one's White side," but interacts with other factors to influence an individual's choice of racial identity (Wijeyesinghe 1992).[4]

## Identity: Fluid and Changing over Time

Dill and Zambrana (2009) indicated that intersectional scholarship sought to "capture and convey dynamic social processes in which individual identities and group formations grow and shift in continuous interaction with one another, within specific historical periods and geographical locations (2009, 5). The Multiple Dimensions of Identity model by Jones and McEwen (2000) and the Factor Model of Multiracial Identity by Wijeyesinghe (2001) do not present identity as a fixed or essential part of one's being. Instead, identity is a sense of self that evolves and changes, based on the interaction and changing level of salience of numerous factors.

The larger social, historical, and political forces in which individuals form and experience identity are in constant flux. Identity formed within this macro context must also be seen as fluid and complex (Weber 1998). In describing their model, Jones and McEwen indicated that "influences of sociocultural conditions, family background, and current experiences cannot be underestimated in understanding how participants constructed and experienced their identities" (2000, 410). Wijeyesinghe (1992, 2001), Root (1992), and Renn (2003) also incorporated the impact of social and historical context on Multiracial people and identity into their models of Multiracial identity.

## Whose Voices and How to Hear Them

By placing the experience of women who encounter oppression on multiple, intersecting levels at the center of analysis, Dill and Zambrana (2009) noted that "intersectional knowledge is distinctive knowledge generated by the experiences of previously excluded communities and multiply oppressed groups" (2009, 6). Models of Multiracial identity are also distinctive frameworks based on experiences of a racially group not studied in earnest before the 1980s. They added new foundational perspectives to the literature on racial identity development by framing racial identity as a choice (Root 1992; Wijeyesinghe 1992, 2001) that changes over time. Multiracial models, such as those by Root (2002), Wijeyesinghe (1992, 2001), and Renn (2003) also point to the complex interaction of variables that influence how individuals name and live their racial identity in everyday life.

The exploration of how individuals *experience* their identity is best served by qualitative and grounded approaches to research.[5] Early studies on Multiracial identity relied on qualitative measures (Wijeyesinghe 1992; Kich 1992), as did models that represented Intersectional perspectives on identity such as those by Jones and McEwen (2000) and Abes, Jones, and McEwen (2007).

*Linking Theory to Social Change*

In addition to providing a more holistic picture of identity and highlighting the experience of previously overlooked and excluded groups, Intersectionality is a tool for promoting social justice and eradicating social inequality (Dill and Zambrana 2009; Jones and Wijeyesinghe 2011). Dill and Zambrana outlined several avenues for this work, including "advocacy, analysis, policy development, theorizing, and education" (2009, 12). Early literature on Multiracial identity helped raise awareness of the experiences of Multiracial people and the need to change social constructions of race and racial identity, as well as institutional practices. Multiracial organizations such as AMEA and MAVIN were formed as advocacy and resource groups for Multiracial and Multiethnic people. Conferences on race and ethnicity began including seminars on Multiracial topics.[6] Greater media attention was paid to the experience of Multiracial people. Social and political groups for Multiracial students appeared and increased on college campuses. Through grass roots advocacy, institutional practices changed so that individuals could check more than one box to indicate race in the 2000 and 2010 national Census.

Intersectional scholars, including Dill and Zambrana (2009) and Luft and Ward (2009), saw Intersectionality as a vehicle for changing higher education, where knowledge is created and conveyed. Jones and Wijeyesinghe (2011), and Goodman and Jackson (this volume) offered specific strategies for implementing Intersectional strategies in college teaching and faculty development. Higher education is a location where change related to Multiracial identity is particularly evident, with departments, courses, academic conferences, as well as student organizations, covering the experience of Multiracial people.

The chapter now reviews three models of Multiracial identity that acknowledged that multiple factors influence choice of racial identity.

Multiracial Models Depicting Multiple Influences on Identity

The influence of multiple factors on racial identity development was noted in some early Multiracial identity models (Wijeyesinghe 1992, 2001; Root 2002), and a more recent contribution by Renn (2003).[7] Although these three models are not intersectional, as the term is understood today, in their approach, they describe a single social identity, race, as multiply influenced,

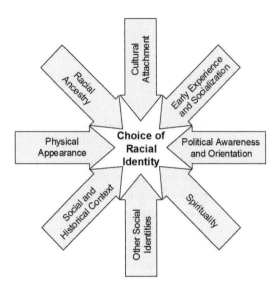

Fig. 4.1 The Factor Model of Multiracial Identity (FMMI) © Charmaine L. Wijeyesinghe, Ed.D. 2001

complex, and evolving, and affected by larger social constructs. These models also attend to the influence of other social identities, such as gender, class, and sexual orientation, on racial identity development.

## The Factor Model of Multiracial Identity Development

The FMMI (Wijeysinghe 1992, 2001) framed racial identity in Multiracial people as a choice made by an individual. This choice was affected by a number of factors and reflected an internal meaning-making process of the individual, which takes place within broad external social and political contexts.[8] The FMMI consists of eight factors that affect choice of racial identity. A Multiracial person's choice of identity at a given point of time was usually based on some, but not all, of these factors. Each factor is briefly reviewed in this section.[9]

### RACIAL ANCESTRY

Some people who identify as Multiracial base their identity in large part on the racial makeup of their families of origin. However, Multiracial people who choose Monoracial identities may rely on all of their racial ancestry to a lesser degree, if at all, when establishing their racial identity. Unlike other Multiracial models (Poston 1990; Kich 1992), choosing an identity based on part and not all of one's family makeup is not assumed to be accompanied by feelings of guilt, embarrassment, or conflict in the FMMI.

## EARLY EXPERIENCES AND SOCIALIZATION

Early socialization and experiences often provide Multiracial people with overt as well as subtle messages about their racial identity, racial ancestry, or racial group membership. It can include parental assignment of a child's early identity, for example when a parent tells a child, "You are Multiracial because your mother is Latino and I am White." This factor is related to social and historical context, since living under the legacy of the "one-drop rule" the majority of Multiracial people born prior to the last two decades of the twentieth century could only identify with their "minority" ancestry

Early socialization can also include exposure to extended family and cultural aspects of one or more of the racial groups represented in a person's background (such as food, music, celebration of various holidays, and languages spoken). Racial identities assigned in childhood can be retained throughout one's lifetime, or changed due to experiences that occur later in life.

## CULTURAL ATTACHMENT

Aspects of culture that Multiracial people are exposed to in their past and present environments can affect their choice of racial identity. A Multiracial person's choice of a Multiracial identity may reflect, in part, exposure and attachment to cultural traditions that encompass all of a person's racial background. The relationship between cultural attachment and choice of racial identity can be affected by at least some of the other factors represented in the FMMI. For example, claiming a Black identity based on a strong preference for Black culture may be less of an option for a Multiracial person who appears to be White, than for a Multiracial person who is seen as Black by others based on appearance.

## PHYSICAL APPEARANCE

Physical appearance creates a strong context in which Multiracial people choose their racial identities. Characteristics such as skin color and tone, hair color and texture, eye color and shape, size and shape of facial features, and body structure are used by the general public and society to make assumptions about people's racial ancestry, racial group membership, and racial identity. Physical appearance can support some Multiracial people's choice of racial identity, and facilitate their acceptance into a particular racial community, for example when a person "looks Black" and identifies as Black. However, appearance can also create barriers to the choice of certain racial identities.

## SOCIAL AND HISTORICAL CONTEXT

The various options for how Multiracial people identify are affected by social responses to issues of race, racism, interracial relationships, and Multiracial people at a given time in history. Prior to the 1990s people with Multiracial ancestry had little opportunity to claim Multiracial identities. Multiracial rights movements, the increase in the number of people who identify as Multiracial, as well as the election of Barack Obama have increased the awareness of Multiracial issues and discussion of how Multiracial people choose to identify. With these changes come greater options—personally, culturally, and institutionally—to claim a Multiracial identity.

## POLITICAL AWARENESS AND ORIENTATION

Choice of racial identity for some Multiracial people is influenced by their awareness and experiences of race, racism, and racial identity in larger historical, political, economic, and social contexts. Within this context, choosing a particular racial identity, whether Multiracial or Monoracial, can represent a form of personal political action or commitment. Multiracial identity as a political force is evident in aspects of Multiracial literature,[10] and the use of terms such as Critical Mixed Race in descriptions of courses and conferences.

## OTHER SOCIAL IDENTITIES

Racial identity for Multiracial people may reflect an integration of racial and nonracial social identities, such as gender, ethnicity, sexual orientation, and socioeconomic class. Some of these other identities may be more salient than race to a Multiracial person's sense of self based on her current concerns or circumstances. For example, when a Multiracial person has just become independent, he may be concerned with class and economic resources, as opposed to his racial identity. A Multiracial woman who is a lesbian may seek support and services that are attentive to both her race as well as sexual orientation. Taken with the impact of social and political context to individual identity, the interaction between the experience of racial identity and other social identities provides the strongest link between Multiracial identity models and Intersectionality

## SPIRITUALITY

While often associated with religious practice, spirituality is defined broadly in the FMMI as the degree to which individuals believe in, seek meaning from, or are guided by a sense of spirit or higher power. Spiritual beliefs or practice can provide individuals with a source of strength and refuge from racism, sustain them through the process of racial identity development, or assist them in deriving greater meaning from their racial ancestry or identity. In addition, spirituality can create a sense of connection between people that transcends racial labels and differences.

## Summary

While identified individually, many of the factors in the FMMI have an overlapping relationship. For example, racial ancestry has some effect on a Multiracial person's appearance, which in turn may affect his early socialization. In another instance, active involvement in racial justice causes may result in a Multiracial person seeking a cultural and political community that supports her work and choice of identity.

Interaction between factors can raise questions of how well various factors "fit" together in a particular Multiracial person's life. When there is congruence between factors, few if any intrapersonal or interpersonal conflicts may emerge. Greater possibilities for internal conflict may exist when there are wide discrepancies between factors underlying choice of racial identity, and possibly external perceptions or forces. For example, a woman may identify as Multiracial based on her racial ancestry, early socialization, and political orientation. However, other people may see as her as Black based on their view of her physical characteristics. The Multiracial woman may have to reconcile her chosen identity with the racial group membership ascribed to her by others, and this situation may or may not cause a conflict for her.

Another example of the impact of perceptions of others on Multiracial people and identity is a study by Khanna (2004). Khanna explored the impact of appearance on the identity of Multiracial Asians by focusing on the concept of "reflected appraisals" (2004, 116), or how individuals interpreted how others saw them. In this study participants were more likely to identify as Asian if they believed that others saw them appearing to be Asian. In addition, Khanna noted that "physical characteristics often dictate acceptance into ethnic/racial groups. For those who attempt to assert an identity that differs from their physical appearance, reactions by others may constrain their choices and influence their identity formation" (2004, 125).

The FMMI assumes that there is no one right or more appropriate choice of racial identity for a Multiracial person. Racial identity in this model is determined by each Multiracial individual, and this individual can change his identity based on which factor or set of factors underlies this choice at any given point.[11]

The FMMI presents racial identity in Multiracial people as complex and evolving, reflecting one of the core features of Intersectionality. However, the graphic used to represent the model does not adequately capture the interrelationship of, and interaction between, factors. In addition, the varying levels of salience of individual factors to choice of identity is not shown, since the model implied that all factors were at the same distance from the center, even though for each person a subset of factors can have a more significant influence on identity at a given point in time.

*Ecological Framework for Understanding*
*Multiracial Racial Identity Development*

The Ecological Framework for Understanding Multiracial Identity Development (Root 2002) identified numerous factors that affected choice of racial and ethnic identity in Multiracial people. The model included factors generally seen as influencing identity, such as physical appearance and family socialization, as well as factors that were less apparent but that created "a background invisible context" (Root 2003, 35) in which identity development occurred, such as generation, geographical region, gender, and sexual orientation.

Root's Ecological Framework identified aspects of family, including family socialization, level of function, and physical appearance as overarching influences on identity. *Family socialization* could include assignment of a racial identity to the young Multiracial person, discussions (or lack of discussion) of family makeup and racial dynamics, and exposure to various aspects of culture (such as language, traditions, and extended family interaction). Family function referred to "the quality of the emotional sustenance and stability that a family provides" and affected "how a child negotiates many aspects of his or her developmental years, with racial identity being just one aspect of his or her development" (2003, 37).

In Root's model, *physical appearance* based on a range of traits could lead a person to choose a particular identity, and was used by others to place individuals into different racial groups. In the Ecological Framework, appearance interacted with other factors in that it would "predict some of the life experiences a child is likely to have based upon the communities in which she or he is raised, the part of the country in which she or he lives, his or her social attractiveness, and the family socialization to understand others'

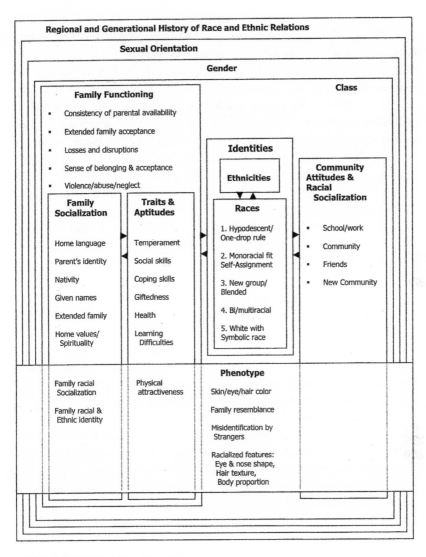

© Maria P. P. Root, Ph.D., 2002     Used with permission

Fig. 4.2 Ecological Framework for Understanding Multiracial Identity Development

reaction to their appearance and its congruence or incongruence with their declared identity" (2003, 40).

Several factors contributed to an invisible context that affected identity: the *region* where a person lived; the *historical period* in which they developed; and the other social identities of *gender, sexual orientation, and class.*[12]

The interrelationship between race and other identities within the Ecological Framework clearly echoes aspects of Intersectionality. For example, given discrimination against gay, lesbian, and bisexual people within communities of color, Root noted that finding support based on sexual orientation may take a Multiracial person into more White environments and interactions. Root described gender as affecting trends in coupling, socialization of Multiracial children, and parent-child dynamics. Class affected how racial groups experience and are experienced by others and the larger culture. In addition, Root noted that class often affected the communities in which Multiracial children and interracial families lived, and thus were socialized.

The representation of the Ecological Model for Understanding Multiracial Identity Development has similar limitations to those of the FMMI: while factors are displayed near or around each other, the dynamic nature of their interaction is not captured in the graphic. In addition, the impact of the salience of factors on choice of identity is not clearly evident.

### The Ecological Approach to Multiracial Identity

Using the framework of developmental ecology, Renn (2003) examined the impact of different campus environments on Multiracial students' choices and fluidity of racial identity. In particular Renn studied "the cumulative, interactive influences of overlapping social settings, some or all of which may be sending contradictory messages regarding racial identity and identification" (2003, 386). Examples of these influences were: previous experiences and existing characteristics, including *other social identities* (such as gender, sexual orientation, and class), *political and social orientations, prior academic achievement*, and *family background*.

In addition to looking at various influences on identity, the Ecological Approach to Multiracial Identity incorporated different levels of "developmental influences arrayed [around an individual] in a series of nested contexts called *microsystems, mesosystems, exosystems*, and *macrosystems*" (2003, 387). Renn described each system as contributing information and messages about racial identity, and "the systems themselves interact in important ways, as well, to create congruent, non-conflicting settings; incongruent, conflict-free settings, or something in between" (2003, 388). Campus climate regarding race and racial groups, institutional practices such as allowing students to check only one box to designate race on forms, and the extent to which courses included Multiracial people contributed to the overall environment in which individual students chose and experienced their racial identity.

Additional Factors Affecting Racial Identity in Multiracial People

This section explores factors that influence choice of racial identity in Multiracial people that were not included in the FMMI. These new factors include: region of the country where an individual lives (geographic region) and different situations or environments that an individual encounters (situation). In addition, the impact of living in an increasingly global world can affect a person's early and ongoing environment. For example, exposure to international travel or direct exposure to a "home country" outside the United States enhances the context in which a person understands and experiences her race and ethnicity. Therefore the factors of global experiences and generation are also discussed in this section.

*Geographic/Regional Environment*

During a presentation of the FMMI at the National Conference on Race and Ethnicity in American Higher Education (NCORE) in the early 1990s, a woman at the back of the audience stood up and shouted, "This has no relevance to us in Hawaii! We're all Multiracial there!" This sentiment was echoed by another seminar participant who lived in Alaska.[13] From this session, and others where participants expressed similar perspectives, it became apparent that the regional and geographic area where a Multiracial person lived and/or was raised could influence choice of racial identity.

In discussing social identity development McEwen (2003) indicated that "where one grows up, forms basic values, currently resides, and envisions oneself in the future are rarely considered in discussions of identity development. Yet if identity is socially constructed, then one's region or place may be a salient part of such social constructions. Place may also reflect the social dimension of urban, suburban, or rural" (2003, 223). More specific to Multiracial identity, Root (2003) noted that "a geographical region's and generation's history of race and ethnic relations provides a critical format for understanding what identity options are available and how relations are transacted" (36). In their study of individuals from a range of racial backgrounds who identified as Multiracial, Miville, Constantine, Baysden, and So-Loyd (2005) noted that "critical places," including "settings where participants grew up and attended school also had great impact on racial identity development" (2005, 513).

The factor of geographical region appears in the new model of Multiracial identity in order to acknowledge the impact of different histories and cultural norms around race, interracial families, and Multiracial people found in various regions of the United States.

## Situational Differences

Everyday interactions provide smaller environments in which identity is enacted and transacted.[14] Within these closer, more immediate contexts, Root (1996a) described Multiracial individuals and families as employing "situational ethnicity and situational race as one might manipulate the extent to which any other aspect of identity—such as parent, worker, partner—is foregrounded or backgrounded in different contexts" (1996a, xxi).

In her study of Multiracial college students, Renn (2003) noted that "the ability to move freely between and among academic and social microsystems enhanced students' degree of exploration of multiple identity patterns, including the option not to identify along racial lines" (2003, 400). Building on the work of Renn, Chaudhari and Pizzolato (2008) conducted a study of Multiracial college students which found that some research participants displayed a "situational ethnic identity pattern" (2008, 449), in that individuals shifted identity in different environments and situations based on appearance and interaction with peers. Chaudhari and Pizzolato defined *cognitive identity* as "the process by which individuals understood their identity and identity shifting [identity claims] across contexts," which represented "an ability to mentally process and balance the external (interpersonal) and internal (intrapersonal) influences on one's identity" (2008, 451).

## Global Influences and Generation

Globalization, immigration, and interaction with the language, place, and culture of another country provide new lenses for understanding racial identity development. The meaning and influence of these factors will continue to change in response to evolving social and political dynamics.

In the Intersectional Model of Multiracial Identity presented later in this chapter, generation is defined less by the particular time period in which one is raised, such as "the Baby Boom Generation" or "Generation X," than by the number of years or life cycles between the time of immigration to the United States and the present. The impact of generational status in the United States has received most attention in writings and study of Multiracial Asians. Root (2001) indicated that younger Asians with Multiracial ancestry differed from individuals born around the time of the Korean War. The older generation lived in the United States when exposure and knowledge of Asian cultures and diversity was limited, and as children these Multiracial Asians were "often viewed as foreigners and not Americans" (2001, 66). In contrast, younger Multiracial Asians often have two American-born parents and a better understanding of themselves as "Asian Americans." Root noted that this latter group had more options in terms of identity, attention to race, and attachment to Asian culture. In Root's research, this was seen when "some of the mixed-race persons, like many white persons, said they had not thought much about race. Simultaneously, other participants described a symbolic identification with their Asian heritage that had an element of choice to it and that often promoted a positive uniqueness about themselves that suits the American struggle for individuality" (2001, 67).

Both Wijeyesinghe (1992, 2001) and Root (2003) indicated that languages spoken in the home environment were part of the cultural environment that could influence a person's choice or experience of racial identity. In a study of Multiracial individuals of Asian and White ancestry, Khanna (2004) found that knowledge of and ability to speak the language of participants' Asian ethnic group influenced level of acceptance and "strengthen the respondent's identity as Asian" (2004, 126). However, Khanna indicated that Multiracial Asian and White individuals who visited or lived in their family's country of origin could feel a greater distance between themselves and their Asian ethnic group, and were actually less likely to identify as Asian due to their experiences of being seen as different by the monoracial populations of that country.

The chapter now turns to the task of constructing a new model of Multiracial identity that includes the factors discussed in this section and approaches a more Intersectional representation. A model that provides guidance on the latter charge is reviewed next.

## The Model of Multiple Dimensions of Identity

The Model of Multiple Dimensions of Identity by Jones and McEwen arose from a study of college women where researchers sought to "engage in dialogue with participants to elicit their descriptions and perceptions of themselves and their understandings of identity development" (2000, 407).[15] In the Multiple Dimensions of Identity Model (MMDI), "identity was defined and understood as having multiple *intersecting* dimensions. The particular salience of identity dimensions depended upon the contexts in which they were experienced" (italics added, 2000, 408). The MMDI has several features and premises:

1. A center point that represented a person's core, internal, almost private sense of self; personal identity was achieved through an internal process and experience;
2. A set of "externally defined dimensions" (2000, 409) of identity that included race, gender, sexual orientation, and other social groupings. Occurring around the core, these factors differed in their level of connection to or influence on the core sense of identity (defined as salience) at a specific time and in a particular context;
3. Dimensions of identity, such as race, class, gender, and sexual orientation were "both externally defined and internally experienced" (2000, 410), linking larger social and environmental contexts with personal experience of identity;
4. Aspects of identity were understood through their relation to each other and "various identity dimensions are present in each individual" (2000, 410). The extent to which individual identity dimensions were acknowledged by an individual related to its level of salience or closeness to the core sense of identity.

In addition to highlighting the multiple aspects that contribute to a person's overall sense of identity, the MMDI reinforces the sense of fluidity of identity. Jones and McEwen noted that "the model is a dynamic and fluid one, representing the ongoing construction of identities and the influence of changing contexts on the experience of identity development" (2000, 408). Differences in the way individuals name and experience their personal sense

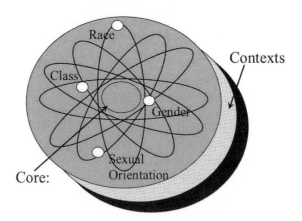

(Jones & McEwen, 2000)
Used with Permission

Fig. 4.3 Multiple Dimensions of Identity Model

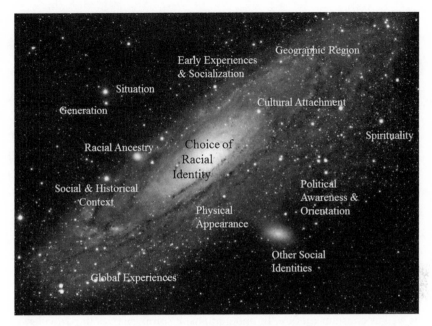

Fig. 4.4 The Intersectional Model of Multiracial Identity. © Charmaine L. Wijeyesinghe, Ed.D., 2011. Background galaxy photo © Robert Gendler, 2002. Used with permission.

of identity was understood by examining which identities were felt to be more salient to the core. For example, a White, middle-class lesbian may feel that her identity is based more on her gender and sexual orientation whereas a Black, heterosexual, middle-class, and Christian student may feel that race, gender, and faith tradition are the foundations of her personal identity.

The graphic used to represent the MMDI more readily communicates the dynamic interplay of various factors representing identity at any given point of an individual's life. The design of the Intersectional Model of Multiracial Identity, presented in the next section of the chapter, was informed and inspired by the representation of the MMDI.

## The Intersectional Model of Multiracial Identity

The Intersectional Model of Multiracial Identity is based on a number of core premises/assumptions:

- Choice of identity in a Multiracial person is influenced by a number of factors that vary in level of salience or significance at any given point.
- Choice and experience of racial identity can change over time based on the factor or factors that form the basis of that identity.

- No choice of racial identity is more valid or legitimate, or evidence of greater psychological health. A Multiracial person may choose to identify with some or all of his racial ancestries, without necessarily experiencing feelings of dissonance, anxiety, or confusion.
- Other social group memberships, such as gender, class, age, or faith tradition, can influence how a Multiracial person identifies in terms of race, or how he experiences and lives his racial identity.

Many of the factors represented in the model are interrelated and affect choice and experience of racial identity, and in some cases, each other.

The graphic representation of the IMMI portrays the influence of multiple variables on choice of racial identity in a more fluid and interactive manner than the FMMI. The IMMI is modeled on the image of a galaxy because aspects of galaxies capture many of the themes inherent in the IMMI. Galaxies have many features, only some of which are currently known.[16] Many galaxies start out small, and build over time as more stars are born within them. Within galaxies there is continuous activity and interaction between bodies, as well as constant motion. In photographs of spiral galaxies in particular, a haziness surrounds the core or center area. Lastly, some galaxies have within them smaller galaxies.

In the Intersectional Model of Multiracial Identity there are many factors surrounding the center, which in the model represents choice and experience of racial identity. The level of influence or salience of a particular factor or group of factors to a Multiracial person's choice of identity is measured by how close it or they are to the center area. Choice of identity may change over time in response to the factor or factors closest to this area.

A Multiracial individual's "personal galaxy" of factors that influence her choice and experience of racial identity grows and expands as she encounters new experiences and situations. A young Multiracial person may experience only a few factors, such as early socialization, assignment of racial identity, and early cultural experiences. However, other factors can appear in this person's "galaxy" as he or she has additional experiences later in life. Take, for example, the experience of a Multiracial woman of Black and White ancestry who identifies as Black before entering college, based on appearance, family socialization, and growing up in a Southern state. Upon enrolling in a large university in California, this student becomes active in a campus group for Multiracial students where exposure to other Multiracial people, their experiences, and social and political networks may lead her to change her identity to Multiracial. For this individual, the factors of appearance and early socialization move from a place that is close to the center (representing choice of racial identity), to a place that is further away. The factors of situation, cultural attachment, family ancestry, and perhaps political and regional differences move closer to the center, replacing the previous factors, and resulting in a change in racial identity.

The IMMI uses the clouded nature of galaxies to represent interaction across factors, their mutual influence on each other, and the "process in action" of identity. In the new model, the representation of a "galaxy within a galaxy" is most useful in conveying the impact of other social identities (such as gender, class, and sexual orientation) on racial identity. While these other aspects of self are integrated into the experience of racial identity, they also have their own processes that are influenced by various life circumstances and experiences. Lastly, since material can be added to galaxies, as additional research uncovers new factors influencing racial identity, these items can be added to the IMMI.

Multiracial Identity, Racial Identity, and
Intersectionality: Looking Ahead

This chapter offers a preliminary analysis of the overlap between the Multiracial identity literature and Intersectionality. Reflecting on existing theories of racial identity through an Intersectional lens holds the promise of uncovering new insights from models that may be years or even decades old. One of the challenges of moving to more intersectional and interrelated models of social identity development is how to address aspects of each identity that are unique, while linking aspects that are shared.[17] Understanding how race and racial identity are experienced at the personal, cultural, and societal level can assist Intersectionality scholars develop models and strategies that acknowledge areas that are relevant to race, and less so to other social identities. Future research and analysis will yield additional and more nuanced understanding of what Multiracial identity (in particular) and racial identity (in general) can offer Intersectionality, and how Intersectionality can inform existing and future models of racial identity.

In offering strategies for the integration of Intersectionality into college teaching, Jones and Wijeyesinghe (2011) note that "as we look to the future, it is important to acknowledge that we are just beginning to grapple with how such an analytic framework may be applied to the day to day life in the classroom, and used to dismantle inequality and promote social justice within that classroom, higher education, and larger society" (2011, 18). A foundation of intersectional models of racial identity development or broader social identity development is in the process of construction. Jones and McEwen (2000),

Abes, Jones, and McEwen (2007), Holvino (this volume), and the Intersectional Model of Multiracial Identity presented in this chapter all offer specific tools to be used, analyzed, and critiqued. The analysis, research, and refinement of these models will yield insights to be incorporated in future paradigms.

As future research and writing yield more intersectionally based models of racial identity, the challenge of how to best represent these models in terms of diagrams or graphics must be addressed. Both the Multiple Dimensions of Identity model and the Intersectional Model of Multiracial Identity advance the presentation of identity beyond stages or phases of development. By adopting images that people can generally envision beyond their representation on paper, these two models can be transformed into three-dimensional images. The use of technology holds promise for the development and use of models that that go beyond two dimensional representations, and that can better portray the dynamic interplay of various influences in the constant evolution of identity. In a sense, the contribution of the IMMI is less about the inclusion of additional factors that affect choice of identity in Multiracial people, and more about how to advance the discussion of how to represent and interpret intersectional identity models.

Being mindful that the model presented in this chapter is based on the identity of Multiracial people, the chapter concludes with three areas that relate to this population. First, in 1992 and 2001, Wijeyesinghe framed racial identity as a choice made by Multiracial individuals. Positing racial identity as a choice was met with controversy and skepticism. With the passage of time, this perspective on identity has been more widely accepted, and framing racial identity as choice appears in numerous essays and research studies (Rockquemore 2002; McEwen 2003; Torres, Jones, and Renn 2009; Stets and Burke 2000; Renn 2003, 2000; Root 1996a; and Gallegos and Ferdman, this volume). Yet, as evidenced by the discussion around Barack Obama's ancestry, how he identifies in terms of race and how he is identified by others, framing racial identity as a choice continues to fuel lively debate.

Within the context of the experience of Multiracial people, the perspective that identity results from a choice made by an individual can have an empowering effect. However, for social groups such as gay, lesbian, bisexual, and transgender communities, the labeling of identity as a choice has often come from people working to sustain LGBT oppression and maintain social privileges accorded to heterosexuals. In exploring more inclusive and intersectional models in the future, we must be mindful that factors that are essential to the experience of identity for some groups and seen as central to their efforts to achieve basic rights can be used to advance exactly the opposite goals for other groups.

The second area to note is the size and diversity of the Multiracial population. The 2010 U.S. Census indicated that over 9 million people, or 2.9 percent of the U.S. population, reported two or more races to describe their racial backgrounds (Humes, Jones, and Ramirez 2011). Three-quarters of the people who identified as Multiracial indicated that they were White and one other racial group (1.8 million White and Black, 1.7 million White and Some Other Race, 1.6 million White and Asian, and 1.4 million White and American Indian and Alaskan Native). Of the respondents indicating they were Asian, a full 15 percent indicated Asian with one or more other race. Over half the people who identified as Native Hawaiian and Other Pacific Islander indicated that their ancestry also included one or more other races. Over 7 percent of individuals within the Black or African American population identified as Multiracial, with 59 percent of this group indicating they were Black and White. The statistics indicate that Multiracial Americans are a diverse group, and present in every racial community in the country. These facts offer many opportunities for investigation as research on Multiracial people and identity continues, leading to the investigation of pressing questions, such as: what experiences, if any, do Multiracial people share, regardless of their actual racial makeup? How differently do factors such as culture and social and political context affect various Multiracial groups? How do the experiences of Multiracial people with some White ancestry differ from the experiences of Multiracial people whose backgrounds are based in communities of color? And how does the issue of appearance affect different Multiracial groups?

Lastly, social and political processes related to race, Multiracial people, and the larger climate around multiracial issues continue to evolve more rapidly than in historical eras of the past. Therefore, how Multiracial people develop, experience, and live their racial identities within this changing context will remain a relevant area of study in the coming years. This much is clear, since the 1980s inclusion of Multiracial people in discussion of race in the United States has moved from total absence or denial to a regular and necessary component of the American landscape related to race and identity. Regardless of the direction and rate of social and political change, there is no going back.

NOTES

1. The author notes that her analysis and reflection over the course of writing this chapter was significantly affected by the work of Susan Jones, and her recent collaborations with Dr. Jones on publications and presentations. In addition, the author thanks Michael Cooper and Christian Lietzau for their assistance in creating the graphic for the Intersectional Model of Multiracial Identity.

2. See Root and Kelley (2003) and Winters and DeBose (2003) for essays on a diverse range of Multiracial populations; Williams-León and Nakashima 2001 edited a volume focused solely on the Multiracial Asian experience; See Ifekwunigwe 2004 for essays on Multiracial issues from diverse national perspectives, and the volume by Winters and DeBose.

3. See also Weber 1998 for overview of historical antecedents of Intersectionality.

4. The author acknowledges that Multiracial people as a whole are a diverse group that includes Multiracial individuals whose backgrounds do not include White ancestry. See note 2 for examples of writing on or by these populations.

5. See Hesse-Biber 2007 for an excellent review of philosophical underpinnings, history, and methodology related to feminist research theory and practice.

6. In 1995, Wijeyesinghe presented the first seminar on Multiracial identity held at the annual National Conference on Race and Ethnicity. Since that year, the program of this conference has included sessions on Multiracial people, and caucuses and social events for Multiracial participants.

7. The FMMI is discussed in greatest detail as many of its factors also appear in the Intersectional Model of Multiracial Identity presented later in this chapter.

8. See Abes, Jones, and McEwen 2007 for fuller discussion of the interaction of personal meaning making, context, and level of salience in a revised version of the Model of Multiple Dimensions of Identity (Jones and McEwen 2000).

9. A more extensive description of the FMMI, including discussion and examples of individual factors is presented in the Multiracial chapter by Wijeyesinghe (2001) in *New Perspectives on Racial Identity Development: A Theoretical and Practical Anthology*, the first edition of this volume.

10. Root's "A Bill of Rights for Racially Mixed People" (1996b, 3) is a specific example of literature in which claiming a Multiracial identity is described as a political act of resistance against oppressive systems related to race.

11. See citation under note 9 for discussion of managing bias related to the different factors in relation to legitimate indications of race.

12. See Root 2001 and 2003, for fuller discussion of influence of these and factors from this model described in this section.

13. See also Rosa 2001, and Rooks 2001 for essays based on Hawaiian and Alaskan Multiracial experience, respectively.

14. See Renn 2003 for discussion of varying levels of environments that individuals encounter; framed by Renn as microsystems, mesosystems, exosystems, and macrosystems (p. 393). Cross (this volume) discusses a model of identity management that is enacted across, and in response to, social situations.

15. See Jones and McEwen (2000) for full discussion of aspects of the model and research underlying its development.

16. The following resources provided information on the properties of galaxies and images that inspired the choice of a galaxy for the representation of the IMMI: DK Publishing, 2010; Aguilar, Pulliam, and Daniels 2007; and the Jet Propulsion (California Institute of Technology)/NASA website: http://www.jpl.nasa.gov.

17. See Luft 2009 and and Goodman and Jackson, this volume, for additional perspectives on the strategic and selective use of intersectional strategies in social justice education.

## REFERENCES

Abes, Eliza .S., Susan R. Jones, and Marilu K. McEwen. 2007. "Reconceptualizing the Model of Multiple Dimensions of Identity: The Role of Meaning-Making Capacity in the Construction of Multiple Identities." *Journal of College Student Development* 48: 1–22.

Aguilar, David A., Christine Pulliam, and Patricia Daniels. 2007. *Planets, Stars, and Galaxies: A Visual Encyclopedia of Our Universe*. Washington, D.C.: National Geographic Society.

Chaudhari, Prema, and Jane E. Pizzolato. 2008. "Understanding the Epistemology of Ethnic Identity Development in Multiethnic College Students." *Journal of College Student Development* 49 (5): 443–458.

Crenshaw, Kimberle. 1989. "Demarginalizing the Intersection of Race and Sex: A Black Feminist Critique of Antidiscrimation Doctrine, Feminist Theory and Antiracist Politics." *University of Chicago Legal Forum*: 139–167.

———. 1991. "Mapping the Margins: Intersectionality, Identity Politics, and Violence against Women of Color." *Stanford Law Review* 43 (6): 1241–1299.

Cross, William E. 1971. "Discovering the Black Referent: The Psychology of Black Liberation." In *Beyond Black and White: An Alternative America*, edited by V. J. Dixon and B. G. Foster, 96–110. Boston: Little, Brown.

Dill, Bonnie T., Amy E. McLaughlin, and Angel D. Nieves. 2007. "Future Directions of Feminist Research: Intersectionality." In *Handbook of Feminist Research: Theory and Practice*, edited by S. N. Hesse-Biber, 629–637. Thousand Oaks, Calif.: Sage.

Dill, Bonnie T., and Ruth E. Zambrana. 2009. "Critical Thinking about Inequality: An Emerging Lens." In *Emerging Intersections: Race, Class, and Gender in Theory, Policy, and Practice*, edited by B. T. Dill and R. E. Zambrana, 1–21. New Brunswick, N.J.: Rutgers University Press.

DK Publishing. 2010. *Space: A Visual Encyclopedia*. New York: Dorling Kindersley, Inc.

Hardiman, Rita. 1982. "White Identity Development: A Process Oriented Model for Describing the Racial Consciousness of White Americans." Ed.D. dissertation, School of Education, University of Massachusetts, Amherst.

Helms, Janet E. 1984. "Toward a Theoretical Explanation of the Effects of Race on Counseling: A Black and White Model." *Counseling Psychologist* 17 (2): 227–252.

Hesse-Biber, S. N. 2007. Ed. *Handbook of Feminist Research: Theory and Practice*. Thousand Oaks, Calif.: Sage.

Humes, Karen A., Nicholas A. Jones, and Roberto R. Ramirez. 2011. "Overview of Race and Hispanic Origin: 2010." 2010 Census Briefs. www.census.gov/prod/cen2010/briefs/c2010br-02.pdf

Ifekwunigwe, Jayne O., ed. 2004. *Mixed Race Studies: A Reader*. New York: Routledge.

Jackson, Bailey, W. 1976. "The Function of a Theory of Black Identity Development in Achieving Relevance in Education for Black Students." Ed.D. dissertation, School of Education, University of Massachusetts, Amherst.

Jones, Susan R., and Marilu K. McEwen. 2000. "A Conceptual Model of Multiple Dimensions of Identity." *Journal of College Student Development* 41 (4): 405–414.

Jones, Susan R., and Charmaine L. Wijeyesinghe. 2011. "The Promises and Challenges of Teaching from an Intersectional Perspective: Core Components and Applied Strategies." In *Understanding the Intersections: An Integrative Analysis Approach to Diversity in the College Classroom*, edited by Mathew L. Ouellett, 11–20. San Francisco: Jossey-Bass.

Khanna, Nikki. 2004. "The Role of Reflected Appraisals in Racial Identity: The Case of Multiracial Asians." *Social Psychology Quarterly* 67 (2):115–131.

Kich, George K. 1992. "The Developmental Process of Asserting a Biracial, Bicultural Identity." In *Racially Mixed People in America*, edited by M. P. P. Root, 304–317. Newbury Park, Calif.: Sage.

Luft, Rachel E. 2009. "Intersectionality and the Risk of Flattening Difference: Gender and Race Logics, and the Strategic Use of Antiracist Singularity." In *The Intersectional Approach: Transforming the Academy through Race, Class, and Gender*, edited by M. T. Berger and K. Guidroz, 100–117. Chapel Hill: University of North Carolina Press.

Luft, Rachel E., and Jane Ward. 2009. "Toward an Intersectionality Just Out of Reach: Confronting Challenges to Intersectional Practice." In *Perceiving Gender Locally, Globally, and Intersectionally*, edited by V. Demos and M. T. Segal, 9–37. Bingley, U.K.: Emerald Group Publishing.

McEwen, Marylu K. 2003. "New Perspectives on Identity Development." In *Student Services: A Handbook for the Profession*, edited by S. R. Komives and D. B. Woodward Associates, 203–233. San Francisco: Jossey Bass.

Miville, Marie L., Madonna G. Constantine, Matthew F. Baysden, and Gloria So-Loyd. 2005. "Chameleon Changes: An Exploration of Racial Identity Themes of Multiracial People." *Journal of Counseling Psychology* 52 (4): 507–516.

Poston, Carlos W. 1990. "The Biracial Identity Development Model: A Needed Addition." *Journal of Counseling and Development* 69 (November/December): 152–155.

Renn, Kristen A. 2000. "Patterns of Situational Identity among Biracial and Multiracial College Students." *Review of Higher Education* 23 (4): 399–420.

———. 2003. "Understanding the Identities of Mixed Race College Students through a Developmental Ecology Lens." *Journal of College Student Development* 44 (3): 383–403.

Rockquemore, Kerry, A. 2002. "Negotiating the Color Line: The Gendered Process of Racial Construction among Black/White Biracial Women." *Gender and Society* 16: 485<N<503.

Rooks, Curtiss, T. 2001. "Alaska's Multiracial Asian American Families: Not Just at the Margins." In *The Sum of Our Parts: Mixed Heritage Asian Americans*, edited by T. Williams-León and C. L. Nakashima, 71–80. Philadelphia: Temple University Press.

Root, Maria P. P. 1992. "Within, Between, and Beyond Race." In *Racially Mixed People in America*, edited by Maria P. P. Root, 3–11. Newbury Park, Calif.: Sage.

———. 1996a. "The Multiracial Experience: Racial Borders as a Significant Frontier in Race Relations." In *The Multiracial Experience: Racial Borders at the New Frontier*, edited by Maria P. P. Root, xiii–xxviii. Thousand Oaks, Calif.: Sage.

———. 1996b. "A Bill of Rights for Racially Mixed People." In *The Multiracial Experience: Racial Borders at the New Frontier*, edited by Maria P. P. Root, 3–14. Thousand Oaks, Calif.: Sage.

———. 2001. "Factors Influencing the Variation in Racial and Ethnic Identity of Mixed-Heritage Persons of Asian Ancestry." In *The Sum of Our Parts: Mixed Heritage Asian Americans*, edited by T. Williams-León and C. L. Nakashima, 61–70. Philadelphia: Temple University Press.

———. 2002. "Ecological Framework for Understanding Multiracial Identity Development." http://www.drmariaroot.com/doc/Ecological Framework.pdf

———. 2003. "Racial Identity Development and Persons of Mixed Race Heritage." In *Multiracial Child Resource Book: Living Complex Identities*, edited by M. P. P. Root and M. Kelley, 34–41. Seattle: MAVIN Foundation.

Root, Maria P. P., and Matt Kelley, eds. 2003. *Multiracial Child Resource Book: Living Complex Identities*. Seattle: MAVIN Foundation.

Rosa, John P. 2001. "The Coming of the Neo-Hawaiian American Race: Nationalism and Metaphors of the Melting Pot in Popular Accounts of Mixed Race Individuals." In *The Sum of Our Parts: Mixed Heritage Asian Americans*, edited by T. Williams-León and C. L. Nakashima, 49–56. Philadelphia: Temple University Press.

Stets, Jan E., and Peter J. Burke. 2000. "Identity Theory and Social Identity Theory." *Social Psychology Quarterly* 63 (3): 224–237.

Thomas, Charles W. 1971. "Boys No More: Some Social-Psychological Aspects of the New Black Ethic." In *Boys No More*, edited by C. W. Thomas, 16–26. Beverly Hills: Glencoe Press.

Torres, Vasti, Susan R. Jones, and Kristen A. Renn. 2009. "Identity Development Theories in Student Affairs: Origins, Current Status, and New Approaches." *Journal of College Student Development* 50 (6): 577–596.

Weber, Lynn. 1998. "A Conceptual Framework for Understanding Race, Class, Gender, and Sexuality." *Psychology of Women Quarterly* 22: 13–32.

———. 2010. "Introduction." in *Understanding Race, Class, Gender, and Sexuality: A Conceptual Framework*, 2nd ed., 1–19. New York: Oxford University Press.

Wijeyesinghe, Charmaine. 1992. "Towards an Understanding of the Racial Identity of Bi-Racial People: The Experience of Racial Self-Identification of African-American/Euro-American Adults and the Factors Affecting Their Choices of Racial Identity." Ed.D. dissertation, School of Education, University of Massachusetts, Amherst.

———. 2001. "Racial Identity in Multiracial People: An Alternative Paradigm." In *New Perspectives on Racial Identity Development: A Theoretical and Practical Anthology*, edited by C. L. Wijeyesinghe and B. W. Jackson III, 129–152. New York: NYU Press.

Wijeyesinghe, Charmaine L., Pat Griffin, and Barbara Love. 1997. "Racism Curriculum Design." In *Teaching for Diversity and Social Justice: A Sourcebook*, edited by M. Adams, L. A. Bell, and P. Griffin, 82–109. New York: Routledge.

Williams-León T., and Cynthia L. Nakashima, eds. 2001. *The Sum of Our Parts: Mixed Heritage Asian Americans*. Philadelphia: Temple University Press.

Winters, Loretta L., and Herman L. DeBose, eds. 2003. *New Faces in a Changing America: Multiracial Identity in the 21st Century*. Thousand Oaks, Calif.: Sage.

5

# Twenty-First Century
# Native American Consciousness

## A Thematic Model of Indian Identity

PERRY G. HORSE

## Introduction

In the first edition of *New Perspectives* I presented a paradigm of American Indian consciousness based on at least five psychosocial influences (Horse 2001). Such influences occur at the individual or group levels. I revisit these briefly as part of this introduction. Additional commentary will follow. Indian identity issues are bound to be affected in significant ways due to the passage of time. Succeeding generations of Indian people may see identity from a different perspective than we who are products of the twentieth century. Nevertheless, the topics covered herein are cross-generational in terms of historical analysis.

Usually, three descriptors have been used when discussing the aboriginal people of this land. One that is commonly used now is Native American. Along with Indian and American Indian, all three descriptors are used interchangeably in this chapter.

Five Influences on Indian Consciousness—A Review

In 2001 I observed that contact with our native consciousness is influenced in at least five ways:

1. How well one is grounded in the native language and culture;
2. Whether one's genealogical heritage as an Indian is valid;
3. Whether one embraces a general philosophy or worldview that derives from distinctly Indian ways, that is, old traditions;
4. The degree to which one thinks of him- or herself in a certain way, that is, one's own idea of self as an Indian person, and
5. Whether one is officially recognized as a member of an Indian tribe by the government of that tribe.

In the world community of humankind we Indians like everyone else understand ourselves in relation to other races of people wherever they are. That is, we know we are not White, Asian, African, or Middle Eastern, for example. Aside from that we tend to identify first as members of our own tribal nations. Our identity as such lies in our tribal languages and cultures.

One's tribal heritage and the influence of one's tribal culture play a significant role in forming one's identity as an American Indian. However, we recognize that Indian cultures have gradually changed through succeeding eras of contact with non-Indian cultures. The attrition of older generations of Indians is a huge factor in the changes that have taken place, including the loss of native languages.

We Indians know that we must also understand ourselves in relation to the modern world. What is it that helps us navigate comfortably through this techno-multicultural world while retaining essential aspects of our "Indianness"? That is the question we must explore when talking about a native perspective on race and ethnicity. Our sense of Indianness is rooted in the past. However, I believe we arrived where we are now through certain stages of consciousness— which is what frames this discussion.

Eras of Change in Indian Consciousness

One's critical awareness of one's own identity and situation is influenced in different ways. The consciousness of American Indians in this century, for example, is influenced by our respective tribal histories and cultures and the tension between our past and current situations. Just as societies in Western culture went through the era of Enlightenment and into the era of postmodernism, Indian cultures evolved through different eras and situations. That is what I have in mind when taking a very broad perspective on what got us to where we are now in terms of identity themes and issues.[1]

The consciousness of people is affected or influenced by their individual and/or group situation. Situations change over time. Modern-day Native Americans can look back at our respective historical situations and see some clear demarcations where profound transitions were made from one era to another.

From the broadest historical perspective one can identify the first era, or epoch, when Indians were totally independent; that is, before non-Indians immigrated to North America. That was a time predating the establishment of European/American colonies. The second broad era began with the U.S. Declaration of Independence and the subsequent westward expansion of the new nation. The third era covered the latter part of the nineteenth century and continued throughout the twentieth century. During the latter era Indians were adjudicated by the Supreme Court as being *domestic dependent nations*.[2] We can anticipate a new era in the twenty-first century when Indians can strive to break the bonds of dependency. Such dependency is represented by the old model of racism, paternalism, and economic oppression.

A twenty-first century Native American consciousness would be a natural transition; a time of recovery from the old model. This will occur generation by generation. In the meantime the contemporary influences of racial awareness, the legal status of Indians, and potential loss of native languages and cultures will all figure into the Indian identity equation.

Orientation to Race Consciousness

Everyone's perception about race is linked, consciously or unconsciously, to race relations. One cannot ignore blatant racist attitudes and practices, for example. Nor is racism the exclusive domain of White people. The driving forces that inform our racial sensibilities begin at an early age. For example, research has shown that racial stereotypes are found in every culture and every people. Even children three years old prefer their own group (Spiegel 2010).

How did the Indian concept of race evolve? I cannot state unequivocally that Indians were unaware of other races in pre-Columbian times. People develop a collective consciousness based on past events or conditions. If pre-Columbian contact with other races was in their memory chain, our ancestors would have coined descriptors.

The first mention of my tribe by early White explorers in America was made by LaSalle.[3] That would have been the time when our people lived along the upper Missouri and along the Platte River in Colorado. Much later, military expeditions made contact with my forebearers in what are now Oklahoma and Kansas. Thus the existence of a White race of people was noted in our tribal history for the first time. A story is told by our tribe's historians that the White explorers had mules and donkeys as pack animals. A Kiowa word meaning long ears was used as a quick reference to Whites. It is still used in the slang version of Kiowa.

Indians who served in the armed forces in World Wars I and II had to choose which race they were from among the classifications of White, Yellow, Red, or Black. Such color coding was unfamiliar to Indians. It is recorded that "Indians in the military in World War I were classified as White, except in the segregated south, where they were classified as 'colored'" (Viola 2008, 100). Thus began the Indian introduction to race as one aspect of their identity. The aforementioned classification of Red devolved from an earlier racist stereotype whereby White soldiers and settlers called us Redskins.

Institutional and personal racism worked insidiously against the best interests of Indian people almost before they could discern what was happening in that regard. A good example of that is pointed out in a book about White settlement in Oklahoma Territory. White people gradually took over lands that had once been reserved exclusively for tribes in Oklahoma. Government agricultural agents, railroads, and banks encouraged White settlers to convert the land to market economies while discriminating against Indians and Blacks. In fact, "most people, even today, are not aware of the ways in which that discrimination played itself out socially and environmentally" (Lynn-Sherow 2004, 145).

The way we see ourselves as tribal nations or Indian people is not based on race per se. Most Indian tribes that I know of simply describe themselves as *the people*. In the Kiowa language the translation or explanation in reference to humans would be *people of life*. Tribe-specific names do exist. The current Kiowa word for ourselves is *Kcoy-gu*, but its exact meaning is not known. In this book's first edition I noted that "some geneticists believe that the concept of race is so vague that practically any of the hundreds, even thousands, of subdivisions in the human species could be called a race" (Horse 2001, 94).

From a global perspective American Indians have much in common with non-White races worldwide. European colonists left indelible social marks on the continents of Africa, Australia, Asia, India, the Middle East, the Island nations, and, of course, in South and North America. In all those places there is a blend of cultures and mixing of ethnicities. In our country the state of

Hawaii provides the most striking example of interracial mixing. Native Hawaiians are now included under the official rubric of Native American. They are now linked with American Indians in legislation previously limited to federally recognized tribes on the mainland.

Globally, we are now linked with other formerly colonized Indigenous Peoples through membership in the World Indigenous Nations Higher Education Consortium or WINHEC. The WINHEC organization grew out of the 1999 World Indigenous Peoples Conference on Education. This international conference is held every three years. It is partially modeled on the American Indian Higher Education Consortium, AIHEC, which is an umbrella development and advocacy organization that serves the thirty-seven tribal colleges and universities in the United States and Canada.

The term postracial is now used in the dialogue on race and ethnicity. The question is, Does race still matter? And if so, how do we discuss it? Such questions will no doubt be raised and debated for years to come. It is tempting to speculate whether we may be moving toward a new social construct where race is not strictly limited to visual clues when we interact with one another.

Indian sensibilities about race will evolve as each succeeding generation comes to know themselves in relation to their tribal affiliations and in relation to the larger modern society. Adoption of the English language in place of native languages will be a significant factor in that evolution, as we will see later in this chapter. A common issue among the world's Indigenous People is concern about language retention and/or revitalization.

Orientation toward Political Consciousness

No discussion of Indian identity can overlook either the legal aspects or the political identifiers. The legal status of Indian tribes as sovereign nations is critical to how we Indians see ourselves. It is critical to how others can better understand us. It is a political rather than a racial distinction.

The U.S. federal government officially recognizes tribal nations as being sovereign political entities with the inherent right of self-governance. Such status is still being sought by many tribes who are not so recognized (Bordewich 1996). The Six Nations or Iroquois Confederacy in New York State aggressively asserts its right to self-governance, including the issuance of passports, for example.[4]

Well before their Declaration of Independence the English colonists were mindful of the need for a federal policy that would guide their dealings with Indians. That need is addressed in the Constitution. Article 1, Section 8, enumerates the powers of Congress and states in part, "To regulate Commerce with foreign nations, and among the several states, and with the Indian Tribes."

Migrating westward, the White American settlers met fierce resistance. This resulted in the Indian Wars that eventually resulted in the treaty-making period that lasted until 1871. In 1924 Congress passed the Indian Citizenship Act. That law granted U.S. citizenship to America's indigenous peoples. Indians did not have to give up tribal citizenship. This, in effect, created a dual citizenship status. Thus began a lengthy, complex set of laws and regulations, a body of law known as Federal Indian Law.[5]

The Indian treaties were never abrogated. This means that, legally, the relationship between the United States and Indian tribes is one of government-to-government. It is also known as the federal Indian trust relationship, whereby Congress is the trustee. The Executive Branch is in charge of administrative aspects of the treaties.

A plethora of congressional legislation was enacted throughout the twentieth century to deal with the "Indian problem." Throughout the 1900s federal Indian policies were carried out with the following emphases:

- eradication of Indian languages and cultures;
- termination of Federal obligations to Indians;
- relocation of Indians from reservations to cities;
- benign neglect, paternalism; and (now)
- self-determination.

The Indian Reorganization Act of 1934 sought to improve conditions on the reservations. It emphasized the strengthening of tribal governing structures via written constitutions. Many tribes reformed their governments accordingly; others did not.

Governmental reform in some tribes continues to this day. Sovereignty is the touchstone of Indian governance. Its relevance to this discussion is that Indian sovereignty gives tribal governments the exclusive right to determine who is or is not a tribal member. Those seeking to reinforce their identity as Indians by enrollment in a federally recognized tribe are affected accordingly.

The right of self-governance for Indian tribes is well established in law. Other aspects of sovereignty, such as jurisdictional issues, may not be as clear.

Federal Indian law is complex and requires legal specialization. Legal advocacy organizations were created in the 1970s to protect and preserve Indian rights across a broad range of issues. The work they do protects our land and natural resources as well as our fundamental right to exist as Indian tribes.

## Orientation toward Linguistic Consciousness

"When a people loses its language, they have lost who they are," said a prominent Kiowa tribal member (Hall 2000, 263). Language as identity is a common theme across Indian Country. Native speakers invariably point out that the true identity of Indians is in their respective languages. While others may not necessarily agree, the power of language cannot be over-stated. Throughout Indian Country it is perhaps *the most potent aspect of one's tribal identity.*

We know from applied research currently being done that children who are learning their native tongue gain an identity that connects them with their past while empowering them to succeed in the modern world. This is being studied in immersion schools on several Indian reservations (Ogden 2008).

Early in my life I grew up in a bilingual setting. I heard and felt the power of words in the prayers and songs of my kinfolk. I noticed a certain healing quality in our language that I took for granted. One went to prayer meetings, healing ceremonies, and ritual dances expecting everything to be conducted accordingly.

To me, at that time, English was the language of schooling, commerce, and entertainment. Speaking and writing English had a different kind of power and appeal. It was a power derived from a non-Indian epistemology. It provided a different way to express oneself in poetry, stories, and song, for example. I came to appreciate that fluency in two languages opens the door for deeper intellectual exploration that would otherwise not be possible. It instills a respect for all languages.

When I left home in 1961 I did not hear or attempt to use the Kiowa lan-guage consistently for almost thirty years. My professional career took me to regions of the country where few if any other Kiowa speakers lived. During my adult life English became my first language, Kiowa my second. I do not think the shift in primary languages changed my sense of identity. I did lose some Kiowa-speaking proficiency, though, because language has a use-it-or-lose-it quality. Now I feel like I am reversing the process by reimmersing myself in the Kiowa traditions of old. I can see clearly now the contradictions that were imposed on me as a result of the aforementioned colonialist prac-tices. I am not resentful, though, because I feel that my experience in two worlds has made me a stronger person.

Immigrants to America provide another example of the hold that language has on nationalities from all over the world. In the sociopolitical scheme of things there has been much debate about immigration reform in the United States. English-only advocates add fuel to that debate. They seem to think that declaring English as the official language of the country will somehow mitigate their fear of foreign language incursion.

The myth of America as a melting pot is now part of history. Instead there is much discussion about the value of diversity in American life. Bilingual education is not a new idea any more. Distinct ethnic communities exist in all of America's great cities. Language is the glue that holds those communities together. The poet Czesław Miłosz is quoted as having said, "Language is the only homeland" (Miłosz 2011).

Across Indian Country I have noted growing concern about language extinction. It can happen. It can happen in one generation. A case in point is that of the Wichita people, a small tribal nation in southwestern Oklahoma. Realizing, too late perhaps, that the language was dying the Wichita tribe enlisted the help of a linguist to capture as much as they could of their vocabulary and grammar. In the beginning the linguist noted that there were fewer than one hundred people who knew the language. He used them as his informants and advisers. His work ended when attrition left only one speaker in 2008 (Stewart 2008).

One of the most salient issues for Indian tribes is the dwindling number of fluent native speakers. They tend to be middle-aged or older. Often they do not have academic credentials. Life expectancy is another factor. It is conceivable that remnants of my generation could live to be over eighty or ninety. That would mean that by 2020 to 2030 the number of native speakers will have dwindled significantly.

It is estimated that twenty-five languages die each year. At that pace half of the world's five thousand languages will disappear by the end of this century. The driving forces associated with the life and death of languages were analyzed by French linguist Claude Hagege. One of his conclusions is as follows, "All the factors in the death of languages, whether they are political, economic, or social are capable of acting to the detriment of any language other than English, and to the benefit of this one language" (Hagege 2009, 331). And, "most importantly, due to modern techniques of communication, the power and speed that characterize the diffusion of English in the entire world far surpass that which permitted other idioms in the past, like Latin two thousand years ago, to bring about the total extinction of a great number of languages" (Hagege 2009, 331). These factors are now at work in all Native American communities.

For American Indians the metaphor of language as homeland is not a literary device. America, after all, *is* our homeland. Language is a vital part of our living heritage. Succeeding generations of Indians will make their choices about the importance or efficacy of language retention. They will discern for themselves the relevance of ancient languages amid the social complexities and economic imperatives of the modern world.

### Orientation toward Cultural Consciousness

The elders I knew in the twentieth century felt that language and culture go hand in hand. They lamented the potential loss of our language. They placed great emphasis on cultural integrity. This was most evident among traditional Indians. Many felt the old ways were superior to the new. While this was not exactly cultural solipsism, I think they feared that our identity as Indians would be irretrievably lost. It was primarily an emotional response among older Indians who were never comfortable with the White Man's ways.

Actually the grudging acceptance of a new era in the Indian world began around 1900. "The old roads are passing away," one elderly Kiowa man said in November of that year (Lassiter, Ellis, and Kotay 2002, 56). The early twentieth century was a traumatic time for my tribal nation. The transition to reservation life was under way. Our identity as a truly free and independent people had slipped away, along with the old belief systems.

About that time a new type of cultural power emerged. It had a transforming effect on our religious beliefs. It was introduced by Christian missionaries from different denominations. Christianity became known in my tribe as the Jesus Road. Its appeal was the personal power it brought to adherents. Kiowas practice a unique expression of Christianity in that new beliefs were blended with some of the old. Scholars have studied the way in which Kiowas wove the faith into their identity. They note the power of Christian hymns that were composed and sung in the Kiowa language as one potent example (Lassiter, Ellis, and Kotay 2002).

During the 1900s some very old Kiowa traditional societies were revived. Others were "put away," as the elders explained, because they were specific to a totally different time and environment. They belonged in the ancient culture that had changed dramatically. The experience of tribes who lost their culture is a poignant reminder that what we think of as culture is fragile. Not only is it susceptible to change, but under certain circumstances it can be lost entirely. Or, as with the Kiowa experience, some aspects of culture can be deliberately "put away" while generating new ones.

Those who have studied collective trauma among Native peoples think that cultural renewal can be done in positive, useful ways. It does not mean that everything need be brought back intact from the past, but some selective revival of cultural elements and generation of new ones could and should be done (Lambert 2008). Throughout Indian Country something along those lines is taking place. One example is that people are reverting to the use of tribal-specific names for themselves or for their institutions and edifices.

The cultural consciousness of Indians ultimately depends on the extent to which individuals take responsibility for learning and maintaining cultural elements, whether old, renewed, or new. Indians who practice the Plains Culture know intimately about the power of song and dance. They know the profound feeling of pride among our people that emanates from the dance ceremonials or religious worship. The emotion that comes out at such times is virtually indescribable.

That is the emotion that individuals, once they experience it, seek out consciously. Indians take comfort and protection in the old ways. Those ways give us a shared sense of belonging. They define us in ways that Western culture cannot. In 2010 we are still close enough to our traditional native cultures for them to remain meaningful. *Meaningfulness* is what people seek in their quest for cultural identity as Native Americans.

## Recovery: An Emerging Paradigm of Indian Identity

It is very likely that Indian people will shift their sense of identity in a way that fits the new era of recovery from dependency. For some it will not be easy. In fact it may take several generations to break free from the cycle of dependency and poverty that is so debilitating in many communities. But positive change will come with better health care, better living conditions, and an educated, well-informed populace. Discarding the restraints of dependency is a precondition for a different paradigm of Indian identity.

In my view recovery from dependency is akin to nation-building. Formerly colonized nations around the world rebuilt their countries once they gained independence. Recovery for them was not easy. But it was their only option, if not their destiny. Native Americans face a similar situation, albeit as domestic political entities.

Strengthening tribal governing structures will be a key factor. New leaders, those yet to be born, will be from generations that have no firsthand knowledge of oppressive federal government policies that were endured by their twentieth-century counterparts. They will indeed have a new perspective vis-à-vis the themes discussed in this chapter.

Throughout history Native Americans were perceived in simplistic ways by non-Indians. For example, other people viewed us as noble savages, indomitable warriors, or as the iconic Red Man who was imbued with some sort of innate mystical wisdom. "Good Indians" were those who in some way either helped or supported the White Man in his endeavors. That romantic image was reinforced in literature, movies, and other media. It is/was the Indian who never really existed except in someone else's imagination.

Strengthening our identity as Indians is intertwined with economic recovery. The experience of wealthy tribes demonstrates that native people can bring themselves out of poverty. They can develop education and cultural retention programs that preserve the best of their heritage, including language recovery.[6]

Knowledge of one's native language in Indian communities is an important part of the identity equation. However, we might be losing ground in recovering or retaining our languages. Some have even lamented that our native Indian languages may disappear by the end of this century. Earlier in this chapter I noted that the Wichita tribe of Oklahoma provides a case in point.

In the digital age of texting, twitter, and Facebook it may be challenging for our young Indian people to think realistically about learning native languages. Such languages, after all, came from a totally different time. On the other hand, the new technologies could be conducive to enhancing dialogue about Native American cultural preservation. Tribal songs and stories abound on YouTube. News about happenings in Indian Country is readily accessible on the internet. Our cultures are alive and dynamic. Thus, Indian identity in the twenty-first century need not be threatened by technological innovations.

In 2001 I discussed identity as a sense of self that derives from a particular tribal consciousness of self. One thinks of himself or herself as a tribal member first, then as a Native American. I pointed out that it is an individual issue but large groups of people guided by a common ethic can create a tacit collective consciousness about themselves. One's own experience in that regard informs one's sensibility about being an Indian person; as being from a specific tribe or nation. Indians feel they are Indian because they have earned that entitlement in some way. Only they can tell you how that came to be. Such is still the case, I believe.

It is possible to blend old elements of culture with new ones. Cultures and languages are dynamic in whatever form they are created; they are man-made. People depend on culture for the particular knowledge and skills that are embedded therein. Cultures are defined by the generations that succeed one another. So too are the *identities* of the people who live those cultures.

Like all human groups the Kiowa people constructed a culture that fit the environments of the different eras of consciousness they passed through. Such adaptation will no doubt continue because, as noted by Lassiter, "To speak only of cultural loss is to ignore the fact that culture is a human condition that changes as a matter of purpose" (Lassiter, Ellis, and Kotay 2002, 116). Cultural change is more than mere deviation from fixed models of assimilation. It occurs as a result of complex interactions between and among different races of people over time.

American Indians of the future will define *Indianness* in their own time and as circumstances may dictate. Cultural adaptation will motivate them to preserve the useful aspects of their societies while moving beyond things that may have limitations. We simply cannot know at this time what those might be.

In closing, we must ask: What does it mean to be Indian in the twenty-first century? I believe that the themes discussed herein provide an overall framework to explore that question. To me, when recovery from colonization and dependency eventually occurs Indian tribal nations will experience economic prosperity; they will have made great inroads in the fight against poverty; and they will have reduced or eliminated many of the social ills that plague our communities.

We who survived the twentieth century are responsible for handing down what we know in terms of our cultural integrity. We must reinforce those traditions that still fit within the modern framework of our lives. Our cultures are subject to change. But we can guide those changes in ways that make sense to us. That idea, in terms of defining ourselves, is the touchstone for Indian identity now and for generations to come.

NOTES

1. See chapter 5 in *New Perspectives on Racial Identity Development* (Wijeysinghe and Jackson 2001) by Horse for a discussion of Native American consciousness in relation to certain eras of consciousness identified for Whites by Charles Reich in 1971 (Reich 1971).

2. See *Cherokee Nation v. Georgia* (1831). In this early Supreme Court decision the court stated that the Cherokee people, not being a state, and claiming to be independent of the United States, were a "denominated domestic dependent nation" over which the Supreme Court had no original jurisdiction. The court held open the possibility that it might rule in favor of the Cherokees on an appeal from a lower court. Chief Justice John Marshall wrote that "the relationship of the tribes to the United States resembles that of a "ward to its guardian."

3. Robert D. LaSalle was a French explorer who claimed the entire Mississippi River Basin for France, circa 1682. In that year he mentioned "Mahroats," probably the Kiowas (Mayhall 1984, 12).

4. This incident made news worldwide. Prior to 2010, members of the Iroquois team were permitted to use their tribal nation passports to travel abroad. See Chen 2010.

5. See Title 25, U.S. Code, for a complete listing of all federal Indian laws.

6. Good examples of this are found among the Mississippi Choctaw, the Rumsey Band of Wintu Indians in California, and the Assiniboine (Nakoda) and Gros Ventre (White Clay) tribes in Montana.

REFERENCES

Bordewich, Fergus M. 1996. "We Ain't Got Feathers and Beads." In *Killing the White Man's Indian*. New York: Doubleday.

Chen, Michelle. 2010, July 17. "Passport Flap Keeps Iroquois Out of World Lacrosse Championship." Accessed April 5, 2011. http://colorlines.com/archives/2010/07/grounded_iroquois_lacrosse_team_bows_out_but_upholds_dignity.html

Hall, Harlan. 2000. *Remember, We Are Kiowas: 101 Kiowa Indian Stories*. Bloomington, Ind.: Authorhouse.

Hagege, Claude. 2009. *On the Death and Life of Languages*. New Haven: Yale University Press.

Horse, Perry G. 2001. "Reflections on American Indian Identity." In *New Perspectives on Racial Identity Development: A Theoretical and Practical Anthology*, edited by C. L. Wijeyesinghe and B. W. Jackson III, 91–107. New York: NYU Press.

Lambert, Craig. 2008, March–April. "Trails of Tears and Hope." *Harvard Magazine*, 39–43.

Lassiter, Luke Eric, Clyde Ellis, and Ralph Kotay. 2002. *The Jesus Road: Kiowas, Christianity, and Indian Hymns*. Lincoln: University of Nebraska Press.

Lynn-Sherow, Bonnie. 2004. *Red Earth, Race and Agriculture in Oklahoma Territory*. Lawrence: University Press of Kansas.

Mayhall, Mildred. 1984. *The Kiowas*. Norman: University of Oklahoma Press.

McKenzie, Parker, and John P. Harrington. 1948. *Popular Account of the Kiowa Language*. Albuquerque: University of New Mexico Press.

Miłosz, Czesław. 2011. Czesław Miłosz quotes. Accessed April 5, 2011. http://www.goodreads.com, www.goodreads.com/author/quotes/84259.

Ogden, Karen. 2008, Fall. "Kipp's Trip." *Magazine of the Harvard Graduate School of Education* LII (1): 29–33.

Reich, Charles. 1971. *The Greening of America*. New York: Bantam.

Spiegel, Alex. 2010, April 12. "Without Fear, Racial Stereotypes Fail to Take Root." National Public Radio. Accessed April 5, 2011. http://www.npr.org/blogs/health/2010/04/without_fear_racial_stereotype.html.

Stewart, Alison. 2008, January 30. "The Last Living Speaker of Wichita, Doris McLemore." National Public Radio Interview. Accessed April 5, 2011. http://www.npr.org/templates/story/story.php?storyId=18532656

Tocakut. See Hall, Harlan.

Viola, Herman J. 2008. *Warriors in Uniform: The Legacy of American Indian Heroism*. Washington, D.C.: National Geographic.

# 6

## White Identity Development Revisited

*Listening to White Students*

RITA HARDIMAN AND MOLLY KEEHN

## Introduction

Research and writing on White racial identity development has been located in the disciplines of Education and Counseling Psychology and includes the early models of Hardiman (1982) and Helms (1984) and subsequent models by Sue and Sue (2003), Rowe, Bennett, and Atkinson (1994), and Sabnani, Ponterotto, and Borodovsky (1991),which articulated stages similar to those of Hardiman and Helms. As discussed in "Reflections on White Identity Development Theory" in *New Perspectives on Racial Identity* (Hardiman 2001), the Hardiman and Helms models emerged in the years following the resurgence of the civil rights and Black power movements of the 1960s and 1970s. Helms's model and subsequent variations remained the focus of research efforts through the 1980s and into the middle part of the 1990s. Most of this research focused on the development of a White racial identity assessment instrument and various attempts to validate Helms's stages, or as she later described them, statuses.

While research on White racial identity by counseling psychologists has abated in recent years, theories of whiteness and research on White people's views of their race and race privilege has exploded in a variety of fields, including critical race theory, cultural studies, feminist theory, and other social science disciplines. These various disciplines have been part of a multidisciplinary, ongoing dialogue in which scholars challenge each other to define and clarify what we are describing when we investigate race, racism, and oppression, and the meaning of White identity and whiteness. Varying by discipline, whiteness is seen as a position, an identity, a discourse, and more, but a common goal in most writing is the intention of understanding whiteness in order to dismantle White privilege and racial dominance. The more recent examination of whiteness and challenge to the notion of White identity is based on poststructuralist concepts of subjectivities. As Kellington (2002, 157) states, this is because

> [a]n exploration of White subjectivities, rather than White identities, thus seems particularly appropriate to the study of Whiteness precisely because Whiteness is not a thing (Frankenburg 1997, 1) which exists outside of the ways it is thought and talked about. It is however, a constantly shifting and evolving process of becoming and defining oneself and one's racial group as White (Frankenburg 1993, 6). An exploration of White subjectivities allows for the examination of Whiteness, as a set of evolving, multiply layered and potentially contradictory discourses than as a set of attitudes towards a unified, stable "thing" called Whiteness.

The study of whiteness and White identity has also been influenced by theorists such as Crenshaw (1991) and Collins (2000) who focus on the Intersectionality of identities rather than on a singular focus on one dimension. Whiteness as seen in this view is one of many social identities that do not exist independent of other identities such as class, gender, sexual orientation, ethnicity, or religion.

In addition, since the creation of the first models of White Identity Development, the United States has undergone substantive changes in the way race is construed, how racism is enacted, and a number of public milestones regarding race. These milestones include the rising population of people of color in the United States and the election of the first Black, or depending on who defines him, Biracial Black/White president. How race and other social identities are construed by laypersons and scholars alike has changed substantially since the early writings on White identity, as well as more recent works, such as the discussion presented by Hardiman in the first edition of this book.

Among the major critiques in the field of counseling psychology of the Helms and Hardiman models and works derived from them, is that the models focus primarily on the racist attitudes and consciousness of Whites, and their views of people of color. Less attention, however, is paid to how Whites experience or name their own identity in a racialized society. Notably, the most recent work of Chesler, Peet, and Sevig (2003), Doane and Bonilla-Silva (2003), Bush (2004), and McKinney (2005) examines Whites' experience of their whiteness in terms of both race privilege and power, as well as their cultural identification or attachment to an identity or sense of belonging with the White group. This research focuses on how, or if, White people view themselves as White; how, or if, they see themselves as privileged by their whiteness or having any advantage based on race, and how they view the current state of racism in the United States.

Our research, presented in this chapter, focused on similar questions. In the in-depth interviews that we conducted as preparation for this chapter, we were most interested in exploring both the phenomenon of race identity for Whites and how, or if, Whites view themselves as having White privilege and advantage in U.S. society. We were interested in examining these questions through the lens of Hardiman's model of White Identity Development (1982, 2001). This model includes five stages of White racial identity development in which a person begins with no awareness of him- or herself as a racial being and eventually moves to creating an antiracist White identity (Hardiman 1982, 2001). The first stage, *Naivete*, is characterized by a lack of awareness and consciousness about race and racism, and occurs in very young children. Once White people discover and begin to internalize racist programming they enter the *Acceptance* stage. While in this stage, White people often believe in the myth of meritocracy, White supremacy, and the innate inferiority of people of color, and exhibit these beliefs both actively, consciously and purposefully promoting racist beliefs, and passively, colluding with the system in place in an unconscious and subtle manner.

Some White people may have an experience that leads to some sort of critical incident or "aha" moment connected to the topic of race, or experience a series of events that leads them to question their prior beliefs (for example, developing a friendship with a person of color, taking a class on social justice that discusses race and racism, etc). These experiences may lead a person to enter the third stage of Hardiman's model, *Resistance,* in which White people begin the process of unlearning racism. This stage is characterized by a number of negative feelings such as guilt and shame which lead people to want to distance themselves from their whiteness, and spend time most of their time with people of color. In the next stage, *Redefinition*, people become less estranged from their whiteness, and begin to honestly examine their White privilege and the ways they enact racism while being connected to both White people and people of color. The final stage, *Internalization*, is when a person integrates their new nonoppressive White identity into their entire being, and becomes committed to taking action against racism.

## Current Study

To pursue the notions of racial identity and how White people are experiencing and reflecting upon their race, the authors chose to focus on traditional age college students at a small public college in a rural part of Massachusetts. We were not looking to test the original WID model, but rather were interested in having conversations with young White students to take a fresh look at how racial identity, privilege, and understanding of racism was experienced by this generation, who came of age a half century after the 1960s. The choice of college students was not only due to proximity (both authors work at colleges in western Massachusetts) but also to focus on how the current generation of White young people are focusing on themselves as White.

## Methodology

We solicited participants via the student email system, noting that we were interested in exploring White students' views of their race and racism in the United States. To select our interviewees we asked students to complete a one-page questionnaire which solicited basic information such as gender, age, major, and prior courses they had taken on the subject of race and racism. We had a brief phone interview with each student who responded and selected ten students (out of thirty-eight) to interview based on their willingness to be recorded and their availability. Interviews were conducted during the winter of 2010. The interviews were conducted by the authors, two White women, one of whom was in her early thirties, the other in her fifties. While the interviews included questions developed by the authors, each interviewer also varied from the protocol at times, by asking follow-up questions when a student was vague or a response needed further explanation. Interviews lasted from roughly an hour to an hour and a half and participants received nominal compensation for their time. Although we are aware of the limitations of this small sample, we chose a qualitative approach to investigate the phenomenon of how White students view their own race, rather than to test a hypothesis. We were hoping for a balance of female and male students. We had nine students participate for the complete interviews, as one student dropped out of the interview early in the process. There were four men and five women.

## Themes and Outcomes

Our interviews focused on two major themes: the students' sense of racial identity and its meaning to them; and their understanding of White privilege and racism as an evolving phenomenon in the United States. Within these larger contexts we asked several questions to probe White students' views of their own race and its meaning to them. We expected students to know that they were White but weren't sure how they would feel about their race: proud, ashamed, empty, guilty, embarrassed, and/or confused? Expecting an absence of attachment to whiteness as a cultural identity, we also wanted to explore whether these students identified with any cultural heritage or national, ethnic, or religious identity. We also wanted to focus on whether they saw racism, their understanding of how it works, how they might impact it, and how they are impacted by it. The first set of interview questions asked students how they identified themselves racially, and not surprisingly, the first theme that emerged was that students either did not identify as White, or knew that they were White but felt no attachment to that identity. Students reported that their race is not central to their experience or their life story and they feel no real identification with that identity.

For example, one White woman said, "I don't see myself as belonging to a particular racial or ethnic group," but when required to identify in school or on a form, she identified as "White, Caucasian, you know, just who I am I guess." She went on further to say that "[This] is not something that comes up in my everyday life. You know, the people I hang out with are just the people I hang out with. . . . everyone is just kind of 'hey, we are people.'" Another student articulated a different position, that of adopting the race of people of color she is with. For example, when asked whether she saw herself as belonging to a particular race, or having a racial identity, she said, "Not really, I guess I've been involved in so many, like I've worked in an Indian restaurant . . . a Chinese restaurant . . . so I kind of tend to . . . I guess I become kind of family with them. So I don't see things from just a pure like White standpoint and it's [pause] I guess it's just not clear-cut for me." Another student framed his race in physical terms, saying he identifies as "Caucasian or White because that's the color of my skin. I think it's hard to identify race in that, that sort of definition is so robotic, it's off-putting for me but, yeah, I guess Caucasian or White. . . . it's not a huge part of my life."

It was not surprising that these students did not identify as White or feel a strong attachment to their race. This is consistent with other research (Chesler, Peet, and Sevig 2003) and is reflective of White privilege, being unmarked by race in a White racist society. While expecting these responses, we were interested to note the ease with which two of the students described themselves as being able to adopt or choose another racial identity (Indian or Chinese), in a superficial manner such as partaking of the food, and also feeling that this is something that a White person can elect to do, with no apparent awareness of whether the Indian or Chinese friends were involved in this process of "adoption." Also, not surprising was the response from a student who highlighted her Native American ancestry, which has become a familiar phenomenon among Whites when the discussion of whiteness presents itself. This flight away from whiteness to the miniscule percentage of those with American Indian ancestry despite no knowledge of tribe, ancestry, or culture is a relatively common occurrence.

While lack of awareness or attachment to whiteness is a familiar finding in recent research, we were intrigued as to whether participants in our interviews identified with any cultural heritage, or national, ethnic, or religious identity. We allowed for the possibility that while White privilege obscured awareness of whiteness, the presence of strong religious, ethnic, or cultural identity may also be a factor in the failure to see oneself as White and to attach meaning to that identity. In other words, ethnicity for some individuals, or religion for others, may be in the foreground of one's thinking about self, overshadowing his or her awareness of race. Our findings revealed that several of the students knew that they had an ethnic background or some ties to a cultural group, but they were almost unanimous in describing that understanding on an intellectual level, not a personal or emotional one. It was very much another academic exercise: I know I am this race, White, but I don't relate to it.

For instance, one male student said, "as far as belonging, I don't really feel like I belong to any certain group, if anything it would be just White, with no cultural background, pretty much, no ties. . . I feel like I am different from other people. I'm American, so, I guess I relate to Americans well." Or another student, who said, "I feel like I'd be fake if I was really tied to my Mom's Irish background. . . . it's not really my thing." One student who expressed interest in culture and genealogy said, "but I don't feel like I really identify with a certain group. . . . I'm from Vermont and people tend to tell me that it's a totally different world and I guess that I don't really realize it until I'm there." Another White woman, responding to the question "Do you feel like you belong to a racial group?" said, "I kind of feel like I don't come from anywhere because there is just so many White people and because I didn't really grow up with like going to church. . . . I almost feel like I don't have a culture, even though I know I do." One of our interviewees was a young Jewish man who explained his connection to his culture and religion this way: "I had my Bar Mitzvah when I was fourteen. . . . But my brother, training to be a rabbi, had made me reconsider my beliefs. I don't recognize myself as Jewish anymore which is kind of a shift from what I used to be." He later clarified his remarks and identified more with being Jewish as "not just a religion but an element as culture . . . which is what I identify with more than the religion." A White woman, who described her grandmother as having traced her family lineage back to the eleventh century (1000 C.E.), said she didn't identify with her ethnicity or her race. She said, "I'm just kind of here I guess. That's really all I've been. I don't really have a religious identity either. It's just like, 'Hi, I'm Jennifer,' that's about it" [Note: name changed].

Thus, the majority of the students interviewed felt no connection to a national, ethnic, or religious identity, except for the one student who was from a religious minority (Jewish). A clear undertone in most of the interviews was the feeling that students saw the recognition of their own race and that of others as an undesirable thing, or as a racist thing, although the word "racist" wasn't directly used. For example, students said things like, "I don't notice things like that." In describing their friendships or interaction with students of color, there was a defensive quality to their responses, and a desire to see themselves and have us as interviewers see them as color-blind, although again, that particular word was not used. Noticing the race of friends was seen as something that would separate them from their friends. The students did say they noticed race frequently when we moved into questions about discrimination or racism and if they had ever witnessed racist episodes or events happening.

We were also interested in investigating how these young people viewed other Whites, particularly ones of their age group, who adopt or emulate other cultures, particularly Black, urban culture, portrayed in mass media as "hip-hop" or "gangsta."

Young people at this age are very immersed in popular culture and are particularly tuned into music and contemporary artists. Many are well-versed in rap/hip hop artists and are aware of the way in which Black, urban hip hop culture has impacted the music industry, appealing to people of all backgrounds. Additionally, they are aware of the phenomenon in which White youth emulate or copy these artists or the commercial style of these artists that is represented in dress, shoes, jewelry, and the like. They also see White peers who go beyond just dressing "gangsta" but adopt speech and affectations of Black musicians and celebrities. When asked about White kids in rural areas who go "gangster" or the White version "wangsta," many of the students were familiar with this phenomenon and found it strange, weird, or embarrassing, noting, "I don't know. I guess they have a different perception on life than I do. Like, I don't identify as a wigger[1] at all. I actually probably close to the opposite of a wigger. So, I guess I just don't understand the way that they think." And, "In high school I had friends that kind of dressed with baggy clothes and stuff like that, used ebonics, but . . . I don't really know what to say about them. I guess it's just a choice of style. A way to dress and a way to act I guess."

Another student, who was a musician, identified this behavior as confusing and problematic, stating, "Well I think for myself, I identify that sort of phenomenon because of the music. I don't think that it is just recently that this happened. If you look at all through history, music has played a role in culture. You know, blues originated as slave music and once that became popular it became connected and brought together people of different races. I mean I'm aware that people are identifying with a specific race, based on music." He went on to say that "Personally I think it's ridiculous looking, but then again I don't think that's Black culture really. I think it's something itself because I've seen lots of White people like with the Yoga and everything, go towards more Indian lifestyle and that's okay, but the Wigger thing it just confuses me and I don't . . . I don't really understand why they are doing it, it doesn't show respect, it doesn't show talent . . . so I don't even understand where they even get the idea that doing that will make them seem more like the group that they want to be like, cause it's more than that. It's not just a way of dress. It's not. . . It's kind of almost disrespectful actually. . . . It's almost like they are taking on a history that they don't belong to and taking personal offense to it but they're White so they don't even have that. . . . I think that they are missing something and they are grabbing onto something that is very eccentric . . . to find a group, to find placement."

Another student noted that the phenomenon is "White people trying to act like they are ghetto/gangsta when they're like 15. And they put their hat on sideways and they have no idea of what it means to be like, you know, some of those people. I think it is bad because they're adopting it for the wrong reasons." She went on to explain that they think they are acting Black and being cool but they don't understand Blacks or Black culture at all, or that not all Blacks are into hip hop. Some of the students saw this behavior as simply a form of teenage rebellion or an individual choice of what to wear and how to act, not connected to anything in particular.

Beyond identification with their race and/or ethnicity and cultural background, we also wanted to explore if students viewed being White as conferring advantage or disadvantage to them as individuals and members of a group. One way this idea was explored was through our question: "Have you experienced discrimination because of your race, or have you felt disadvantaged by your race?" One male student said, "I think that people . . . some people hate, not like hate all White people, but I think there is a lot of hostility toward White people because it's just assumed that we are racist because of our past history . . . and that kind of bothers me a little bit, but I don't know, I don't really think about belonging to the White group." This same student said that he didn't think he had any advantages being White, and believed that he might have had some disadvantages. He felt that he may have been discriminated against as a White person because "back in high school, middle school, or maybe elementary school, there were two Black kids and they called me a cracker." He also indicated, "I feel like I have disadvantages. I feel like I am less apt to get jobs and less apt to get financial aid for school." A White female student felt that Affirmative Action might be a disadvantage, stating that "I've always worried about being passed over because they need to fill a quota . . . but then again I really like Affirmative Action because it kind of evens the playing field." Additionally, she acknowledged that it might benefit her as a woman. Absent in most students' minds was an awareness of discrimination or racial disadvantage occurring as a result of policies or practices imbedded in laws or institutional behavior. Discrimination was viewed typically as a result of individual action and sometimes it was individual people of color who were acting against them. One female student, describing how she is disadvantaged by being White, said, "Yes, because if you think about the hip hop culture and rappers it would take a lot for, for me to be accepted into that culture." Another student mentioned being discriminated against because she had a Black male friend and received "dirty looks" that seemed to suggest to her that her relationship was inappropriate.

When asked about the privilege of whiteness or having an advantage by being White, students were mixed in their points of view. Some individuals who were aware that people of color face racism in some situations, were unable to see the other side of racism: unearned privilege conferred on Whites, as with the male student who said he didn't think he had any advantages, but thought he might have had disadvantages. The only student among our interviewees who was of a religious minority, Jewish, imagined that he was in a position of privilege "because I am not persecuted against, at least not actively," but he was clear that he was discriminated against as a Jew. He was also aware of his White privilege but felt that when people realized he was Jewish, their anti-Semitism was apparent, resulting in him being treated differently than non-Jewish White people. Interestingly, one woman said,

"I've been told that I have advantages but I've never really thought of myself as having advantages [as a White person]. I mean I might see myself as having more advantages being a woman than White." She added, "I don't see advantages or disadvantages to being White. It's just the way I was born, you know. There is not much I can do about it."

Many students' responses about racial matters involved a focus on their somewhat limited interactions with people of color. We wanted to shift the focus a bit and explore whether the students experienced issues with other White people—did they experience racial conflict with other Whites because of racism or differences in attitudes, beliefs, and behaviors when it came to race? We asked participants, "Have you had conflict with White people because of your views or behavior regarding race and racism?"

In response to this question, one White woman said, "Yeah . . . my friends . . . my grandparents, they're accepting but their arms aren't reaching around people." The student went on to describe some tension in her family and the gradual acceptance of her previous boyfriend who was from Africa and a Muslim. Another student described a rift that occurred between himself and a White friend over the friend's attitudes toward Blacks and Latinos which emerged when they both attended a campus party where a number of Black and Latino students were present. The interviewee described his friend this way: "He kept saying, I don't feel safe when realistically there wasn't any danger, so I think that put a sort of wedge in between our friendship because I realized that he had an insecurity [around people of color] that I didn't share." Another student described conflicts when she has challenged racist jokes or assumptions about other races, noting a conflict she got into at a holiday party when an uncle said that abortion encourages Black people to be more sexually promiscuous and behave badly. Finally one student identified conflict not with White people, but potentially with people of color because of his beliefs. He said, in response to our question about conflict with Whites, "No, never . . . because I keep my opinions to myself. If I ever did have an opinion about race I probably wouldn't be the one to say it, because it could cause conflict easily, like if there was a minority complaining about how they are a minority and they don't get anything out of life, then I would probably like to say that they get a lot out of life and they have more chances than most people."

It was important to us to explore how students saw racism now and if they understood how it has morphed and changed its forms. Contemporary racism has become in some ways less visible or coded in different language, or hidden in institutional practices that are portrayed as postracial. We asked, "How do you see racism now, do you think that there is more racism now, less now, or about the same?" One theme we found in the responses was that students saw racism as something that happens one-on-one, or in discrete settings like a mall, rather than as a pervasive phenomenon. A White woman said, "I think that, I definitely think that there is some racism out there . . . and I still think that in a class, or in a store setting I have those advantages over people of a different race." Some students reflected an internal debate while thinking out loud about this question, noting that while in some areas racism has abated, and that Obama is president, they were also aware of its continuing presence. "I think it's not really changing. It's less acceptable formally on paper, in the laws it is not OK to discriminate if you are interviewing for a job or something . . . but I think that doesn't really change much. It's become more of a private problem and less of a public problem."

Another student reflected the belief that the behavior of people of color contributes to racism. She commented, "It's hard to say, um I kind of think it's more of a problem because I feel like there is a bigger separation between people . . . and it's kind of almost because of media, things like rap, they are just like for every one Obama there are 20 rap artists that kind of let the stereotypes fly. It would die down if people would stop being so focused on it but because everybody is so hyperfocused on it, it's more of a problem . . . also Affirmative Action is still being kind of racist because you're demanding people choose people." One of the students made a comment that was echoed by several others, which centered on an unwillingness or inability to challenge racism when it is seen. She said, "I never really challenge things. I feel like, I don't know. It's not worth challenging it, I don't think. There is just not a big enough reward, I guess. . . . I can't challenge something just for self-righteousness. Just because I am content with what I have and who I am. So, I don't see a point to challenging something. Cause it doesn't bother me if it goes, how things go. Yeah, nothing would really bother me, I don't think. Cause I don't identify with a group I guess."

### Reflection on White Identity Development (WID) Stages

If one reviews the early WID stages of Hardiman and Helms's model of WRID it appears that most of the students from this study are in the early stages of White identity development. Their understanding of racism was primarily described as the attitudes and behaviors of individuals acting upon race prejudice, with little mention of political or economic power structures affecting the lives of people of color. Similarly, their views of the privileges and advantages conferred on White people are quite limited. Most of what was mentioned was either the absence of being hassled in a store, or being followed by a White cop. Racism was largely seen as individual actions rather than as a systemic power structure. Participants acknowledged the history of bad things that Whites have done to Blacks and American Indians in particular, for example, slavery and the theft of land, but lack the awareness of the ongoing nature of racial oppression in the United States. Because they tended to see racism as individual actions rather than as a system of advantage, the students interviewed for this chapter saw themselves as discriminated against by name-calling or isolated incidents of being picked on by people of color. Similarly some students had a sense that racism had abated because we have a Black president, while others believed that racism isn't changing and won't change because there will always be racist people. Most of the interviewees made statements that reflected the Passive Acceptance stage in Hardiman's model and the Contact stage in Helms's model.

We also saw a familiar pattern of Whites not understanding how their view of themselves as individuals who can choose whether or not they focus on race is reflective of their privilege as people unmarked by race. The students we interviewed were from rural areas, living in very White small towns. Yet while all the participants had some interaction with people of color, most of them also had limited exposure to serious study of U.S. history and, in particular, the racial history of this country. Several students seemed to accept the notion that Affirmative Action favored people of color and made life harder for them as Whites. When we asked them what the basis was for this view, they said they believed it was so and didn't seem interested in investigating whether this belief is borne out by the facts. Sadly, these students don't seem connected to a history or to a culture from which they derive meaning, be it a local, ethnic, or religious culture. In describing family traditions they talked about food or rituals that have little significance to their lives. What replaces a group heritage is a view of themselves as unique individuals. This mirrors the myth of the rugged individual, a familiar U.S. archetype which obscures the way that race, gender, and class affect people differently based on their identity.

Some of the students voiced evidence of the markers of the passive and active acceptance stage in the WID model. They had some awareness of their White privilege and some awareness of the racism that their friends of color were experiencing, but were either unwilling or unable to know how to interrupt racism in their midst.

The ways in which these students described themselves as White and discuss White privilege and racism reflects other recent research that suggests that explicit racism, or perhaps the awareness of overt racism, is less prevalent and that racism has not disappeared but has become more hidden. Almost all the researchers we looked at agree that "old fashioned racism"—which included outright expression of prejudice and hate for people of color— is on the decline (Chesler, Peet, and Sevig 2003; Dovidio and Gaertner 1998; Feagin 2000). This explicit form of racism has "largely disappeared from the American scene or has gone underground as it is no longer acceptable as public speech" (Chesler, Peet, and Sevig 2003, 219). People are now less likely than in the past to come out and state that they think Black people are lazy, that they think that interracial marriages should be forbidden, or that they would not vote for a Black leader because of race (Dovidio and Gaertner 1998). Because of this decline in explicit racist views and speech, it is easy for White people to point to these examples of reported tolerance, and argue that racism no longer is a problem. Eduardo Bonilla-Silva has done a great deal of research on the new ways that White people express racist thoughts and feelings. He cites five central elements of this new type of racism, which he refers to as "color-blind" racism— (1) racist thoughts and actions have become increasingly subtle and covert, (2) Whites try to avoid talking about race and racism, and frequently claim that they are victims of "reverse racism," (3) institutional and cultural racism are often invisible, (4) "safe" or token minorities are incorporated into institutions and are used to support the claim that racist policies are absent, and (5) the racial patterns of the Jim Crow era are now replicated in a subtle form (Bonilla-Silva 2003, 272). We found all these elements represented in the interviews with this small group of White students. These students believed that there is an "equal playing field" and everyone can attain the "American Dream." It also appears that our participants are fearful of being labeled "racist" and try to avoid conversations about race. This fear compounds the problem because institutional and cultural racism cannot be brought to light.

Bonilla-Silva and Forman (2000) conducted a study that directly examined this new type of racism. The study involved having White students take a brief survey measuring racial attitudes and then interviewing the participants in detail about similar questions to the material covered on the survey. The rationale of this methodology was that, in recent times, possessing racist attitudes has become so taboo that White people will typically choose what they perceive to be the most tolerant answer on a survey. The researchers hoped that by using interviews they could get at more subtle racist beliefs. What they found was that students were much more likely to express racist attitudes in the interviews than in the surveys. They also discovered that even though the participants seemed to be more prejudiced in the interviews, they used a new "racetalk" (2000, 50) to avoid sounding racist. This "racetalk" enabled participants to avoid directly talking about racial issues while protecting the racial privileges that they have (Bonilla-Silva and For-man 2000, 52). The findings of this study support the existence of color-blind racism and demonstrate some of the ways in which it operates.

Another label used by researchers to describe contemporary racism is "aversive racism," which involves an internal conflict between beliefs in equality and unconscious feelings of prejudice toward people of color (Chesler, Peet, and Sevig 2003, 219). According to Dovidio and Gaertner (1998), this type of racism often involves White people who see themselves as nonprejudicial and it is a very subtle, and usually unintentional, form of bias. Feelings associated with this type of racism "involve discomfort, uneasi-ness, disgust and sometimes fear" (Dovidio and Gaertner 1998, 6). One com-ponent of aversive racism outlined by Dovidio and Gaertner is the fact that even though White people may consciously reflect on these racist thoughts, unconscious negative feelings often do not go away. Thus, White people in our study who expressed the sentiment, "I don't have a prejudiced bone in my body" may be operating out of aversive racism—and not aware of what is really going on.

Although this study only incorporated the thinking of nine White stu-dents, it gives a glimpse into how some college students experience and name their racial identity, and the ways they think about racism and White privilege. The lack of identification with and/or resistance to identifying with a racial, ethnic, or cultural identity expressed by the participants connects with the work of others (Bush 2004; Kendall, 2006; McKinney 2005). It is also interesting to note how this void leads White students to take on the cul-ture of others, whether it is the Black "hip hop" culture they have seen in the media, the culture of distant Native American ancestors, or that of friends of color. Thus, not only is being seen as an individual and not needing to be connected to a racial or ethnic identity an example of White privilege, but it simultaneously demonstrates loss or a cost of racism to White people (Kivel 2002). Our study also echoed the findings of other research that found that White participants may see racism on an individual level, but do not see rac-ism as a systemic phenomenon (Bush 2004; McKinney 2005).

The interviews that we conducted for this chapter suggest a number of areas for additional research on White identity. One area would explore the intersection of whiteness with other social identities and explore the varia-tions of experience of how race impacts White people from different reli-gions, socioeconomic statuses, ethnicities, and other social identities. It was interesting, but not surprising, that the one student in our interviews of a Jewish background was most aware of the ways in which he was privileged by race, but not privileged by religion, and was also connected to, albeit in a complex way, his cultural heritage as a Jew. Another area to explore is Kel-lington's notion of White subjectivities, rather than White identities, and to look at the "shifting and evolving process of . . . defining oneself and one's racial group as White" (2002, 157). The students we interviewed described moving in and out of awareness of race and racism, and in and out of aware-ness of their White and other group identities, depending on their location, peer group, family dynamics, and more, thus suggesting a less static "stage" of development and a more fluid process of racial identification and race priv-ilege. This fluidity is consistent with our more recent thinking about indi-viduals occupying more than one stage of racial identity at any given time, and experiencing the thoughts, feelings, and behaviors of multiple stages, depending on the issues that present themselves. It could be interesting to look at White college students who identify as antiracist in the context of the WID model stages, to see if the stages that were originally created (based on antiracist adults) would still hold. It would also be important to not only look at what students are saying in the interviews, but how they are saying it through discourse analysis, examining the ways coded language can be used to bring up racist views ("crime," "welfare," "urban areas") (Bush 2004).

The interviews with students in this study also raise broader questions about the salience of any cultural or religious identification for young White men and women at this moment in history. While we expected students not to identify strongly with their whiteness, it was surprising to hear them voice almost no group affiliation or heritage with which they identified. Finally, a more sobering concern that we took away from these conversations was a sense that these young White people were ill-equipped to understand or fully participate in an increasingly multicultural society. They had a limited understanding of how the politics of race continue to shape U.S. society and their privilege as White people. They also appear to have limited cultural competence to interact effectively with individuals and institutions that are culturally diverse and to compete in a global economy where cross-cultural understanding is essential. This demonstrates the importance of educating college students about the racial history of the United States and around the world, and using pedagogies, such as intergroup dialogue (Zúñiga et al. 2007), that help students to grasp how racism plays out on an institutional as well as a personal level.

NOTE

1. A male Caucasian usually born and raised in the suburbs who displays a strong desire to emulate African American hip hop culture and style through "bling," fashion, and generally accepted "thug life" guiding principles.

## REFERENCES

Bonilla-Silva, Eduardo. 2003. "'New Racism,' Color-Blind Racism, and the Future of Whiteness in America. In *White Out: The Continuing Significance of Racism*, edited by Ashley W. Doane and Eduardo Bonilla-Silva, 271–284. New York: Routledge.

Bonilla-Silva, Eduardo, and Tyrone A. Forman. 2000. "'I Am Not Racist but . . .': Mapping White College Students' Racial Ideology in the USA." *Discourse and Society* 11 (1): 50–85.

Bush, Melanie. 2004. *Breaking the Code of Good Intentions: Everyday Forms of Whiteness*. New York: Rowman & Littlefield.

Chesler, Mark, Melissa Peet, and Todd Sevig. 2003. "Blinded by Whiteness: The Development of White College Students' Racial Awareness." In *White Out: The Continuing Significance of Racism*, edited by Ashley W. Doane and Eduardo Bonilla-Silva, 215–230. New York: Routledge.

Collins, Patricia Hill. 2000. *Black Feminist Thought: Knowledge, Consciousness and the Politics of Empowerment, Revised 10th Anniversary Edition*. New York: Routledge.

Crenshaw, Kimberle. 1991. "Mapping the Margins: Intersectionality, Identity Politics and Violence against Women of Color." *Stanford Law Review* 43 (6): 1241–1299.

Doane, Ashley W., and Eduardo Bonilla-Silva, eds. 2003. *White Out: The Continuing Significance of Racism*. New York: Routledge.

Dovidio, John F., and Samuel L. Gaertner. 1998. "On the Nature of Contemporary Racism: The Causes, Consequences, and Challenges of Aversive Racism." In *Confronting Racism: The Problem and the Response*, edited by Jennifer L. Eberhardt and Susan T. Fiske, 3–32. Thousand Oaks, Calif.: Sage.

Feagin, Joe R. 2000. *Racist America: Roots, Current Realities, and Future*. New York: Routledge.

Frankenberg, Ruth. 1993. *White Women, Race Matters: The Social Construction of Whiteness*. Minneapolis: University of Minnesota Press.

Hardiman, Rita. 1982. "White Identity Development: A Process-Oriented Model." Dissertation Abstracts International.

———. 2001. "Reflections on White Identity Development Theory." In *New Perspectives on Racial Identity Development: A Theoretical and Practical Anthology*, edited by Charmaine L. Wijeyesinghe and Bailey W. Jackson III, 108–128. New York: NYU Press.

Helms, Janet. 1984. "Toward a Theoretical Explanation of the Effects of Race on Counseling: A Black/White Model." *Counseling Psychologist* 12 (4): 153–165.

Kellington, Stephanie. 2002. "Looking at the Invisible: A Q-Methodological Investigation of Young White Women's Construction of Whiteness." In *Working through International Perspectives*, edited by Cynthia Levine-Rasky, 153–178. Albany: SUNY Press.

Kendall, Frances E. 2006. *Understanding White Privilege: Creating Pathways to Authentic Relationships across Race*. New York: Routledge.

Kivel, Paul. 2002. *Uprooting Racism: How White People Can Work for Racial Justice*. Gabriola Island, B.C., Canada: New Society Publishers.

McKinney, Karyn. 2005. *Being White: Stories of Race and Racism*. New York: Routledge.

Rowe, Wayne, Sandra K. Bennett, and Donald R. Atkinson. 1994. "White Racial Identity Models: A Critique and Alternative Proposal." *Counseling Psychology* 22 (1): 129–146.

Sabnani, Haresh B., Joseph G. Ponterotto, and Lisa G. Borodovsky. 1991. "White Racial Identity Development and Cross-Cultural Counselor Training: A Stage Model." *Counseling Psychologist* 19 (1): 76–102.

Sue, Derald Wing, and David Sue. 2003. *Counseling the Culturally Diverse,* 4th ed. New York: John Wiley & Sons.

Zúñiga, Ximena, Biren A. Nagda, Mark Chesler, and Adena Cytron-Walker. 2007. "Intergroup Dialogue in Higher Education: Meaningful Learning about Social Justice." *ASHE Higher Education Report:* 32 (4).

7

# Asian American Racial Identity
# Development Theory

JEAN KIM

This chapter reviews the theory of Asian American racial identity development (AARID) that was created by the author in the early 1980s and updated in the context of the evolution of social identity theories over the past thirty years.

An overview of how researchers approach social identities starts the chapter, followed by a discussion of the importance of the social context and the impact of racism on Asian American racial identity development. The review of the AARID is followed by a section that examines the relevance of the AARID theory to Asian Americans today. The chapter explores changes in the political and economic climate and how those changes may impact Asian American racial identity development. Given the large percentage of Asian American immigrants among Asian Americans as a whole, the chapter also examines the relevancy of AARID to different generations of Asian Americans and outlines current issues for future research in the area of racial identity development for Asian Americans.

## Identity Lenses

There are several ways to explore an individual's identity. While it is generally acknowledged that an individual's identity is comprised of multiple dimensions (race, gender, sexual orientation, socioeconomic class, religion, roles in life, personality, etc.), a traditional approach has been to explore identity through a single lens or dimension such as race. There is general agreement on race as a social construct and phenomenon that has taken on an important meaning. It describes not only how outsiders view members of a different racial group, but also how members of a given racial group view themselves (Atkinson, Morten, and Sue 1993).

Racial identity describes a person's identification with membership in a socially designated racial group, and this identification is largely influenced by socialization around race (Alvarez, Juang, and Liang 2006; Helms and Talleyrand 1997). In short, racial identity describes how people deal with the effects of racism, eventually disowning the dominant group's views of their own race and developing a positive self-definition and positive attitude toward their own group. As the model presented in this chapter is a theory of racial identity development for Asian Americans, and to further clarify the distinction between racial and ethnic identities, the title of this theory has been changed from AAID (Asian American Identity Development)[1] to AARID (Asian American Racial Identity Development).

Unlike racial identity, ethnic identity is not so closely tied to oppression and racism. Ethnicity can be defined as the culture, traditions, and customs of a group of people. For many Asian Americans ethnic group membership is related to their country of origin and expectations they are aware of, based on various aspects of their cultural heritage. An Asian American individual can have different levels of identification with, or rejection of, cultural expectations and values. The essence of ethnic identity is about resolving any tension between how an individual is expected to be and how the person wants to be perceived as an ethnic being (Chang and Kwan 2009). Most research has focused on ethnic identity development theories for Asian Americans rather than race. Some examples are Phinney's Three Stages of Ethnic Identity Development (1989) and Smith's Four Phases of Ethnic Identity Conflict (1991). In Smith's framework, conflict related to an individual's ethnic identity begins when contact with others leads to the realization that there are majority and minority statuses. When a minority person feels rejected by the majority, he or she attempts to identify with the majority. Of the various ethnic minorities in the United States, the study by Phinney (1989) indicates that a higher percentage of Asian American adolescents would change their race to White if they could and that they feel less ethnic pride than African Americans or Hispanics.

Both racial and ethnic identity development theories are related to the concept of social identity. Social identity theory (Tajfel and Turner 1986) postulates that racial and ethnic groups are social groups that have varying status within society. The evaluation of the prestige of one's social group influences the extent to which an individual identifies with that group in order to enhance his or her self-esteem. Researchers generally believe that individuals have both ethnic and racial identities, both of which develop continuously. The primacy of ethnic or racial identity varies depending on many factors such as social context, group membership, and so on. Chang and Kwan (2009) postulate that for Asian Americans ethnic/cultural identity may develop before racial identity, especially for the immigrant (first) generation where the needs of acculturation trump understanding oneself as a racial being. Another reason for racial identity having less primacy among Asian Americans may be that the discrimination and racism many of them experience is more subtle than that directed toward other groups of color, and because of the prevalent stereotype of Asian Americans being the model minority (Chen et al. 2006; Inman 2006).

The saliency of a person's ethnic and racial identity may also vary depending on the social context and individual's stage of identity development. Since typically people have multiple identities, depending on the situation or relationship context, whether race or ethnic identity is primary may depend on who is around and the nature of the situation (Yip 2005). For example, an Asian American woman of Chinese heritage may express a stronger connection with her ethnic identity as Chinese when interacting with her family, but express a stronger racial identity as an Asian American person when interacting with her White peers in class. Individuals may also reject racial identity in favor of their ethnic identity, especially if they feel marginalized even within their own racial minority group.

There are other theoretical models that explore how individuals manage multiple social identities either by compartmentalizing social identities or integrating identities. Conflict can arise if an individual identifies with more than one social group. Compartmentalizing is one way to manage the potential conflict among multiple social identities (Chen 2009). For example, knowing that there is stronger bias against homosexuality within Asian cultures than in U.S. culture, gay Asian American men and women may keep their sexual orientation identity separate from their racial or ethnic identity when interacting with Asian ethnic communities. Other researchers conclude that some individuals do not identify with any social group and focus mostly on personal identity. such as their roles as parent, student, worker, friend, sibling, and so on. Such focus on personal identity may be due to personal characteristics such as personality traits being more salient in their lives or it could be a means of denying or avoiding dealing with the social realities of their group membership.

For some Asian Americans, particularly the immigrant generation, the most pressing challenge and objective is related to surviving and establishing themselves in the new country, assimilating as quickly as possible into mainstream America. Contemplating their minority status may seem like a type of navel gazing for this group, one they can ill-afford. Focusing on their personal rather than social identity may also be due to the fact that most Asian American immigrants come to the United States after their formative years when their personal identity and self-concept have solidified. Therefore, the social political climate and racism in the United States may have less of an effect on their personal identities than on those Asian Americans who are coming of age in the White dominant society.

When I have shared my AARID theory with Asian American professionals, they recognize and connect to the stages of AARID, but they believe it is more relevant to the experiences of their children who were born and raised in the United States. This is understandable, given the fact that the majority of these professionals are immigrants who came to the United States after completing their college educations and with a more fully developed personal identity. Historically, it has also been true that for some Asian Americans, like the Japanese Americans during and after World War II, their survival was dependent on their downplaying their minority status (less focus on race and ethnicity). This may also explain why this group has a higher rate of mixed marriages (mostly with Whites) than any other Asian ethnic group.

## Social Context and Asian Americans

One cultural trait that Americans of Asian heritage share regardless of their specific ethnic group membership is group orientation. This orientation distinguishes them from the dominant White population and the individual orientation more prevalent in the dominant society. Through this propensity for group orientation, Asian Americans learn to be sensitive to the expectations of the group they are with and their social environment.[2] For example,

Asian people's view of themselves (*the private self*) is primarily influenced by what other people (*the public*), and particularly what a specific group of people (*the collective*) think of them. Consequently, the development of individual identity is largely influenced by messages that are external to Asian Americans in both the collective and public environments. Given Asian Americans' tendency to be externally rather than internally focused, their racial identity development is especially affected by the social environment. In particular, the impact of White racism and the attendant oppression of Asian Americans by European Americans are critical factors in Asian American identity development (Chan and Hune 1995; Kim 1981; Moritsugu and Sue 1983; Smith 1991). However, before we can discuss the impact of racism on Asian Americans, it may be helpful to clarify how race is conceptualized in the United States and how racism is defined.

Discussions about race tend to be very emotional, and it is difficult to have a common understanding of what race is and why it matters. But many scholars, especially those associated with the Critical Race Theory movement (Begley 1995; Crenshaw 1995; Delgado 1995) have argued persuasively that the phenomenon of race is a social and legal construct.[3] A growing number of Asian American legal scholars also support this view, arguing that race is not simply an immutable biological attribute (as in skin color) but represents a complex set of social meanings which are affected by political struggle (Omi and Winant 1994). Understanding that race is socially and politically, rather than biologically, determined may help us to understand how racial prejudice and racial dominance operate in U.S. society.

Racial prejudice is created by inaccurate and/or negative beliefs that rationalize the *superiority* or *normalcy* of one race. Racial dominance, on the other hand, describes the control of societal structures by a single racial group which enforces that group's racial prejudice and maintains its privileges. Racism occurs when racial prejudice and racial dominance occur simultaneously (Wijeyesinghe, Griffin, and Love 1997). In the United States the White race is racially dominant and racial prejudice is taught to everyone, including members of racially oppressed groups. In addition, race often tends to be seen in Black and White terms, and we are most familiar with racial prejudices directed against Black Americans. We are less aware of the experiences of other groups of color (Asian, Latino, and American Indian). We also assign a specific set of stereotypes to each racial group (Wijeyesinghe, Griffin, and Love 1997).

Since the mid-1960s, when the Black civil rights movement was gaining momentum, the media began depicting Asian Americans as the "model minority." Articles appeared in popular magazines portraying Asian

Americans as one minority group who had made it in this country through hard work (Kasindorf 1982; Chan and Hune 1995). These stories cited higher academic attainments and combined family earnings of Asian Americans as indicators that Asians are a model minority. Several positive generalizations—that Asians work hard, are technological nerds, are good at math, are focused on education, and the like—were added to the negative stereotypes of Asians—for example, that Asians are sly, ruthless, untrustworthy, submissive, quiet, foreigners, and lack communication skills and leadership potential. Given this "model minority" myth and the so-called "positive" stereotypes of Asian Americans, some people are unaware of the fact that White racism is also directed against Asian Americans. In fact, the history of racism against Asians began with the first wave of Asian immigrants from China almost one hundred fifty years ago. Subsequent to this early period, Asians have been subjected to massive and intense discrimination, including the denial of citizenship, the segregation of schools and housing, lynching, massacres, internment in concentration camps, random acts of violence, and subtle forms of unfair treatment in employment.[4]

In spite of this history, there is a pervasive myth accepted by many, including Asian Americans themselves, that Asian Americans have overcome all these obstacles and have succeeded in finding a place for themselves in the American dream through hard work, perseverance, and quiet suffering. It is true that many Asian Americans have obtained higher levels of education than the general population and have achieved middle-class status (Carnevale and Stone 1995). However, the model minority myth[5] ignores both the significant psychological cost of acculturation into a White racist society and the reality of continuing discrimination against Asian Americans. One such psychological cost is racial identity conflict.

Racism and Identity Conflict

Of the many problems faced by Asian Americans in the psychological arena, racial identity conflict is the most critical and severe (Sue and Sue 1971; Suzuki 1975; Sue and Sue 1990). Conflict about one's identity can be said to exist when individuals perceive certain aspects or attributes of themselves which they simultaneously reject. In the case of Asian Americans, awareness of oneself as an Asian person is rejected in favor of the White models that are so pervasive in our society. The issue here is not the lack of awareness of one's racial self but rather how one feels about and values that part of oneself.[6]

The phenomenon of identity conflict is manifested in a number of ways, with varying degrees of severity (Kohatsu 1993; Huang 1994). An Asian

American may experience identity conflict as a belief in his or her own inferiority (as well as the inferiority of other Asian Americans), perhaps coupled with deep-seated feelings of self-hatred and alienation. At some point in their lives, many Asian Americans have both consciously or unconsciously expressed the desire to become White, and tried to reject their identity as Asians (Kim 1981; Suzuki 1975; Huang 1994). A painful expression of this identity conflict among Asian American women is the practice of creating double-folded eyelids (many Asians have single-folded eyelids) either through surgery or by using scotch tape in a vain attempt to meet the beauty standards of White society. This practice of "Americanizing" Asian eyes is reminiscent of the practice among Blacks of straightening their hair and bleaching their skin to look whiter in appearance (Suzuki 1975). Such experiences of denial and/or rejection of their Asian heritage contribute toward Asian Americans' negative self-concept and low self-esteem, both hallmarks of negative racial identity (Sue and Sue 1990).

The experience of identity conflict among Asian Americans is a direct result of living in a society that has institutionalized racism throughout its major structures, cultures, and value systems, as noted in Knowles and Prewitt's original work in 1969. Examples of institutional racism are stereotypes of Asians evident in film and television. The history of the U.S. legal and political system also contains voluminous pages of violence and discrimination directed at Asian Americans (Takaki 1989; Chan and Hune 1995). Although the racism experienced by Asian Americans today may be more subtle than in prior decades, its effects have been shown to have a negative impact on Asian Americans' psychological well-being (Chin 1970; Sue and Kitano 1973; Sue and Sue 1971, 1990). Various manifestations of identity conflict can be seen as the result of Asian Americans' attempts to make it in a White society, which, for the most part, devalues racial minorities and considers people of color to be aliens and foreigners even though many have been here for generations. Identity conflict as experienced by Asian Americans seems inevitable in a society where being different is synonymous with being inferior.

Asian American Racial Identity Development (AARID): The Model

This theory is comprised of five stages which explore how Asian Americans gain a positive racial identity in a society where they must deal with various negative messages and stereotypes about who they are. Each stage is characterized by the basic components of an identity: a self-concept that includes evaluation and meaning attribution (ego identity). The cultural tendency for

Asian Americans to have a group and public orientation and to avoid shame contributes to the assimilation strategy evident in the White Identification stage. Access to information and increased understanding about White racism can help an Asian American to move out of the White Identification stage and start on the road to a positive racial identity. Although the process is not linear or automatic, the five stages are conceptually sequential. For example, it is possible for an Asian American to get stuck in a certain stage and never move to the next stage. Whether Asian Americans move on to the next stage in their racial identity development is dependent primarily on their social environment, and various factors in this environment determine both the length and the quality of experience in a given stage.

*Stage One: Ethnic Awareness*

Ethnic Awareness is the first stage of AARID, and represents the period prior to Asian Americans entering the school system. Awareness of their ethnicity comes primarily from interactions with family members and relatives. Asian Americans who live in predominantly Asian or mixed neighborhoods have greater exposure to ethnic activities and experience more ethnic pride and knowledge of their cultural heritage. One benefit of membership in a larger Asian community is that Asian Americans experience what it is like to be in the majority and have a sense of security and positive ethnic awareness. Asian Americans who live in predominately White neighborhoods and have less exposure to ethnic activities are not sure what it means to be a member of an Asian ethnic group and feel neutral about their ethnic membership. Furthermore, greater exposure to Asian ethnic experiences at this stage leads to a positive self-concept and clearer ego identity while less exposure is related to a neutral self-concept and confused ego identity (Kim 1981, 2001). For most Asian Americans, this stage lasts until they enter the school systems. When they begin school, most Asian Americans' social environment changes from a protective secure home setting to a more public arena. It is this change in social environment that heralds a period of increased contact with the dominant White society, a key factor that moves individuals to the next stage.

*Stage Two: White Identification*

The beginning of the White Identification stage is marked by Asian Americans' strong sense of being different from their peers. They acquire this sense mostly through painful encounters such as being made fun of, being the object of name-calling, and the like. Such experiences tell Asian Americans that being different is bad. Given the Asian cultural values of quiet suffering and avoiding public shame, most Asian parents are not able to help their children cope with this other than by telling them to ignore these slights and hurts. The significance of shame in Asian cultures may also influence Asian Americans to try at all costs to fit into White society in order to avoid publicly embarrassing themselves. Gradually they internalize White societal values and standards and see themselves through the eyes of the White society, especially regarding standards of physical beauty and attractiveness.

Although their reference group is White, Asian Americans in the White Identification stage often feel socially isolated from their White peers and enjoy little closeness or meaningful contact with them. Many Asian Americans compensate for this by becoming involved in formal organizational roles and responsibilities in school such as becoming class presidents, class officers, club leaders, and by excelling academically. However, this is a very painful period when Asian Americans' self-concept begins to change from positive or neutral to negative. They also experience alienation from self and other Asian Americans while feeling inferior and believing they are at fault and responsible for racial incidents that happen to them.

ACTIVE WHITE IDENTIFICATION

There is some variation as to how the White Identification stage is experienced, depending on the degree to which Asian Americans identify with White people. Asian Americans who grow up in predominantly White environments are more likely to experience what is called *Active White Identification*, and repress negative feelings and experiences associated with their Asianness. In actively identifying with White people, these Asian Americans consider themselves to be very similar to their White peers and do not consciously acknowledge any differences between themselves and Whites. They especially do not want to be seen as an Asian person and do all they can to minimize and eliminate their Asian physical features or preferences for Asian food.

PASSIVE WHITE IDENTIFICATION

Asian Americans who experience a positive self-concept during the first stage of Ethnic Awareness and who grow up in predominantly Asian or mixed neighborhoods are more likely to experience *Passive White Identification*. In Passive White Identification, Asian Americans do not consider themselves to be White and do not distance themselves from other Asians.

However, they experience periods of wishful thinking and fantasizing about being White. Like Asian Americans in Active White Identification, Asian Americans in Passive White Identification also accept White values, beliefs, and standards, and use Whites as a reference group.

Whether experienced actively or passively, White Identification is a stage marked by negative attitudes and evaluations of self as Americans of Asian ancestry and include behaviors that reflect turning one's back on other Asian Americans and ethnic minorities. These behaviors and attitudes are accompanied by a lack of political understanding that could help them to make sense of their experiences. At this stage, Asian Americans personalize their experiences and are not conscious of social injustice or racism. They are likely to say that there is no racism and that they have not encountered any discrimination. The goal of Asian Americans at the White Identification stage is to fit in, to pass for a White person, or at least not be seen as Asian. As long as Asian Americans believe they can be fully assimilated into White society, they remain in this stage of White Identification.

*Stage Three: Awakening to Social Political Consciousness*

It is during stage three of the AARID that some Asian Americans are able to shift their worldview and realize that they are not personally responsible for the way White racism has impacted them. In moving their paradigm from personal responsibility to social responsibility, Asian Americans at this stage acquire social and political understanding that enables them to transform their self-image. This transformation begins with a realistic assessment of Asian Americans' social position and a clear realization of the existence of societal blocks and the futility of trying to "pass" or to strive for acceptance within the White world. The awareness of White racism also provides alternative perspectives for Asian Americans which allow them to reinterpret their lives and lets them know that things could be different. Prior to the Awakening to Social Political Consciousness stage, Asian Americans blamed themselves for their negative racial experiences and believed these were the result of personal failings. An alternative perspective that these negative encounters have societal rather than personal roots releases the individual from unnecessary guilt and feelings of inferiority. Another major change during stage three is a reaction against White people. For Asian Americans at this stage, White people are no longer the reference group to which they aspire. Rather, White people become the antireferent group, people they don't want to be like.

*Stage Four: Redirection to an Asian American Consciousness*

Although in the previous stage Asian Americans changed their affiliation from Whites to minorities, they had not yet identified with Asian Americans. With support and encouragement from friends, Asian Americans begin to feel secure enough in themselves to look at their own experiences via immersion in Asian American culture, history, and environment. Asian Americans discover that while they had some knowledge of their Asian cultural heritage, they don't really know very much about the Asian American experience. As they learn more about the history of Asian Americans, they feel anger and outrage toward the dominant White system for the acts of racism directed toward Asians in this country. Eventually Asian Americans are able to move out of this reactionary state into a more realistic appraisal of both themselves and other Asian Americans and figure out what parts of themselves are Asian and what parts are American.

The ego identity of Asian Americans in stage four is centered on being an Asian American, which entails knowing they belong in the United States, having a clear political understanding of what it means to be Asian American in this society, and no longer seeing themselves as misfits. They acquire racial pride and a positive self-concept as Americans with an Asian heritage.

*Stage Five: Incorporation*

The key factor in stage five of the AARID is confidence in one's own Asian American identity. This confidence allows Asian Americans to relate to many different groups of people without losing their own racial identity as Asian Americans. Having been immersed in Asian American history and culture in the previous stage and resolving their racial identity conflict, Asian Americans who are in Incorporation stage no longer have a driving need to be exclusively with other Asian Americans. They also recognize that while racial identity is important, it is not the only social identity of importance to them. The hallmark of this last stage is the blending of individuals' racial identity with the rest of their social identities.

AARID Overview

The Asian American Racial Identity Development theory (AARID) falls under psychological theories of racial identity and describes a developmental process that progresses through five stages of perception and relation to one's

*Table 7.1: AARID Stage Summary*

| | Social environment | Critical factor | Self-concept | Ego identity | Primary reference group | Hallmark of the stage |
|---|---|---|---|---|---|---|
| Stage I: Ethnic Awareness | home with family | amount of participation in ethnic activities | participation leads to positive; participation leads to neutral self-concept | participation = clear sense as a person of Asian heritage, participation = less clear about being | Family | discovery of ethnic heritage |
| Stage 2: White Identification | public arenas such as school systems | increased contact with White society leading to acceptance of White values and standards | negative self-image, especially body image | being different, not fitting in, inferior to White peers, feel isolated and personally responsible for negative treatments | White people and dominant society | alienated from self and other Asian Americans inability to connect experience with racism |
| Stage 3: Awakening to Social Political Consciousness | social political movements and/or campus politics | gaining political consciousness related to being a racial/political minority and awareness of racism | positive self-concept | identification as a minority in the United States, oppressed by but not inferior to Whites | people with similar politics, anti-establishment perspectives | gain new political perspective, political alienation from Whites |
| Stage 4: Redirection to an Asian American Consciousness | Asian American community | immersion in Asian American experience | positive self-concept as Asian American | proud of being Asian American, experience a sense of belonging | AAs at similar stage of racial identity development | focus on Asian American experience, anger towards Whites on treatment of Asian Americans |
| Stage 5: Incorporation | general | clear and firm Asian American identity | positive self-concept as a person | View self as a whole with race as a part of their significant social identities | people in general | blending of racial identity with the rest of one's social identity |

racial group and the dominant group.[7] As with other developmental models, AARID views racial identity development as a lifelong process wherein individuals may have completed a stage in their identity development but their behavioral response to situations/events may appear to push them back to a previous stage. As such, a stage could be revisited or some stage experienced so subtly or for such a short period of time that it would appear as if they have skipped it altogether.

*Relevance of the Racial Identity Stage Development*
*Model for Asian Americans*

Beyond the more traditional approach to understanding identity through a single lens—whether that of race, gender, ethnicity, or sexual orientation—more recently identity scholars have been considering other factors that influence one's identity, such as identity salience, social context, and internal versus external definitions of identity (Chen 2009). As is the case in AARID, most research on Asian Americans presumes that race or ethnicity are the salient factors in their identity development, given the existence of White racism in this country. It is therefore assumed that the oppression of racial minorities has a psychological impact on Asian Americans.

Some scholars have argued that this assumption limits our understanding of Asian Americans as it does not consider the diversity of social class, gender, ethnicity, religion, sexual orientation, and the like among them. They argue that depending on the individual's situation, a different identity dimension may be more salient than race/ethnicity (Fouad and Brown 2000; Rotheram and Phinney 1987). Specifically, Helms (1994) has suggested that race may not be the salient dimension of identity development for Asian Americans because of the existence of the "model minority" myth. The model minority myth can place Asian Americans in opposition to other visible racial minorities. The myth encourages Asian Americans to believe that they can be fully accepted into the White majority society, and can live more privileged lives as an "exception" to other racial minorities if they act more "White." The belief in the model minority myth could lead Asian Americans to overlook racial discrimination directed against them and White Americans to be more tolerant and less discriminatory against Asian Americans. If Asian Americans believe racial discrimination is not a significant factor in their lives, their racial identity may not be the most salient identity for them. When individuals identify with a single social identity, it tends to be the social identity most salient to them at the time. Saliency is influenced by the degree of struggle, pain, or conflict that one has to deal with in that identity dimension. Thus, if a person's racial membership presents the most challenge and pain then racial identity will have salience over other aspects of self. However, for some Asian Americans who are also gay, the most salient social identity could be sexual orientation rather than racial membership, since homophobia is stronger and more prevalent within Asian ethnic cultures than in the United States.

Some researchers have questioned the usefulness of stage development theories and models of identity development for Asian Americans (Yeh and

Huang 1996). They consider stage theories to be too restrictive and individually focused. In addition, stage models are seen as being unable to incorporate more group-oriented Asian culture and the Confucian philosophy that
are salient to understanding Asian American development. In their research
Yeh and Huang collected visual data from projective drawing exercises and
concluded that Asian Americans were more focused on collectivism than
individualism in their identity development and that avoidance of shame is
a stronger driver in Asian American identity development than anger. The
Asian cultural tendency to conform to group expectations and the desire
to avoid the shame of being different may lead Asian Americans to more
readily accept mainstream American standards. In summarizing the AARID
theory, I see this dynamic as playing a role during the White Identification
stage. I believe the cultural context of a group orientation versus an individual one presents a potential mitigating factor in the quality of the identity
stage experienced, but it has no impact on whether individuals experience
identity development stages.

Results from a qualitative study by Chen and Guzman (2003), which
explored identity saliency and the multiple identities of Asian Americans,
suggests that a multidimensional model of identity may be more applicable
for this population. Their outcomes indicate that while ethnicity and race
are the most salient social identities for "many" Asian Americans, other
dimensions like gender, religion, and socioeconomic class are more salient
for "some" Asian Americans, and still others listed personal identity characteristics such as personality or a career as being the most salient identity for
them. While the Chen and Guzman study did not include this, I am guessing
that for the "some" who identified with social dimensions other than race
and ethnicity, generational status could be a factor. As stated earlier, first-
generation, immigrant Asian Americans are more likely to be in the "some"
category than would Asian Americans who have multiple minority social
identities such as being gay.

Other researchers have confirmed the efficacy of the stage development
models for Asian Americans (Ibrahim, Ohnishi, and Sandhu 1997; Phinney
1989; Tse 1999). Through analysis of thirty-nine previously published personal stories by Asian Americans, Tse (1999) advanced stages of identity
development for Asian Americans comprised of ethnic emergence (identity search) and ethnic identity incorporation (achieved identity). Tse also
found two substages within ethnic emergence: "Awakening to Minority Status" and "Ethnic Exploration." In the first of these substages, Asian Americans become more sensitive to issues of race and to the visibility of their
minority status and realize how their minority membership has affected

their self-perceptions and may express anger at mainstream society for their treatment. This description is very similar to stage three in AARID theory: "Awakening to Social Political Consciousness." It is during the stage of Awakening to Social and Political Consciousness that some Asian Americans are able to shift their worldview and realize that they are not personally responsible for their situation and experiences with White racism. In moving their paradigm from personal responsibility to social responsibility, Asian Americans acquire social and political understanding that enables them to transform their self-image.

In Tse's second substage, "Ethnic Exploration," Asian Americans explore their Asian culture, seeking friendships with members of their own culture and learning their language. This is very similar to stage four in AARID theory, "Redirection to an Asian American Consciousness." In both the Tse and Kim models Asian Americans begin to look at their own experiences and immerse themselves in the Asian American experience. Through related activities, Asian Americans discover that while they had some knowledge of their Asian cultural heritage, they don't really know very much about the Asian American experience.

## Future Research

While I have received much anecdotal information from Asian Americans of different ethnic backgrounds that the theory is applicable to their personal experience, it has not been tested by formal research among different Asian ethnic groups. This could be a fruitful area for future examination. In fact, a study of college students by Yeh and Huang (1996) which focused on ethnicity found that Asian Americans explicitly separate race and ethnicity, and concentrate on ethnicity. This research indicated that Asian Americans are largely affected by external forces and relationships in determining their affiliation with their cultural group and ultimately in forming ethnic identity. Yeh and Huang highlight the importance of acknowledging the collectivistic nature of ethnic identity development among Asian Americans. In addition, on college campuses today there are more Asian ethnic associations, such as organizations for Korean students or Chinese American students, than Asian American associations. This shift implies a greater ethnic rather than racial orientation among modern college students. Future research could examine the factors that influence whether race or ethnicity has salience for different generations of Asian Americans, including college students. A related area of exploration could look at the psychological impact on international students from Asia studying in the United States when they are mistaken for being Asian American.

## AARID and the Changing Social Political Context

Although Ethnic Awareness is a stage of AARID, Asian American racial identity development is not primarily a process of finding one's heritage, although this does occur for some Asian Americans. As is evident in the AARID theory, understanding and proclaiming one's Asian heritage is a necessary but not a sufficient condition for developing an Asian American racial identity. A critical factor is the acquisition of a coherent political point of view and a new paradigm, which are often gained through involvement in political movements. That new perspective recognizes the subordination of people of color in this country, including Asian Americans.

The political climate in the United States has changed significantly since the 1960s and the 1970s.[8] There is more acceptance of the racial status quo, more political backlash about affirmative action, and more resistance to dealing with social oppression and injustice.[9] Given the importance of the sociopolitical environment in facilitating the development of an Asian American racial identity, how will the current, politically less progressive environment affect Asian Americans? Will Asian American identity evolve as outlined in the AARID theory if there are fewer opportunities to become involved in political movements that challenge the current racial dynamics and institutions? Responses to the AARID theory from college students I've worked with indicate that the shifting of their paradigm during the third stage is much more subtle and at times hard to distinguish from the fourth stage. That is, the Awakening to Social Political Consciousness and Redirecting to Asian American Consciousness may be seamless and felt as one stage. It will be important to study current college students and those in their mid- to late twenties to see how similar or different their experience of racial identity conflict resolution is to the AARID stages.

Another potential impact of the post-1960s and 1970s political environment is that the importance of racial identity is beginning to be questioned. Two books by Asian American writers, Native Speaker by Chang-rae Lee (1995) and The Accidental Asian by Eric Liu (1998), provide some evidence of this. In his own way each author focuses more on the American part of his experience than on the Asian. Both authors are second-generation Asian American males in the White Identification stage, albeit passively, but they do not deny the existence of racial discrimination. One consequence of the changed political environment may be that Asian Americans spend more

time in the White Identification stage, and perhaps never leave it. If this outcome is documented by future research, it would support one of AARID's
theoretical findings, namely, the importance of shifting one's paradigm by
enhancing one's sociopolitical understanding, without which one remains in
the White Identification stage.

AARID and Generational Differences

Responses gained from sharing the AARID model with different generations of Asian Americans indicate that the theory primarily fits the experience of the "1.5" (those born in Asia but raised primarily in this country)
and successive generations. The first generation of immigrants, who come
to this country as adults, seem less affected psychologically by White racism.
Since the theory was developed using second-, third-, and fourth-generation
Asian Americans, it may not accommodate the experiences of the immigrant
generation. This is an important group to research, especially since fully 62
percent of Asian Americans in this country are immigrants. Future research
on Asian American racial identity could also explore the length of time it
takes for White racism to affect the racial identity of Asian Americans and
whether this effect is the same for all generations of Asian Americans. Differences between the experiences of foreign-born and native-born Asian Americans warrant additional attention.

AARID and Changes in the Asian American Family

Another significant social change that has occurred since the AARID theory
was developed relates to the marriage patterns of Asian Americans. Specifically, more Asian Americans are marrying out of their Asian ethnic groups
(for example, Chinese Americans marrying Korean Americans) and especially marrying out of their racial group (for example, Asians with White
partners, Asians with Black partners, and so on). The AARID as currently
written does not account for the experiences of interracial and interethnic
people. Therefore, future research needs to examine the kinds of identity
conflict that arise for Asian Americans who are in interracial marriages, or
who are children of interracial or interethnic marriages. It would be helpful
to know how identity conflict issues are experienced by interracial people,
especially if their background includes the blending of an Asian and another
race of color (that is, Black, Latino, or American Indian), because of their
physical appearance. On the other hand, the mixed Asian ethnic families
and children would probably have similar experiences as Asian Americans

in general and would follow the AARID model because of the saliency of race over ethnicity that was discussed earlier. However, additional research is needed to explore these topics fully.

Another trend since the 1980s is the increased number of Asian ethnic children (mostly Chinese and Korean) that are adopted by White families. While there are more support groups for such blended families to ensure cultural education, it is not clear what the adoptees' experience is with their social identity development either racially or ethnically. Research in this area would add to our understanding of the psychological impact of being different from the dominant social group.

## Synthesis

While there are a number of research topics that could shed light on Asian Americans' racial identity conflict and its resolution, the AARID theory still seems relevant today. In a recent workshop (April 2010) I conducted with seventeen Asian American college students—comprised of six men and eleven women, representing Chinese (11), Filipino (1), Japanese (2), and Vietnamese (3) ethnic groups, and five "1.5" generation and twelve second- generation Asian Americans—fourteen participants confirmed that their experiences mirrored the stages of Asian American Identity Development. Of the fourteen, four experienced the Active White Identification and ten experienced the Passive White Identification stage. All four Active White Identification people grew up in White neighborhoods and went to schools that were mostly White. Of the ten who experienced Passive White Identification, eight grew up in and went to school in either racially mixed or mostly Asian neighborhoods and schools. All three of those who said the Asian American Identity Development stages did not reflect their experiences, were exposed to significant Asian cultural activities (one grew up outside the United States, in Asia) and went to racially mixed schools and reported not experiencing any form of the White Identification stage. The results of this informal research confirm the relevance of the AARID model for understanding the racial identity development process for Asian Americans.

The Asian American Racial Identity Development (AARID) theory specifically focused on racial identity development rather than ethnic identity development. This focus was fueled by the belief that much of what influences AARID is Asian Americans' status as a racial minority in the United States and the social and psychological consequences of this status. This is not to deny the existence of real cultural diversity among Asian ethnic groups. However, the reality of everyday experience is that most Asian ethnic groups, especially those from the East Asian countries of China, Japan, Korea, and the Philippines, are subject to a common set of racial prejudices and stereotypes (Chan and Hune 1995). For the most part, White Americans do not accord a different status or treat an Asian person differently depending on his or her ethnic group affiliation (Chinese, Japanese, Korean, or Filipino). The murder of Vincent Chin[10] in 1982 is a painful example of this reality. In fact, one of the stereotypes of Asian Americans is that we all look alike, with the exception of Asian Indians. Just as a Black person is treated primarily on the basis of the color of his or her skin in this country regardless of ethnic membership (for example, African, Jamaican, Cape Verdean, etc.), most Asian Americans experience a similar social dynamic. It is their racial membership, not their ethnic membership, that impacts how Asian Americans feel about themselves in this country. This is the primary reason for formulating AARID as a racial rather than an ethnic identity theory.

NOTES

1. The AAID was created in the 1980s, based on doctoral dissertation research on the experiences of Japanese American women by the author.

2. Studies that have compared culturally diverse groups found that Asian American subjects provide more collective responses, 20 to 52 percent, than European American subjects whose collective responses were only 15 to 19 percent (Higgins and King 1981). When compared to European Americans, Asian Americans tend to depend more heavily on the situation and values of the host society to define who they are (Triandis 1989).

3. Specifically, Critical Race theorists believe that race is a conceptual mechanism by which power and privileges are distributed in this country. Furthermore, the concept of race was constructed as a political device to keep people of color subordinated to Whites. Therefore, Critical Race theorists believe that progressive racial identity must reflect more than appreciation of common ancestry and include a common political agenda based on a shared worldview. This agenda should seek to terminate the subordination of people of color in this country (Iijima 1997).

4. There are a few books that chronicle the experience of Asian Americans in this country. Ronald Takaki (1989) is a great primer that describes the experiences of the major Asian ethnic groups in America. Another good source is a report of the U.S. Commission on Civil Rights (1992).

5. For further information on the history of racial discrimination suffered by Asian Americans and a critique of the model minority thesis, see Chin et al. (1996: 13–23).

6. Much research in the area of racial identity concludes that a child between the ages of three and six becomes aware of different ethnic groups and begins to identify with the appropriate one. However, both minority and majority children develop a preference for White racial stimuli (Clark 1955; Clark and Clark [1947] 1958; Clark 1980; Brand, Ruiz, and Padilla 1974).

7. Since completing the original study, I have processed the results with hundreds of Asian Americans in different adult stages of development, generations, ethnic

backgrounds, and social environments. These encounters have illustrated that for the most part the theory of five stages is still viable. However, I have become more aware of the interplay between the way Asian Americans experience the various stages and Asian cultural values, especially *of group orientation,* resulting in a greater focus on the external social environment and the role of *shame* as a preferred control mechanism among Asian cultures.

8. The major political influences of this era were the Black liberation movement and Black nationalism. These movements believed that the way to reduce racial domination was to directly transform the power relationship between Blacks and Whites. The birth of the Asian American movement itself coincided with these movements for Black liberation. Asian American activists focused on raising questions of oppression and power rather than on racial pride. To them, Asian American identity was primarily a means of uniting for political struggle rather than acquiring racial identity solely for its own sake (Iijima 1997).

9. It was during the 1990s that we saw the passage of proposition 206 in California that eliminated affirmative action in contracting, selection, and hiring in businesses, and admissions to universities. A number of other states, including Washington State, have followed suit. Other evidence of this changing social climate are the Texas Law School case and the Maryland scholarship case, both of which questioned the legality of affirmative action and the value of diversity in higher education in professional school admissions.

10. In 1982 Vincent Chin was murdered by a group of laid-off auto workers in Detroit. His Asian appearance made him a target. In an area where there was a lot of anti-Japanese feeling due to competition in the auto industry, Vincent was thought to be Japanese, though he was Chinese American. The fact that the White men who murdered Chin received minimum sentences of probation is an example of institutional racism directed against Asian Americans in our legal system.

## REFERENCES

Alvarez, Alvin N., L. Juang, and C. T. H. Liang. 2006. "Asian Americans and Racism: When Bad Things Happen to 'Model Minorities.'" *Cultural Diversity and Ethnic Minority Psychology* 12 (3): 477–492.

Atkinson, D. R., G. Morten, and D. W. Sue. 1993. *Counseling American Minorities: A Cross-Cultural Perspective,* 4th ed. Madison, Wis.: Brown & Benchmark.

Begley, Sharon. 1995, February 3. "Three Is Not Enough: Surprising New Lessons from the Controversial Science of Race." *Newsweek*: 67–69.

Brand, Elaine S., Rene A. Ruiz, and Amado M. Padilla. 1974. "Ethnic Identification and Preference: A Review." *Psychological Bulletin* 81 (11): 860–890.

Carnevale, Anthony P., and Susan C. Stone. 1995. *The American Mosaic: An In-Depth Report on the Future of Diversity at Work.* New York: McGraw-Hill.

Chan, Kenyon S., and Shirley Hune. 1995. "Racialization and Panethnicity: From Asians in America to Asian Americans." In *Toward a Common Destiny: Improving Race and Ethnic Relations in America,* edited by W. D. Hawley, A. W. Jackson, et al., 205–233. San Francisco: Jossey-Bass.

Chang, Tai, and Kwong-Liem Karl Kwan. 2009. "Asian American Racial and Ethnic Identity." In *Asian American Psychology: Current Perspectives,* edited by N. Tewari and A. N. Alvarez, 113–133. New York: Psychology Press.

Chen, G. A., and M. R. Guzman. 2003. "Identity Saliency in Asian Americans." Unpublished manuscript, University of Texas, Austin, Texas.

Chen, G. A., P. LePhuoc, M. R. Guzman, S. S. Rude, and B. G. Dodd. 2006. "Exploring Asian American Racial Identity." *Cultural Diversity and Ethnic Minority Psychology* 12 (3): 461–476.

Chen, Grace A. 2009. "Managing Multiple Social Identities." In *Asian American Psychology: Current Perspectives,* edited by N. Tewari and A. N. Alvarez, 173–192. New York: Psychology Press.

Chin, Gabriel J., Sumi Cho, Jerry Kang, and Frank Wu. 1996. *Beyond Self-Interest: Asian Pacific Americans, Towards a Community of Justice: A Policy Analysis of Affirmative Action.* Los Angeles: UCLA Asian-American Studies Center.

Chin, Pei-Ngo. 1970. "The Chinese Community in L.A." *Social Casework* 51 (10): 591–598.

Clark, Kenneth B. 1955. *Prejudice and Your Child.* Boston: Beacon Press.

———. 1980. "What Do Blacks Think of Themselves?" *Ebony:* 176–182.

Clark, Kenneth B., and M. P. Clark. [1947] 1958. "Racial Identification and Preference in Negro Children." In *Readings in Social Psychology,* edited by T. Newcomb and E. L. Hartley, 169–178. New York: Holt.

Crenshaw, Kimberle. 1995. *Critical Race Theory: The Key Writings That Formed the Movement.* New York: New Press.

Delgado, Richard. 1995. *Critical Race Theory: The Cutting Edge.* Philadelphia: Temple University Press.

Fouad, N. A., and M. T. Brown. 2000. "Role of Race and Social Class in Development: Implications for Counseling Psychology." In *Handbook of Counseling Psychology,* 3rd ed., edited by S. D. Brown and R. W. Lent, 379–408. New York: John Wiley & Sons.

Helms, Janet E. 1994. "The Conceptualization of Racial Identity and Other 'Racial' Constructs." In *Human Diversity: Perspectives on People in Context,* edited by E. J. Trickett, R. J. Watts, et al., 285–311. San Francisco: Jossey-Bass.

Helms, Janet E., and R. M. Talleyrand. 1997. "Race Is Not Ethnicity," *American Psychologist* 52: 1246–1247.

Higgins, E. Tory, and Gillian King. 1981. "Accessibility of Social Constructs: Information-Processing Consequences of Individual and Contextual Variability." In *Personality, Cognition and Social Interaction,* edited by N. Cantor and J. F. Kihlstrom, 69–121. Hillsdale, N.J.: Lawrence Erlbaum.

Huang, Larke N. 1994. "An Integrative View of Identity Formation: A Model for Asian Americans." In *Race, Ethnicity, and Self: Identity in Multicultural Perspective,* edited by E. P. Salett and D. R. Koslow, 43–59. Washington, D.C.: National Multicultural Institute.

Ibrahim, Farah, Hifumi Ohnishi, and Data Singh Sandhu. 1997. "Asian American Identity Development: A Culture Specific Model for South Asian Americans." *Journal of Multicultural Counseling and Development* 25 (1): 34–50.

Iijima, Chris K. 1997. "The Era of We-Construction: Reclaiming the Politics of Asian Pacific American Identity and Reflections on the Critique of the Black/White Paradigm." *Human Rights Law Review* 29: 47.

Inman, A. G. 2006. "South Asian Women: Identities and Conflicts." *Cultural Diversity and Ethnic Minority Psychology* 12 (3): 306–319.

Kasindorf, Martin. 1982, December 6. "Asian-Americans: A 'Model Minority.'" *Newsweek:* 39.

Kim, Jean. 1981. "Process of Asian American Identity Development: A Study of Japanese American Women's Perceptions of Their Struggle to Achieve Positive Identities as

Americans of Asian Ancestry." Ed.D. dissertation, School of Education, University of Massachusetts, Amherst.

———. 2001. "Asian American Identity Development Theory." In *New Perspectives on Racial Identity Development: A Theoretical and Practical Anthology,* edited by Charmaine L. Wijeyesinghe and Bailey W. Jackson III, 67–90. New York: NYU Press.

Knowles, Louis L., and Kenneth Prewitt, eds. 1969. *Institutional Racism in America.* Englewood Cliffs: N.J.: Prentice Hall.

Kohatsu, Eric L. 1993. "The Effects of Racial Identity and Acculturation on Anxiety, Assertiveness, and Ascribed Identity among Asian American College Students." Ph.D. dissertation, University of Maryland, College Park.

Lee, Chang-rae. 1995. *Native Speaker.* New York: Riverhead Books.

Liu, Eric. 1998. *The Accidental Asian.* New York: Random House.

Moritsugu, John, and Stanley Sue. 1983. "Minority Status as a Stressor." In *Preventive Psychology: Theory, Research, and Practice,* edited by R. D. Felner, L. A. Jason, J. N. Moritsugu, and S. S. Farber, 162–173. Elmsford, N.Y.: Pergamon.

Omi, Michael, and Howard Winant. 1994. *Racial Formation in the United States: From the 1960s to the 1990s.* New York: Routledge.

Phinney, Jean S. 1989. "Stages of Ethnic Identity Development in Minority Group Adolescents." *Journal of Early Adolescence* 9 (l): 34–49.

Rotheram, M. J., and J. S. Phinney. 1987. "Introduction: Definitions and Perspectives in the Study of Children's Ethnic Socialization." In *Children's Ethnic Socialization: Pluralism and Development,* edited by J. S. Phinney and M. J. Rotheram, 10–28. Newbury Park, Calif.: Sage.

Smith, Elsie J. 1991. "Ethnic Identity Development: Toward the Development of a Theory within the Context of Majority/Minority Status." *Journal of Counseling and Development* 70: 181–188.

Sue, Stanley, and Harry H. Kitano. 1973. "Stereotypes as a Measure of Success." *Journal of Social Issues* 29 (2): 83–98.

Sue, Stanley, and Derald W. Sue. 1971. "Chinese-American Personality and Mental Health." *Amerasia Journal* 1: 36–49.

———. 1990. *Counseling the Culturally Different: Theory and Practice.* New York: John Wiley.

Suzuki, Bob H. 1975. "The Broader Significance of the Search for Identity by Asian Americans." Lecture presented at the AA Conference held at Yale University, New Haven, Conn., April 12.

Tajfel, Henri, and John C. Turner. 1986. "The Social Identity Theory of Inter-Group Behavior." In *Psychology of Intergroup Relations,* edited by S. Worchel and L. W. Austin. Chicago: Nelson-Hall.

Takaki, Ronald. 1989. *Strangers from a Different Shore: A History of Asian Americans.* Boston: Little Brown.

Triandis, Harry C. 1989. "The Self and Social Behavior in Differing Cultural Contexts." *Psychological Review* 96 (3): 506–520.

Tse, Lucy. 1999. "Finding a Place to Be: Ethnic Identity Exploration of Asian Americans." *Adolescence* 34 (133): 121–138.

U.S. Commission on Civil Rights. 1992. *Civil Rights Issues Facing Asian Americans in the 1990s.* Washington, D.C.: The Commission.

Wijeyesinghe, Charmaine L., Pat Griffin, and Barbara Love. 1997. "Racism Curriculum Design." In *Teaching for Diversity and Social Justice: A Sourcebook,* edited by M. Adams, L. A. Bell, and P. Griffin, 82–109. New York: Routledge.

Yeh, Christine J., and Karen Huang. 1996. "The Collectivistic Nature of Ethnic Identity Development among Asian American College Students." *Adolescence* 96 (31): 645–661.

Yip, T. 2005. "Sources of Situational Variation in Ethnic Identity and Psychological Well Being: A Palm Pilot Study of Chinese American Students." *Personality and Social Psychology Bulletin* 31: 1603–1616.

# 8

## The "Simultaneity" of Identities

### Models and Skills for the Twenty-First Century

EVANGELINA HOLVINO

Two major forces are changing the meanings and models of identity in the twenty-first century. The first force is globalization. With its free flow of goods, capital, labor, and culture across national boundaries and throughout the world, globalization challenges notions of stable and one-dimensional identities (Bauman 1998; Lewellen 2002). The consequence of people crossing national boundaries in search of work and opportunities to live and work in new cultures and nations is that new identities, such as the "international migrant" and the "transnational immigrant" are constructed (Lewellen 2002, 130). In addition, goods, capital, and cultures travel to new locations, with the result that new identities are introduced into "old" cultures with presumed stable identities. An example is "the Japanese Suit," a Western fashion appropriated and made particularly Japanese by invoking a complex identity in-between its historical inferiority and its current economic power (Kondo 1999). Today, one way or another, most people share their time between two or more locations and cultures. The act of frequently moving across those boundaries forms and reforms their identities (Appiah and Gates 1995; Chan 2006; Duany 2002).

The second force is intellectual and political. On the one hand, postmodernism, with its emphasis on the role of language and discourse in creating reality, argues that identity is constructed through language and the social practices of communities. Against linear and progressive models of reality, postmodernism also questions developmental models of identity and suggests that identity is contextual, multiple, malleable, and always in the process of creation (Calás and Smircich 2006; Hall and DuGay 1996). On the other hand, feminists' commitment to theorizing and changing the situation of all women has demanded they address the fact that while women share the social category of sex/gender,[1] there are many ways in which their experience also varies because of their racial, ethnic, and religious differences, for example. Thus, there is not one category of "woman," but many "women" who are different and unequal to men and to each other. Thus, the forces of postmodernism and feminism have also altered the landscape and meanings of identity by focusing on its social construction and the role of discourse[2] in creating identity itself.

As a Puerto Rican scholar and practitioner based in the United States and working internationally I welcome these changes. As a Latina, one-dimensional models of identity have not served me well. For example, when I am given the choice to sit with the women's caucus (my gender identity) or with the Hispanics' caucus (my racial-ethnic identity) I am torn as I cannot separate these aspects of my identity that are inseparable (Holvino 2006). In my diversity consulting, I witness how unidimensional models do not fit the complexity of identities people bring to and experience in organizations. Consequently, I have both a personal and a professional interest in complicating models of identity so that they better explain and help address the challenges of diversity and differences today (Holvino 2001).

In this chapter I present a feminist transnational perspective on differences named *simultaneity* to suggest new ways of seeing and talking about identity. I focus on differences, because like Hall (1996), I believe that identity is "constructed through, not outside, differences" (4). Thus, how we think about differences has important implications for models of racial identity, which is the concern of this book. My interest is both theoretical—to develop new frameworks—and practical—to offer models that can make a difference when applied in daily interactions and work settings.

First, I briefly review the critique of dominant models of identity from a transnational feminist perspective. Specifically, I contrast models of identity commonly used in the practice of diversity in organizations with feminist transnational premises about differences, tracing the historical development of these models: from *one-dimensional* to *intersectional* to *simultaneous*.

Second, I expand on the *simultaneity* model of identity with an example from public practice to illustrate its applicability. Using this example as a heuristic, I discuss assumptions and skills that support simultaneity as well as some of the challenges of working with the simultaneity of identities. I conclude by suggesting the potential of simultaneity to engage with the multiplicity and complexity of identities in today's globalized world and identify areas for future exploration.

## Changing Conceptualizations and Images of Identity: An Exploration

Racial identity development (RID) models in the United States emerged during the civil rights movement of the 1960s, including the struggles for rights and self-definition of African Americans, Chicano/as, and Asian Americans (Adams 2001). Their influences were psychological, humanistic, and developmental (Torres et al. 2009). I will not review these models here, but see Adams 2001 and Renn in this volume. While these identity models have contributed much to acknowledging differences, understanding social identity and identity politics, and articulating its importance in organizations and communities, they have also been critiqued by a variety of practitioners and scholars (Billig 1999; Holvino 1994, 2003b; Spickard and Burroughs 2000; Wing and Rifkin 2001). I summarize these critiques below.

## A Critique of Racial Identity Development Models

Dominant approaches to differences and identity that draw from psychological and sociological theories of human nature have been critiqued, particularly by postmodern scholars, for sharing some of the following premises.

Many models of identity treat differences as essential, innate, and inescapable, as reflected in the phrase, "once a woman always a woman." Because differences are considered to "result from biological destiny" (Yuval-Davis 2006) differences such as gender or race come to be seen as "irreducible" (White 1987). An unintended consequence of this way of thinking is that differences which are seen as "innate" are considered more important and central to identity than others. A categorizing ensues whereby differences are ranked as to which is more important or which creates more privilege or inequality. A hierarchy of oppression results (Lorde 1983). In the United States, for example, gender and race are considered "essential" differences and more important to identity than class and religion, which supposedly can be changed at will.

Loden's "Identity Wheel" (1996), used extensively in diversity training, can be interpreted this way. In this model, two concentric circles list dimensions of differences deemed "primary"—age, sexual orientation, physical abilities, gender, ethnicity, and race—, which appear in the inner circle. Other differences like religion, family status, work experience, and education, appear in the outer circle as "secondary" dimensions. Users of this model could infer that the *primary* differences are more important, hard-wired, and unchangeable, while *secondary* differences are less defining because they can be modified by choice or circumstance. In this model, social class appears in the outer circle as a secondary difference. But this representation of class as a secondary difference does not consider that one of the the best predictor of one's socioeconomic class is one's parents' class, which suggests that class may be partly as predetermined by one's family of origin as race is believed to be determined by one's parents' genes (Holvino 2002). Thus, class should be considered a primary dimension of identity.[3]

Dominant models of differences also tend to study differences as *isolated* and *independent* variables, separate from each other. How differences such as gender and race may relate to and/or mutually constitute each other is usually not considered. But the stereotypes and treatment of women and men are different depending on their race, which has led scholars to explore how race is gendered and how gender is raced and classed (Essed 2001; Valocchi 2005). On the few occasions when race is studied in relation to another identity such as gender, it is done in an additive fashion, meaning race plus gender. This tendency is captured in common phrases like "double whammy," "double jeopardy" (Beale 1970) or "added dimension" (Cross and Fhagen-Smith 2001, 247) to refer to the negative effects of racism and sexism. Figure 8.1 illustrates this approach where a variety of social identities are represented, but in isolation from each other.

Discussing differences independent of each other is particularly problematic for women of color, whose life experience of race and gender interaction is rendered invisible or is misrepresented. As Bowleg (2008) insightfully discusses in "When Black + lesbian + woman ≠ Black lesbian woman," it is not sufficient to consider only one aspect of a person's identity. Latino scholars also point to how Latino/a identity is formed from a combination of geography, culture, race, nationality, and colonialism; all these being seen as inseparable dimensions of identity (Quiñones-Rosado 1998; Ferdman and Gallegos 2001).

In all, while isolating dimensions of difference may facilitate quantitative research or introductions to the topic of identity in educational settings, studying differences separate from each other does not help us understand how they operate in relation to each other at the individual, group, or societal level.

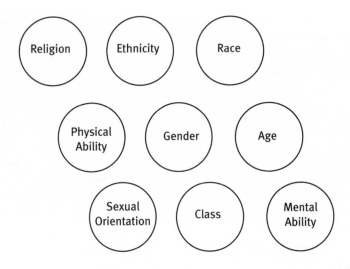

Fig. 8.1 Traditional Models: Social Identity Groups (© 1992 Bailey W. Jackson III).
Used with permission.

Many models of identity also treat differences as if they were *fixed* and *ahistorical*. For example, many White feminists have portrayed gender as *the* universal difference, implying that gender oppression is the same in the United States, China, or Latin America. Race is frequently understood to mean the same thing in all geographical/political contexts. But even in the United States, during the last three centuries race has not meant the same thing and racial categories have shifted for specific racial-ethnic groups (Omi and Winant 1986). My own experience provides a good example. In Puerto Rico, partly because there has been much racial mixing and the "one-drop rule" is not adhered to, I was considered and learned to see myself as a "White" Puerto Rican. When I came to the United States as an adult I had to learn that my racial identity was Brown, "of color," Hispanic, Black, or mixed, but definitely not "White." Then, I worked in northern Nigeria and I was called "bature," that is, a White American.

In all, while not all models of identity share all the above premises, my experience working in diversity initiatives in organizations confirms that assumptions like these dominate the daily practices of diversity profession-als, from the training they offer to the assessments they make to the advice they give: (1) differences are categorized as innate or not; (2) the data on women is not desegregated by race and ethnicity to understand how race and gender may be influencing the experience of different women differently; (3) identity dimensions are discussed serially, as in a workshop on gender and another on race; and (4) while some practitioners acknowledge that differences are *socially constructed*, in the same breath they argue that differences like gender and race are more defining of identities, while other differences like class and religion are less so.

A Transnational Feminist Approach to Differences:
An/Other Perspective on Identity

A transnational feminist approach to differences, which draws from Third World feminist, literary, cultural, and political studies, is based on a different set of premises. I present next an overview of transnational feminism, its assumptions and the contributions it makes to a different understanding of identity.

Transnational feminism consolidates and expands on the important critique of White feminism by Black women like Sojourner Truth and Amy Jacques Garvey, who in the 1800s were already decrying "the evils of imperialism, racism, capitalism, and the interlocking race, class, and gender oppression that Black and other women experienced globally, particularly in colonial context" (Guy-Sheftall 1995,11). Many of these analyses by Third World feminists[4] emerged from critiques of national liberation movements dominated by men, feminist movements dominated by White Western women, Eurocentric academic discourses that privileged theory over community activism, and Marxist analyses of class that ignored gender. They all rendered the lives and experience of women of color and non-Western women invisible (Guy-Sheftall 1995; Hurtado 2000; Mohanty 1991, 2003; Narayan and Harding 2000).

Now embraced by many Third and First World feminists, transnational feminism is even more important in the context of globalization for two major reasons: (1) to understand how movement across nations, transnationalism, impacts women's (and men's) lives differently, and (2) to address the difficulty of forging women's alliances for change taking into account women's many differences. This means going beyond the naive "global sisterhood" (Morgan 1984) and the "global feminism" slogans of the 1980s and 1990s to embrace deeper and more contextual understandings of what unites and divides women (Mendoza 2002).

Transnational feminism conceptualizes gender, class, race, sexuality, and nationality as complex and simultaneous social processes and discursive constructions that produce inequality. Identity is seen as historically and contextually influenced by these specific material and discursive practices. Transnational feminism puts women of color at the center of inquiry,

*Isn't this the same problem but from the opposite perspective?*

trying to understand and rewrite history from their perspective and experience. Women of color are also seen as agents, that is, capable of doing for themselves and changing their situation, instead of just being victims of oppression.

One of the major contributions of transnational feminists is to study the role of the state and the interrelations between colonialism, racism, and gender in the lives of women of color (Mohanty et al. 1991; Otis 2001; Sampaio 2004). For example, in the United States, "draconian provisions" imposed by welfare reform during Clinton's presidency had very negative consequences for poor, poor working, and immigrant women (Hardisty 2010, 16). These new rules include a "family cap" that limits benefits to a five-year period, regardless of whether the woman has found a job or not, and deny food stamps to legal documented immigrants. These are ways in which local and national governments contribute to women's oppression in a complex nexus of power and domination that is gendered, patriarchal, racialized, and (hetero)sexualized (Briggs 1998; Holvino, 2003a; Mendoza 2002; Mohanty 1997).

More specifically, transnational feminism holds the following premises about identity and differences.

First, social differences are seen as *relational*. Discursively, they depend on the formulation of a relation between dichotomized dimensions of differences, whereas the first would not exist in the absence of "an/other." In the West, male exists in relation to female, from which it can be differentiated. In that sense, there is not a female or a male gender, but a relation between men and women, which is constructed in terms of an opposition between the masculine and the feminine "sex." Gender is the term that refers to this particular *relational arrangement,* which may vary throughout the world. For example, one could envision four sets of gender relations: children, females of reproductive age, males of reproductive age, and elders (Gailey 1987) or as Oyewumi (2002) argues, blood lineage, not gender, is the primary relation in Yoruba culture. Queer theory further dismantles these oppositional and relational modes of thinking by demonstrating how the binaries male-female and heterosexual-homosexual are disrupted when we pay attention to the identities of transgenders and drag queens (Valocchi 2005).

Second, differences are *socially constructed.* They reflect the socially attributed meanings to specific dimensions of human differences that have been signaled as important in a given society. Thus, gender or race or ethnicities are not intrinsic or innate physical, psychological, or cultural attributes. Instead, race, gender, and ethnicity are the *meanings attributed to differences* of sex, phenotypes, or culture, *in specific social contexts.* These meanings are shaped by socialization practices, organizational and institutional arrangements, belief systems, and language itself. For example, "white" conveys purity and "black" conveys evil. The meanings we attribute to differences also change over time and are constantly contested and transformed by academic disciplines, social movements, the state, the media, and everyday interactions. For example, there was a time when Irish immigrants in the United States were considered "nonwhite" (Ignatiev 1995). Before the nineteenth century there was no category of "homosexual" and "gay rights" did not exist prior to the 1980s. Today, after enormous political struggle, civil unions granting gays and lesbians the rights enjoyed by married heterosexual couples are legal in some states, illegal in most, and contested in many others in the United States.

Third, differences also construct who we are and are important elements of our *subjective identity* (Calás and Smircich 1992). There is not an essential (ungendered or unraced) "self" that humans possess, which is then "tarnished" by gender stereotypes, socialization patterns, or the media. Subjectivity, how we think of ourselves as social beings, is always in the making and individuals actively participate in constructing their identities. But subjectivity is also shaped by gender beliefs and structures embedded in society, and these beliefs are inseparable from our self-identity. Rosario Morales, a well-known Latina poet, writes about her complex subjectivity, constructed out of her race, gender, ethnicity, language, religion, class, and nationality:

> I am what I am and I am U.S. American . . . I am a Puerto Rican . . . New York Manhattan and the Bronx . . . a real true honest-to-god in college now . . . I really dig the funny way the British speak . . . I'm naturalized Jewish-American . . . Take it or leave me alone. (1981: 14–15)

The fourth premise that transnational feminism brings to understandings of identity refers to how differences *signify relations of power*. In our culture, gender reflects the social organization of the relation between the sexes whereas the male is privileged (one-up, desired, better) and women are subordinated (one-down, less, inferior). This privileging process involves both the material—women earn 74 cents compared to a man's dollar—and the symbolic—the color of girls is pink and the color of boys is blue.

When the difference is *class*,[5] managers are privileged and workers are not. A Latina worker articulates how power and social differences interact:

> The boss tells us not to bring our "women's problems" with us to work if we want to be treated equal. What does he mean by that? I am working here because of my "women's problems." . . . Working here creates my

"women's problems." I need this job because I am a woman and have children to feed. And I'll probably get fired because I am a woman and need to spend more time with my children. (Hossfeld 1990:168–169)

Lastly, differences *intersect with other social processes* like class, race, and ethnicity and *mutually constitute* each other (Dill et al. 2007; Holvino 1994; Shields 2008; Weber 2010). They are interdependent and interactive and cannot be understood in isolation from each other. For example, while stereotypes of White women managers are that they are feminine, bright, and driven (Morrison et al. 1987), Black women managers are perceived as tough, self-sufficient, and caretaking (Bell and Nkomo 2001; Dumas 1985). These different perceptions create different kinds of dilemmas for Black and White women in leadership roles.

Put another way, categories of identity come to be and derive their meaning in relation to other categories in a dynamic, rather than static or fixed, way. Analyses of women of color are not about double oppression "as if [dimensions of difference] were piled one on top of the other" (Oyewumi 1997, 123). Instead, "how one form of oppression is experienced is influenced by and influences how another form is experienced" (Spelman 1988, 123).

In all, transnational feminism conceptualizes differences as a social relation along dimensions of power, which interact with other differences and processes shaping our subjective identity as well as our material existence. Differences like race, gender, and class are also useful *categories of analysis, historical, changing,* and *specific,* not fixed and universal. The assumptions about differences discussed above, but especially the premise that differences intersect with other social processes and need to be studied at their point of intersection, is what is known as multiracial feminism (Zinn and Dill 1996) and Intersectionality (Crenshaw 1989, 1991; Dill 2002; Dill et al. 2007; Luft and Ward 2009; Phoenix and Pattynama 2006; Weber 1998, 2010), which I discuss next.

Intersectionality: The First and the Latest Identity Model?

Today, some feminists declare that Intersectionality is one of the most important contributions of feminist theory to our understanding of gender practices and identities (McCall 2005; Shields 2008). The term "Intersectionality" is attributed to Kimberle Crenshaw (1989), but it is important to note that Intersectionality was already part of a tradition by Black and women of color scholars who posited that race and gender overlapped and changed the experience of gender, which White feminists presented as a universal experience in the first wave of feminism in the nineteenth century (Collins 2000; Guy-Sheftall 1995; Holvino 2010; Hull et al. 1982).

Scholars clarify that Intersectionality is an analytical strategy, a tool to empower people and work for social justice, and a theoretical perspective (Dill 2002; Dill et al. 2007; Luft and Ward 2009). Its purpose is to "transform knowledge and individual lives . . .[and] create a more equitable society that recognizes and validates differences" (Dill 2002, 6). Thus, Intersectionality is both a theoretical framework and a strategy for change based on a multidimensional and discursive and material understanding of identity (Brah and Phoenix 2004; Dill 2002). Intersectionality stresses the qualitative impact of categories of identity which intersect in a variety of ways, creating at the same time both oppression and opportunity. Inequalities are seen as "complex, mutually reinforcing or contradicting processes" (Acker 2006b, 442) as "people live multiple, layered identities and can simultaneously experience oppression and privilege" (Dill et al. 2007, 629). In addition, Intersectionality pays attention to the interplay of macro societal structural inequities and the micro interactions and daily practices that sustain inequality (Essed 1990; Hurtado 2003; Weber 1998, 2010).

In her overview of a conceptual framework for the Intersectionality of race, class, gender, and sexuality, which helps attain a "much richer analysis of people's lives," Lynn Weber discusses five themes that describe an intersectional approach to differences. Weber's five themes match fairly well the transnational feminists' premises discussed earlier. Differences and identity are:

- Historically and geographically contextual;
- Socially constructed;
- Reflective of power relationships;
- Occurring at macro social-structural and micro social-psychological levels; and
- Simultaneously expressed (Weber 2010, 90–92)

Additive models of identity captured in mathematical metaphors like "double or triple oppression" are replaced with more nuanced images like "multiple jeopardy" (King 1988), "matrix of domination" (Collins 2000; Martinez 2000), "border crossing" (Anzaldúa 1987, 1990; Mendez and Wolf 2001) and "cross-border" existence (Hurtado 1999). These metaphors signal an attempt to dismantle hierarchies of oppression and instead articulate and explore complex identities and contradictory subject positions which arise in the context of globalization. Alma, a maquiladora[6] worker and "a thoroughly modern woman" who moves as easily between the fields of Cacahuatepec as

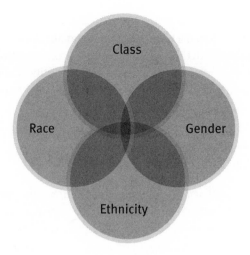

Fig. 8.2 Intersectionality (© 1992, Ella Bell and Stella Nkomo). Used with permission.

among the skyscrapers of Los Angeles, represents this complex identity well (Lewellen 2002, 2).

Intersectionality can be captured in the image of four intersecting circles that meet at a point in the center, stressing the interrelatedness of social differences (Bell and Nkomo 1992) (see Figure 8.2). But considered more carefully, the image of intersections implies "a center," a place in the middle where different identities come together, like different roads meeting at the intersection of a busy traffic light. This center suggests the existence of a core identity, which is still somewhat independent and outside these processes (Jones and McEwen 2000). The metaphor may also suggest a fixed location at the center of the intersecting roads, stable and unitary, which Luft and Ward critique for implying "fixity or stasis" (2009, 25).

I suggest that the figure of intersecting circles does not adequately represent the fluidity of identities, its multiplicity, and the constantly changing process of "identities." The metaphor also misses the dynamic nature of identity relations and its formations and the processes that make for those changes in people's lives (Shields 2008; Kumashiro 2001). While Jones and McEwen (2000) try to capture this dynamic relationship in the representation of cross-cutting ellipses (see Wijeyesinghe in this volume), their model posits the existence of a "center" or "core sense of self consisting of personal attributes, characteristics and personal identity" (Jones and McEwen 2000, 408). But, as we have discussed before, for transnational feminists there is no core identity or inner self because the "self" is always in process, in the making, shaped by those very social and discursive processes that make the subject (Anthias and Yuval-Davis 1992; Calás and Smircich 2009, 2011).

The *simultaneity* model (Holvino 2001, 2010), which I discuss next, suggests that more than intersecting circles, social identity is constructed by a number of coexisting identity-forming *systems of difference always in interaction and transaction with each other at the same time.*

## The Simultaneity of Differences: Towards New Models of Identity and Their Application

There are many similarities between Intersectionality and simultaneity; in fact, many Intersectionality scholars consistently refer in their work to the "simultaneous processes of race, gender, class, and sexuality" (Dill et al. 2007; Dill and Zambrana 2009; Weber 2010). Brewer et al. (2002) trace Intersectionality to "the simultaneity of oppressions" coined by Hull, Scott, and Smith in the pacesetting women of color anthology, *All the Women Are White, All the Blacks Are Men, But Some of Us Are Brave* (1982). Dill et al. describe Intersectionality as "aspects of identity and social relations [that] are shaped by the *simultaneous* operation of multiple systems of power" (2007, 629). Lewellen (2002) talks about self-identity as "simultaneous and overlapping" (92).

Reconceptualizing identity as "simultaneity" also attends to the ways in which race, gender, class, sexuality, ethnicity, and nation are not just about a personal and individual identity, but about the social and institutional processes that determine opportunities, which also produce and reproduce racial, gender, class, and other social differences. Simultaneity thus means the *simultaneous processes of identity, institutional and social practice*, which operate concurrently and together to construct people's identities and shape their experiences, opportunities, and constraints (Holvino 2010).By *processes of identity practice*, I mean the ways in which differences like race, ethnicity, gender, class, and sexuality produce and reproduce particular identities that define how individuals come to see themselves and how others see them. These practices cover the gamut from well-studied early socialization practices to more pervasive societal discourses like the cult of domesticity of the nineteenth and early twentieth centuries, which defined a particular identity for White middle-class women centered on wifehood and motherhood. In contrast, the identity of working-class women of color was constructed as "less than," supporting their roles as domestic servants (Glenn 2001).

By *processes of institutional practice*, I mean the ways in which differences and their social relations and stratification are built into organizational structures and ways of working, which seem normal at the same time that they produce and reproduce particular relations of inequality and privilege. We can further analyze domestic service as a particular type of institution with a particular set of interactions between the domestic worker and her employer, a clear division of labor, poor wages, and a set of practices sustained by the lack of societal regulation of that institution (Glenn 1985, 1986, 1988, 2001; Hondagneu-Sotelo 2001, 2002; Rollins 1985; Romero 1992, 1997).

By *processes of social practice*, I mean the ways in which societal structures, beliefs, and ways of engaging at the societal level produce and reproduce inequalities and identities along the axes of race, class, and gender. For example, analyses of reproductive labor illuminate the complex interrelation between domestic and global market forces that result in a transnational division of the labor of care along lines of race, gender, class, ethnicity, and nationality (Glenn 2001; Parreñas 2002). Specifically, Third World women, like the domestic servants before them, are disproportionately represented in the care-giving jobs of nannies, elder-care givers, and hospital assistants.

The simultaneity model does not refer only to the processes of subjective identity. However, I limit my discussion here to the implications of simultaneity for individuals' identities and propose the image of the hologram to represent its complexity (see Figure 8.3).

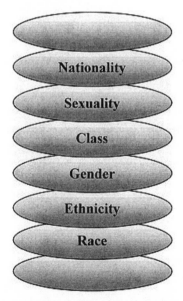

Figure 8.3 Copyright © 2005, Evangelina Holvino. "Theories of Difference: Making a Difference with Simultaneity." http://www.chaosmanagement.com/resources/resources/powerpoint-presentations Chaos Management, Ltd. Used with permission.

The dilemma of simultaneity is that while on the one hand differences such as race, gender, class, ethnicity, nationality, and sexuality coexist and are experienced simultaneously, the importance or salience of specific differences at particular moments varies, given the social context. This makes for identities that are multiple, fluid, and ever changing, instead of stable and one-dimensional. The metaphor of the hologram may convey this movement and multiplicity better than the metaphor of intersecting circles. For example, when I travel in other countries my nationality as an American citizen and a Christian become figural while my "Latinaness" and minority status recede to the background. The opposite is true in the United States, where my Latina identity and Spanish accent are foregrounded, while my Christian privilege and identity are less prominent.

In addition, the hologram suggests that the whole of one's identity contains the various differences that make it, while each difference also reflects the whole. Differences and identity processes work together and inform each other, and thus one dimension of difference also reflects other dimensions of difference, because they mutually constitute and reconstitute each other.

Many identity scholars suggest that subordinated differences or identities are more salient than those that convey privilege. This means that while we all have simultaneous identities, the tendency is to study the identities which are subordinated (Kumashiro 2001; Ward 2004; Warner 2008), maybe because individuals seem to be more aware of those identities in which they experience marginalization and oppression (Hurtado and Sinha 2008). Others argue that people with multiple subordinated identities suffer from "intersectional invisibility," the general societal failure to recognize and understand their experience of intersecting identities, which can be documented historically, culturally, politically, and legally (Purdie-Vaughs and Eibach 2008, 381).

In the following section I apply the simultaneity model to discuss the complexity of identities of a public figure in the recent history of the United States, Judge Sonia Sotomayor, the first Hispanic and third female Justice in the Supreme Court of the United States.

### "A Wise Latina": A Role Model and Application of Simultaneity

In the spring of 2009, Sonia Sotomayor was nominated to the U.S. Supreme Court by President Obama. Born and raised in a housing project in New York of Puerto Rican working-class parents, Sotomayor not only represents the simultaneity of race, ethnicity, gender, and class, but throughout her life she has owned her complex identity as a "Newyorkrican"[7] (Sotomayor 2002, 87) and as a Latina professional woman[8] of working-class background.

While this is by no means an exhaustive analysis of Judge Sonia Soto-mayor and her identity, I do a close reading of one of her speeches, "A Latina Judge's Voice," to apply the simultaneity model. This speech was delivered at Berkeley's School of Law in 2001 to a majority Hispanic audience of law students and was later published in the Berkeley *La Raza Law Journal* (2002). The controversy most noted in the media during the confirmation process of Justice Sotomayor centered on a statement in this speech: "I would hope that a wise Latina woman with the richness of her experiences would more often than not reach a better conclusion than a white male who hasn't lived that life" (2002, 92).

Sotomayor's speech was about the importance of identity, the underrep-resentation of Hispanics, women, and women of color on the bench and the need to have different identities when making judicial decisions. The speech was delivered to an audience of student lawyers with the purpose of helping them "think about these questions [of differences and identity] and to figure out how we go about creating the opportunity for there to be more women and people of color on the bench so we can finally have statistically signifi-cant numbers to measure the differences we will and are making" (2002, 93).

Sotomayor starts this speech by sharing personal stories about her iden-tity. She is a Puerto Rican born and raised in New York. Her parents, like many other Puerto Ricans, came to the United States during World War II, "because of poverty" (2002, 87). Sotomayor talks about her life grow-ing up and the extended-family meetings she attended, her appreciation of Spanish and English as the two languages she learned to speak (though her younger brother did not learn Spanish), and her love of Puerto Rican food. She expands on "the Latina side" of her identity "forged and closely nurtured by my family through our shared experiences and traditions" (2002, 87). A quick reading of the speech may suggest that Sotomayor, not an expert on identity, may have a limited or simplistic understanding of identity in the way she talks of her Latina identity as the food she likes, the music she appre-ciates, and the cultural icons that made her "Latina soul" (2002, 87).

But in the next paragraphs Sotomayor deconstructs this simplistic image of cultural identity and alludes to other identities that enrich who she is: her degrees from Ivy League schools and the historical context of *Brown v. Board of Education* in which she was born. We could add from her biography other experiences and commitments that complicate her identity such as her par-ticipation in Puerto Rican groups on campus, which she says "provided her with an anchor I needed to ground myself in that new and different world" of Princeton (Biography.com); her major in history; her participation in the Puerto Rican community; and her academic success and subsequent stellar career as a lawyer and judge (Lacayo 2009). She admits to no simple answers about what makes for her complex identity.

Sotomayor does not stop with these questions on identity; she wants to discuss what influence her identity "has on my presence on the bench" (2002, 87). Convincing statistics and anecdotes from judges and lawyers of color tell about the existence of race and gender bias in the courts, which Soto-mayor refers to in her speech. There is also compelling data on the biases and injustices that result from ignoring the complex interactions of race, ethnic-ity, class, nationality, religion, gender, and immigrant status in Family Court Proceedings decisions (Driggers 2009). Judge Sotomayor is encouraging her audience to look at these differences and to become lawyers and judges that consider those differences and their impact on court decisions seriously. "Each day on the bench I learn something new about the judicial process and about being *a professional Latina woman* in a world that sometimes looks at me with suspicion . . .we who judge must not deny the differences resulting from experience and heritage but attempt, as the Supreme Court suggests, continuously to judge when those opinions, sympathies and prejudices are appropriate" (93, emphasis added).

For this stance, one that recognizes differences and encourages the use of these differences to make sound professional decisions, Sotomayor was accused of being a racist. Her allusion to the complexity of identities and experience represented in "a wise Latina woman," a phrase taken out of context, drove this accusation. Sotomayor later apologized for the state-ment, something which Monica Driggers (2009) decries, as Sotomayor's statement recognized and encouraged the need for cultural competence in the courts; it was not a mistake, but a statement of need. Cultural knowl-edge should be considered a legitimate and important qualification for being a good judge, concludes Driggers from her extensive research on bias in the courts.

I believe the relentless criticism Somomayor was subjected to by the media and conservative politicians had little to do with the use of the phrase "wise Latina" and a lot to do with her challenge to the ideology of the "melted" American immigrant, who must leave behind and disown her or his com-plex identities in order to become "American." Sotomayor's consistent ref-erence throughout her career to the complex identity which informs her, formed at the intersections of gender, race, ethnicity, and class deprivation and privilege, challenges one-dimensional models of an "American" identity demanded from immigrants to the United States.

With the "wise Latina woman" phrase, Sotomayor was not arguing for the superiority of "a female or people of color voice" (2002, 91). Sotomayor is questioning, like other feminist contemporary lawyers, the supposed impartiality of the law (Crenshaw 1991; Minow 1990) and encouraging her audience to develop a consciousness and a set of skills that can "make a difference in the process of judging" (2002, 91). Because she also recognizes that this difference on the bench is not going to be made by a few isolated individuals, she wants "enough people of color, in enough cases, [to] make a difference in the process of judging" (2002, 91). I suggest that this difference in judging that Sotomayor is looking for comes from having and learning to use a simultaneity perspective; a perspective where events are understood through the complex lens of multiple and sometimes conflicting identities such as that of Sotomayor, a privileged elite educated Latina from the New York projects.

## Skills and Challenges of Embracing the Simultaneity of Identities

The heuristic exploration of Judge Sotomayor as a role model suggests there are important skills, as well as challenges, to acknowledging and enacting the simultaneity of identities. Two important lessons derive from applying the simultaneity lens to the snippets I have discussed in the life of Judge Sotomayor. First, people *can* take up their identities in a complex way that acknowledges the simultaneity of social differences. And second, while taking up the complexity of one's identity can have positive effects, there are also significant challenges to acknowledging complexity and using simultaneity as a lens to approach differences and identities.

On the positive side, few would disagree that "[p]ositive relationships across difference and the ability to dialogue are the cornerstone of a multicultural workforce. . . . These skills must build on a textured understanding both of one's own identity and of the diversity in the groups with which we interact" (Gallegos and Ferdman 2007, 28). Fahim (2009) proposes that understanding ours and others' multiple identities allows us to find commonalities for connecting "to those who seem different at first glance," helping us "overcome global and interpersonal conflict" (4).

One of the most important ways we can apply the simultaneity model is to develop a way of thinking and a set of skills that acknowledges and utilizes such a complex approach to identities. I draw from Sotomayor's example and from Zadie Smith's insightful essay, "Speaking in Tongues" (2009) to propose five skills that support simultaneity.

1. *The Flexibility to speak in two and more voices.* This flexibility comes from understanding and using the plurality of "voices" and ways of seeing that arise from our different identities. For example, Judge Sotomayor

intersperses Spanish words in the delivery of her speech in impeccable English. These are two languages she knows and is not reticent to access. Smith (2009) discusses her initial ability to shift from Oxford English (meaning upper-class English) to the voice of her childhood, the English of her working-class neighborhood and family. She is saddened by the loss of this flexibility and the aliveness she felt when she could speak in these two voices and access these two different identities. "But flexibility is something that requires work if it is to be maintained" (133), she adds.

There is a history of women of color "speaking in tongues" and mixing genres in their writing referred to as "heteroglossia," "multivocality" (Henderson 1989, 22, 36), and code-switching (Anzaldúa 1990). Accessing our different voices does not refer only to the ability to speak different languages, but includes the ability to share the different ways of thinking and seeing that come from our different, and sometimes contradictory, identities. While challenging, it is also a powerful gift that connects us to ourselves and to others (Smith 2009).

2. *Owning complexity and multiplicity.* In their work on Latino identity, Gallegos and Ferdman (2007) describe a frustrated Latino manager, George, who, when asked "where he is from?" answers in a manner that never satisfies his questioner:

Q: Where are you from?
A: Here.
Q: But where are you from?
A: California.
Q: But where are you from?
A: San Diego.
Q: But I mean where are you really from?
A: Well, I grew up in Colorado . . . (27).

While Gallegos and Ferdman use this exchange as an example of the challenges of Latino/a "identity orientations" (2007, 28), simultaneity suggests that George is having difficulty embracing and talking about his complex identities. George is trying to simplify and communicate a very narrow view of who he is, instead of making this exchange an opportunity to own and expand on his multiple identities, and in the process educate his interviewer. Simultaneity also suggests that if George were to be more forthcoming with the complexity of his identities, the questioner would stop badgering George with the simple "where are you from?" question and would have to rise to George's simultaneous identities as well as analyze his or her own complex identities. Sotomayor's role modeling teaches us that even talking about the interaction of three identities—"Latina professional woman"—expands and changes the way we perceive and relate to ourselves and others.

On the other hand, sometimes it is hard to take up one's complex identity because it challenges the myth of authenticity (Smith 2009). Is George a *real "American"*? if he is also a Chicano who speaks only English and was born in Colorado from a family whose lands were in Mexico before they were taken away in the U.S.-Mexican war?

Owning complexity and multiplicity also requires two additional, but linked skills: (3) *managing the expectations and pressure for singularity*, and (4) *making an effort to hold on to the various selves and ones' multiple identities.* Expanding on this point, Smith says that people dread the middle, "the interim place," the in between, thus . . . "[w]hat is double must be made singular" (2009, 135). Whether this aversion to ambiguity and multidimensionality is a human trait, an American sociopolitical tradition, or a result of identity politics, with its demand for unity in the face of oppression, to hold on to one's multiple identities requires resisting this pressure to conform to one-dimensionality. Talking about the "new *mestiza* consciousness," who lives in the in-betweens of race, ethnicity, and the borders between her lands of Mexico and the United States, Anzaldúa also recognizes the importance of "tolerance for contradictions [and] a tolerance for ambiguity" (1990, 379). Holding on to the different selves demands a constant effort not to give up on those multiple identities and its contradictions, which may sometimes be uncomfortable.

5. *Thinking "location" in time and space*, the fifth skill, is one way to hold on to the multiple selves and accept ambiguities and contradictions. Thinking location means paying attention to how identities shift in response to specific social and geographical spaces. Understanding the relation between the particulars of the situation we are in, our situatedness, helps keep us grounded and at the same time flexible. Thus, simultaneity pays attention to the specific moments in which particular identities become more or less salient and under what circumstances. Noticing these moments further increases the capacity to accept and enact multiplicity and simultaneity. This does not mean that anything goes or that those who live by the principles of simultaneity are chameleons. But it means that identities are negotiated in complex interactions with others and the environment; identity is a process, it is not a static "thing" or a fait accompli.

Dhingra (2007), who studied how Asian American professionals in Texas hold on to multiple and contradictory identities, gives many examples of how these professionals constantly negotiate their identities, maneuvering between the apparently nonnegotiable demands and values of their families of origin and their national-ethnic background with the demands and new identities of U.S. middle-class Americans. Dhingra refers to this phenomena as a kind of cultural "lived hybridity in which contradictory identities were attended to simultaneously rather than only in separate spheres or times" (2007, 15). In the face of ambiguity and contradictions, thinking and enacting identities in the context of concrete time and space boundaries helps manage the complexity of it all and allows for life-long learning.

## Conclusions, Reflections, and Questions to Pursue

Globalization and the intellectual forces of postmodernism and transnational feminism suggest new ways of understanding and working with identity. The major shifts in these conceptualizations of identity relate first to moving from a focus on unitary, one-dimensional, and coherent frameworks on "identity" to a focus on differences as the kernel from which *identities* (plural) are constantly coconstructed by the individual and his or her society.

Second, models of identity are shifting from conceptualizing identities as fixed, achieved, and finite to understanding identities as multiple, interacting, changing, and always in process: "What we call identities are not objects but processes constituted in and through power relations" (Brah and Phoenix 2007, 3). "Differences" are seen as encompassing social relations, experience, subjectivity, identity(ies) and power. Thus, attention must be paid to the "contradictory experiences of power, identities (and disadvantage) and to the space 'in between'" (Hurtado and Sinha 2008, 339).

In my review of approaches to differences, I have argued that models of identity and differences can be captured in graphical representations that have changed in the last decades. From representing differences as hierarchical and isolated dimensions of identity, representations that portray differences as intersecting or occurring simultaneously may be more appropriate to these times.

The major challenge that these shifts in conceptualizing identities pose to racial identity development models is the need to consider that interactions of differences like gender, ethnicity, class, nationality, and sexuality shape differences and identities that were previously discussed in isolation from each other. A simultaneity model proposes instead to study the processes by which identities—multiple, contradictory, and changing—form, influence each other, and reform.

The simultaneity model also challenges models of identity which solely focus on an individual's singular identity, as identity is shaped both by the structural political macro forces, over which the individual has little control, as well as by the individual's own subjectivity and agency. Models of racial identity would have to take into account these complex processes in dynamic, iterative ways as opposed to the linear developmental explanations focused on the individual self, which are more common.

Nevertheless, identity scholars are already embracing Intersectionality to expand on their theories of identity development (see, for example, Abes, Jones, and McEwen 2007; Jones and McEwen 2000; Reynolds and Pope 1991; Wijeyesinghe this volume.) Other theories also pose new questions and offer alternatives, such as queer (Butler 1990, 2004; Valocchi 2005) and postcolonial theories (Appiah and Gates 1995; Hall 1996).

What, then, are the future directions for identity research and practice using simultaneity and Intersectionality models? Intersectionality scholars have proposed a variety of research directions in the study of differences and identity (Brewer et al. 2002; Cuadraz and Uttal 1999; Luft and Ward 2009; McCall 2005; Warner 2008). For example, I propose three broad research interventions (Holvino 2010). First, identify and publicize the hidden stories at the intersections of race, gender, class, sexuality, ethnicity, and nation, like the intersectional story of Judge Sonia Sotomayor. Second, identify and untangle the differential and material impact of everyday practices in organizations for different groups across their differences and multiple identities. Acker's (2006a) study of "regimes of inequality," the specific patterns of race, gender, and class relations in organizations, is an example of this strategy. Third, identify and connect internal organizational processes with external societal processes to understand identities within a broader social context and change agenda, such as relating the situation of maquiladora workers in specific factories with the forces of economic global restructuring (Fernandez-Kelly 1994, 2005; Wichterich 2000).

The methodological challenges of researching Intersectionality are now increasingly recognized and articulated (Dill et al. 2007; McCall 2005; Shields 2008; Ward 2004). These challenges also apply to simultaneity. For example, an important challenge is operationalizing Intersectionality so that it helps guide practical interventions in organizations and communities (Luft and Ward 2009). Ward (2004) describes this challenge as "the problem of how to recognize and respond to multiple oppressions simultaneously" (2004, 83).

Another important challenge is how to analyze specific intersections of difference and identities without seemingly excluding other dimensions, which may be as important. On the one hand, analyses cannot be all-inclusive or we end up with the problem of "the infinite regress" (Warner 2008, 455) where mentioning a list of differences does not equate doing Intersectionality (Shields 2008). At the same time, Intersectionality researchers need to be cognizant and explicit about which differences are chosen for study and why (Warner 2008). For example, as a transnational feminist residing in the United States in the era of globalization, the personal and social salience of the dimensions of race-ethnicity, gender, class, sexuality, and nationality leads me to study the simultaneity of these specific dimensions, at least at the moment.

But rather than focus on the challenges, I conclude by suggesting two practical directions for applying simultaneity in higher education: teaching-counseling, and building alliances across differences.

The Intersectionality and simultaneity models of identity suggest new ways and competencies for teaching and counseling. For example, Reynolds and Pope (1991) recommend that counselors and teachers challenge their own assumptions about identity development, especially as they consider the multiple identities of their students and the more complex world of mixed race and bicultural families and communities in which these students live. Jones and Wijeyesinghe (2011) discuss a variety of strategies for teaching from an intersectional perspective, such as developing curricula that integrates multiple identities and employing both single-identity approaches and intersectional approaches to introduce and deepen students' understanding of both privilege and oppression. Kumashiro (2001) goes further to advocate that anti-oppressive education must help "students trouble their own knowledges and identities, trouble the ways they traditionally engage with oppression, and trouble what it means to change oppression" (20). In spite of the challenges, teaching and counseling using simultaneity and Intersectionality models present enormous opportunities for creativity, innovation, and student engagement.

Applying the Intersectionality/simultaneity models of identity to build alliances and coalitions for change is another promising focus for future practice. For example, learning more about the differences and similarities that separate and unite groups makes it easier to build change efforts across different identity groups (Barvosa-Carter 1999); Scully and Segal 2002; Sheridan et al. 2004). Yuval-Davis suggests that this entails moving from traditional perspectives on social movements based on identity politics to social change movements and strategies based on transversal politics (2006). On a similar note, Anner (1996) proposes that community organizers working with youth and their parents become more aware of the "fluid identities of kids," based on a "complicated formula of territory, race, class, and aspirations" (165). She argues for a more inclusive definition of identity politics that reconnects gender, race, and class struggles and goes beyond individual empowerment to building a social justice movement. Students, workers, men, and women across geographical and other borders could all use more alliances to change the conditions of inequality and injustice they face. Embracing and enacting simultaneity may help us do just that.

NOTES

1. Sex gender differentiation is the distinction sometimes made by feminists to refer to sex as the biological and anatomical characteristics of males and females (men and women) while gender refers to the socially constructed meanings and power differentials attributed to those biological differences.

2. Discourse refers to formalized ways of thinking manifested in language and shared by a social group. Lessa (2006) defines Foucauldian discourse as "systems of thoughts composed of ideas, attitudes, courses of action, beliefs and practices that systematically construct the subjects and the worlds of which they speak" (285). Discoursre always embedded in power relations that construct reality and subjectivities through ongoing negotiations of "power-knowledges." Discursive is an adjective that describes the ways in which discourses produce particular effects or results. For example, a discursive analysis examines the specific ways in which a particular discourse becomes dominant in an organization or society.

3. Loden's model has been updated, eliminating the distinction between primary and secondary differences represented in the inner and outer circles and including class in the inner circle. See her website http://loden.com/Site/Welcome.html. But my critique is not so much of the original Loden model as of the way it circulates and is used by others in the diversity and inclusion industry. See for example, Allan Johnson's use of Loden and Rosener's "Diversity Wheel" (2006, 15), where he expands on the challenge of differences and exclusion, which "is especially true of characteristics in the center of the wheel, which have the added quality of being difficult if not impossible to change (except acquiring a disability, which can happen to anyone at any time)" (16).

4. "Third World feminists" is a problematic term, which attempts to distinguish between White feminists from Western, industrialized nations from feminists based in non-Western, industrialized nations. The distinction falls apart when we consider the situation of women of color in Western countries or the situation of privileged women in Third World countries.

5. Class refers to differences in economic and social status, which create inequalities and privileges and which are sustained by class divisions, class interactions, and class symbols and identities.

6. *Maquiladoras* or *maquilas* are factories along the U.S.–Mexico border which export products to the United States under favorable arrangements for the employer. Created by the Border Industrialization Program in 1965 and further supported by the North American Free Trade Agreement (NAFTA), *maquilas* are an important and

contradictory source of income and exploitation, especially for young, single Third World women.

7. Newyorkrican refers to a person born in New York of Puerto Rican parents, themselves born either in the United States or in the island. It can also be spelled Newyorican or Nuyorican.

8. Because of the gendered nature of the Spanish language, "Latina woman" is a redundancy. I use it here to highlight how race and ethnicity combine with gender to actually make up a complex Latina identity at the intersections of race, ethnicity, and class.

9. "American" appears in quotation marks because America is the name of the continents of North, South, and Central America. Naming the citizens of the United States as Americans, as opposed to United Statians, for example, is a colonizing power move representative of the discursive practices transnational feminists challenge.

REFERENCES

Abes, Elisa S., Susan, R. Jones, and Marylu K. McEwen. 2007. "Reconceptualizing the Model of Multiple Dimensions of Identity: The Role of Meaning Making Capacity in the Construction of Multiple Identities." *Journal of College Student Development* 48 (1): 1–22.

Acker, Joanne. 2006a. *Class Questions: Feminist Answers.* Lanham, Md.: Rowman and Littlefield.

———. 2006b. "Inequality Regimes: Gender, Class, and Race in Organizations." *Gender & Society* 20 (4): 441–464.

Adams, Maurianne. 2001. "Core Processes of Racial Identity Development." In *New Perspectives on Racial Identity Development,* edited by Charmaine L. Wijeyesinghe and Bailey W. Jackson III, 209–242. New York: NYU Press.

Anner, Joanna, ed. 1996. *Beyond Identity Politics: Emerging Social Justice Movements in Communities of Color.* Boston, Mass.: South End Press.

Anthias, Fiona, and Nira Yuval-Davis. 1992. *Racialized Boundaries: Race, Nation, Gender, Colour and Class and the Anti-Racist Struggle.* London: Routledge.

Anzaldúa, Gloria. 1987. *Borderlands/La Frontera: The New Mestiza.* San Francisco: Aunt Lute.

———. 1990. "La Conciencia de la Mestiza: Towards a New Consciousness." In *Making Face, Making Soul: Haciendo Caras: Creative and Critical Perspective by Women of Color,* edited by Gloria Anzaldúa, 377–389. San Francisco: Aunt Lute.

Appiah, Kwama A., and Henry L. Gates, Jr., eds. 1995. *Identities.* Chicago: University of Chicago Press.

Barvosa-Carter, Edwina. 1999. "Multiple Identity and Coalition Building: How Identity Differences within Us Enable Radical Alliances among Us." *Contemporary Justice Review* 2 (2): 111–126.

Bauman, Zygmunt. 1998. *Globalization: The Human Consequences.* New York: Columbia University Press.

Beale, Frances. 1970. "Double Jeopardy: To Be Black and Female." In *Words of Fire: An Anthology of African-American Feminist Thought,* edited by Beverly Guy-Sheftall, 1995. New York: New Press.

Bell, Ella L., and Stella M. Nkomo. 1992. "Re-Visioning Women Manager's Lives." In *Gendering Organizational Analysis,* edited by Albert J. Mills and Peta Tancred, 235–247. Newbury Park, Calif.: Sage.

———. 2001. *Our Separate Selves: Black and White Women and the Struggle for Professional Identity.* Boston: Harvard Business School Press.

Billig, Michael, 1999. *Freudian Repression: Conversation Creating the Unconscious.* Cambridge: Cambridge University Press.

Bowleg, Lisa. 2008. "When Black + Lesbian + Woman ≠ Black Lesbian Woman: The Methodological Challenges of Qualitative and Quantitative Intersectionality Research." *Sex Roles* 59 (5–6): 312–325.

Brah, Avtar, and Ann Phoenix. 2004. "'Ain't I a Woman? Revisiting Intersectionality." *Journal of International Women Studies* 5 (3): 75–86.

Brewer, Rose M., Cecilia A. Conrad, and Mary C. King. 2002. "The Complexities and Potential of Theorizing Gender, Caste, Race, and Class." *Feminist Economics* 8 (2): 3–18.

Briggs, Laura. 1998. "Discourse of 'Forced Sterilization' in Puerto Rico: The Problem with the Speaking Subaltern." *Differences* 10 (2): 30–66.

Butler, Judith. 1990. *Gender Trouble: Feminism and the Subversion of Identity.* New York: Routledge.

———. 2004. *Undoing Gender.* New York: Routledge.

Calás, Marta B., and Linda Smircich. 1992. "Re-Writing Gender into Organizational Theorizing: Directions from Feminist Perspectives." In *Rethinking Organization: New Directions in Organizational Research and Analysis*, edited by Michael I. Reed and Michael D. Hughes, 227–253. London: Sage.

———. 2006. "From the 'Woman's Point of View' Ten Years Later: Towards a Feminist Organization Studies." In *The Sage Handbook of Organization Studies*, edited by Stewart Clegg, Cynthia Hardy, Thomas B. Lawrence, and Walter L Nord, 2nd ed., 284–346. Thousand Oaks, Calif.: Sage.

———. 2009. "Feminist Perspectives on Gender in Organizational Research: What Is and Yet to Be." In *The Sage Handbook of Organizational Research Methods*, edited by David A. Buchanan and Alan Bryman, 246–269. London: Sage.

———. 2011. "In the Back and Forth of Transmigration: Rethinking Organization Studies in a Transnational Key." In *Handbook of Gender, Work and Organization*, edited by Emma Jeanes, David Knights, and Patricia Y. Martin, 411–428. London: Wiley-Blackwell.

Chan, Kwok-bun, ed. 2006. "The Stranger's Plight and Gift." In *Social Transformations in Chinese Societies*, vol. 1, 191–219. The Netherlands: Hong Kong Sociological Association.

Collins, Patricia H. 2000. *Black Feminist Thought: Knowledge, Consciousness and the Politics of Empowerment*, 2nd ed. New York: Routledge.

Crenshaw, Kimberlé. 1989. "Demarginalizing the Intersection of Race and Sex: A Black Feminist Critique of Antidiscrimination Doctrine, Feminist Theory and Antiracist Politics." *University of Chicago Legal Forum* 139: 139–167.

———. 1991. "Mapping the Margins: Intersectionality, Identity Politics, and Violence against Women of Color." *Stanford Law Review* 43 (6): 1241–1299.

Cross, William E., and Peony Fhagen-Smith. 2001. "Patterns of African American Identity Development: A Life Span Perspective." In *New Perspectives on Racial Identity Development*, edited by Charmaine L. Wijeyeshinghe and Bailey W. Jackson III, 243–270. New York: NYU Press.

Cuadraz, Gloria H., and Lynet Uttal. 1999. "Intersectionality and In-Depth Interviews: Methodological Strategies for Analyzing Race, Class and Gender." *Race, Gender & Class* 6 (3): 156–175.

Dhingra, Pawan. 2007. *Managing Multicultural Lives: Asian American Professionals and the Challenges of Multiple Identities*. Stanford, Calif.: Stanford University Press.

Dill, Bonnie T. 2002, Fall. "Work at the Intersections of Race, Gender, Ethnicity, and Other Dimensions of Difference in Higher Education." *Connections: Newsletter of the Consortium on Race, Gender, and Ethnicity*. College Park: University of Maryland.

Dill, Bonnie T., Amy E. McLaughlin, and Angel D. Nieves. 2007. "Future Directions of Feminist Research: Intersectionality." In *Handbook of Feminist Research*, edited by Sharlene N. Hesse-Biber, 629–637. Thousand Oaks, Calif.: Sage.

Dill, Bonnie T., and Ruth E. Zambrana, eds. 2009. *Emerging Intersections: Race, Class and Gender in Theory, Policy, and Practice*. New Brunswick, N.J.: Rutgers University Press.

Driggers, Monica. 2009. "The Courtroom in a Diverse Society: Understanding the Need for Cultural Competence." Research & Action Report (Fall/Winter), Wellesley Center for Women. http//www.wcwonline.org/Research-Action-Report-Fall/Winter-2009. Downloaded July 14, 2010.

Duany, Jorge. 2002. *Puerto Rican Nation on the Move: Identities on the Island and in the United States*. Chapel Hill: University of North Carolina Press.

Dumas, Rita G. 1985. "Dilemmas of Black Females in Leadership." In *Group Relations Reader 2*, edited by Arthur D. Colman and Marvin H. Geller, 323–334. Springfield, Va.: Goetz.

Essed, Philomena. 1990. *Understanding Everyday Racism*. Translated by C. Jaffé. Alameda, Calif.: Hunter House.

———. 2001. "Multi-Identifications and Transformations: Reaching Beyond Racial and Ethnic Reductionisms." *Social Identities* 7 (4): 493–509.

Fahim, Urusa. July 2009. "Identity in a Global Context." Unpublished manuscript. California Institute of Integral Studies, San Francisco, Calif.

Ferdman, Bernardo, and Plácida I. Gallegos, 2001. "Latinos and Racial Identity Development." In *New Perspectives on Racial Identity Development: A Theoretical and Practical Anthology*, edited by Charmaine L. Wijeyesinghe and Bailey W. Jackson III, 32–66. New York: NYU Press.

Fernández-Kelly, Maria P. 1994. "Making Sense of Gender in the World Economy: Focus on Latin America." *Organization* 1 (2): 249–275.

———. 2005. "The Future of Gender in Mexico and the United States: Economic Transformation and Changing Definitions." In *The Shape of Social Inequality: Stratification and Ethnicity in Comparative Perspective*, edited by David B. Bills, 255–280. New York: Elsevier.

Gailey, Christine, W. 1987. "Evolutionary Perspectives on Gender and Hierarchy." In *Analyzing Gender: A Handbook of Social Science Research*, edited by Beth Hess and Myra Ferree, 32–67. Bevery Hills, Calif.: Sage.

Gallegos, Plácida I., and Bernardo M. Ferdman. 2007. "Identity Orientations of Latinos in the United States: Implications for Leaders and Organizations." *Business Journal of Hispanic Research* 2 (1): 26–41.

Glenn, Evelyn N. 1985. "Racial Ethnic Women's Labor: The Intersection of Race, Gender and Class Oppression." *Review of Radical Political Economy* 17 (3): 86–108.

———. 1986. *Issei, Nisei, War Bride: Three Generations of Japanese American Women in Domestic Service*. Philadelphia: Temple University Press.

———. 1988. "A Belated Industry Revisited: Domestic Service among Japanese-American Women." In *The Worth of Women's Work: A Qualitative Synthesis*, edited by A. Stathem, E. M. Miller, and H. O. Mauksch, 57–75. Albany: SUNY Press.

——. 2001. "Gender, Race, and the Organization of Reproductive Labor." In *The Critical Study of Work*, edited by R. Baldoz, C. Koeber, and P. Kraft, 71–82. Philadelphia: Temple University Press.

Guy-Sheftall, Beverly, ed. 1995. *Words of Fire: An Anthology of African-American Feminist Thought*. New York: New Press.

Hall, Stuart. 1996. "Introduction: Who Needs 'Identity'?" In *Questions of Cultural Identity*, edited by Stuart Hall and Paul DuGay, 1–17. London: Sage.

Hall, Stuart, and Paul DuGay, eds. 1996. *Questions of Cultural Identity*. London: Sage.

Hardisty, Jean. 2010, Spring. "Commentary. How Women Can Succeed: An Alternative View." *35 Years of Research + Action*, 16–17. Wellesley, Mass.: Wellesley Centers for Women.

Henderson, Mae G. 1989. "Speaking in Tongues: Dialogics, Dialectic, and the Black Women Writers' Literary Tradition." In *Changing Our Own Words*, edited by Cheryl A. Wall, 16–37. New Brunswick, N.J.: Rutgers University Press.

Holvino, Evangelina. 1994. "Women of Color in Organizations: Revising Our Models of Gender at Work." In *The Promise of Diversity: Over 40 Voices Discuss Strategies for Eliminating Discrimination in Organizations*, edited by Elsie Y. Cross, Judith H. Katz, Fred A. Miller, and Eddie W. Seashore, 52–59. Burr Ridge, Ill.: Irwin Professional Publishing.

——. 2001. "Complicating Gender: The Simultaneity of Race, Gender, and Class in Organization Change(ing)." Working Paper #14. Boston: Center for Gender in Organizations, Simmons School of Management.

——. 2002. "Class: A Difference That Makes a Difference." *The Diversity Factor* 10 (2): 28–34.

——. 2003a. "Globalization: Overview." In *Reader in Gender, Work, and Organization*, edited by Robin Ely, Erica Foldy, and Maureen Scully, and the Center for Gender in Organizations, Simmons School of Management, 381–386. Malden, Mass.: Blackwell Publishing.

——. 2003b. "Theories of Differences: Changing Paradigms for Organizations." In *Handbook of Diversity Management: Beyond Awareness to Competency-Based Learning*, edited by Deborah L. Plummer, 111–131. Lanham, Md.: University Press of America.

——. 2005. "Theories of Difference: Making a Difference with Simultaneity." Accessed April 23, 2011 at http://www.chaosmanagement.com/resources/resources/powerpoint-presentations.

——. 2006. "Tired of Choosing: Working with the Simultaneity of Race, Gender, and Class in Organizations." *CGO Insights* 24. Boston: Center for Gender in Organizations, Simmons School of Management.

——. 2010. "Intersections: The Simultaneity of Race, Gender, and Class in Organization Studies." *Gender, Work & Organization* 17 (3): 248–277.

Hondagneu-Sotelo, Pierrette. 2001. *Doméstica: Immigrant Workers Cleaning and Caring in the Shadow of Affluence*. Berkeley: University of California Press.

——. 2002. "Blowups and Other Unhappy Endings." In *Global Woman: Nannies, Maids, and Sex Workers in the New Economy*, edited by Barbara Ehrenreich and Arlie R. Hochschild, 55–69. New York: Henry Holt.

Hossfeld, Karen. 1990. "Their Logic against Them: "Contradictions in Sex, Race, and Class in Silicon Valley." In *Women Workers and Global Restructuring*, edited by Kathryn Ward, 149–178. Ithaca, N.Y.: ILR Press.

Hull, Gloria T., Patricia B. Scott, and Barbara Smith, eds. 1982. *All the Women Are White, All the Blacks Are Men, But Some of Us Are Brave: Black Women's Studies*. New York: Feminist Press.

Hurtado, Aida. 1999. "Cross-Border Existence: One Woman's Migrant Story." In *Women's Untold Stories*, edited by Mary Romero and Abigail J. Stewart, 83–101. New York: Routledge.

———. 2000. "Sitios y Lenguas: Chicanas Theorize Feminisms." In *Decentering the Center*, edited by U. Narayan and S. Harding, 128–155. Bloomington: Indiana University Press.

———. 2003. *Voicing Feminisms: Young Chicanas Speak Out on Identity and Sexuality*. New York: NYU Press.

Hurtado, Aida, and Mrinal Sinha. 2008. "More than Men: Latino Feminist Masculinities and Intersectionality." *Sex Roles* 59 (5–6): 337–349.

Ignatiev, Noel. 1995. *How the Irish Became White*. New York: Routledge.

Johnson, Allan G. 2006. *Privilege, Power, and Difference*. (2nd edition.) Boston, Mass.: McGraw Hill.

Jones, Susan R., and Marylu K. McEwen. 2000. "A Conceptual Model of Multiple Dimensions of Identities." *Journal of College Student Development* 41 (4): 405–414.

Jones, Susan R., and Charmaine L. Wijeyesinghe. 2011. "The Promises and Challenges of Teaching from an Intersectional Perspective: Core Components and Applied Strategies." In *Understanding the Intersections: An Integrative Analysis Approach to Diversity in the College Classroom*, edited by Mathew L. Ouellett, 11–20. San Francisco: Jossey Bass.

King, Deborah K. 1988. "Multiple Jeopardy, Multiple Consciousness: The Context of a Black Feminist Ideology." In *Black Women in America: Social Science Perspectives*, edited by Micheline R. Malson, Elisabeth Mudimbe-Boji, Jean F. O'Barr, and Mary Wyer, 265–295. Chicago: University of Chicago Press.

Kondo, Dorinne. 1999. "Fabricating Masculinity: Gender, Race, and Nation in a Transnational Frame." In *Between Women and Nation: Nationalities, Transnational Feminisms and the State*, edited by Caren Kaplan, Norma Alarcón, and Minoo Moallen, 296–319. Durham: Duke University Press.

Kumashiro, Kevin. 2001. "Queer Students of Color and Antiracist, Antiheterosexist Education." In *Troubling Intersection of Race and Sexuality: Queer Students of Color and Anti-Oppressive Education*, edited by Kevin Kumashiro, 1–25. Lanham, Md.: Rowman and Littlefield.

Lacayo, Richard. 2009, June 8. "A Justice Like No Other." *Time Magazine*, 25–29.

Lewellen, Ted C. 2002. *The Anthropology of Globalization: Cultural Anthropology Enters the 21st Century*. Westport, Conn.: Bergin and Garvey.

Lessa, Iara. 2006. "Discursive Struggles within Social Welfare: Restaging Teen Motherhood." *British Journal of Social Work*, 36 (2): 283–298.

Loden, Marilyn. n.d. http://loden.com/Site/Welcome.html. Retrieved November 8, 2011.

Loden, Marilyn. 1996. *Implementing Diversity*. Chicago: Irwin Professional Publishing.

Lorde, Audre. 1983. *There Is No Hierarchy of Oppressions*. New York: Council on Interracial Books for Children.

Luft, Rachel, and Jane Ward. 2009. "Toward an Intersectionality Just Out of Reach: Confronting Challenges to Intersectional Practice." In *Perceiving Gender Locally, Globally, and Intersectionally: Advances in Gender Research*, vol. 13, edited by Vasilikie Demos and Marcia T. Segal, 9–37. Bingley, U.K.: Emerald Group Publishing.

Martinez, Theresa A. 2000. "Race, Class, and Gender in the Lifestory of Chicanas: A Critique of Nathan Glazer." *Race, Gender, & Class* 7 (2): 57–75.

McCall, Leslie. 2005. "The Complexity of Intersectionality." *Signs* 30 (3): 1771–1801.

Mendez, Jennifer B., and Diane L. Wolf. 2001. "Where Feminist Theory Meets Feminist Practice: Border-Crossing in a Transnational Academic Feminist Organization." *Organization* 8 (4): 723–750.

Mendoza, Breny. 2002. "Transnational Feminism in Question." *Feminist Theory* 3 (3): 295–314.

Minow, Martha. 1990. *Making All the Difference: Inclusion, Exclusion, and American Law.* Ithaca: Cornell University Press.

Mohanty, Chandra T. 1991. "Under Western Eyes: Feminist Scholarship and Colonial Discourses." In *Third World Women and the Politics of Feminism*, edited by Chandra T. Mohanty, Ann Russo, and Lourdes Torres, 51–80. Bloomington: Indiana University Press.

———. 1997. "Women Workers and Capitalist Scripts." In *Feminist Genealogies, Colonial Legacies, Democratic Futures*, edited by M. J. Alexander and C. T. Mohanty, 3–29. New York: Routledge.

———. 2003. "'Under Western Eyes' Revisited: Feminist Solidarity through Anticapitalist Struggles." *Signs* 28 (12): 499–535.

Mohanty, Chandra, Ann Russo, and Lourdes Torres, eds. 1991. *Third World Women and the Politics of Feminism.* Bloomington: Indiana University Press.

Morales, Rosario. 1981. "I Am What I Am." In *This Bridge Called My Back: Writings by Radical Women of Color*, edited by Cherríe Moraga and Gloria Anzaldua, 14–15. New York: Kitchen Table Press.

Morgan, Robin. 1984. *Sisterhood Is Global: The International Women's Movement Anthology.* Garden City, N.Y.: Anchor Books.

Morrison, Ann M., Randall P. White, Ellen Van Velsor, and the Center for Creative Leadership. 1987. *Breaking the Glass Ceiling: Can Women Reach the Top of America's Largest Corporations?* Reading, Mass.: Addison-Wesley.

Narayan, Uma, and Sandra Harding, eds. 2000. *Decentering the Center: Philosophy for a Multicultural, Postcolonial, and Feminist World.* Bloomington: Indiana University Press.

Omi, Michael, and Howard Winant. 1986. *Racial Formation in the United States: From the 1960s to the 1980s.* New York: Routledge.

Otis, Eileen M. 2001. "The Reach and Limits of Asian Panethnic Identity: The Dynamics of Gender, Race, and Class in a Community Based Organization." *Qualitative Sociology* 24 (3): 349–379.

Oyewumi, Oyeronke. 1997. *The Invention of Women: Making an African Sense of Western Gender Discourses.* Minneapolis: University of Minnesota Press.

———. 2002. "Conceptualizing Gender: The Eurocentric Foundations of Feminist Concepts and the Challenge of African Epistemologies." *Jenda: A Journal of Culture and African Women Studies* 2 (1). www.jendajournal.com. Accessed July 23, 2010.

Parreñas, Rhacel S. 2002. "The Care Crisis in the Philippines: Children and Transnational Families in the New Global Economy." In *Global Woman: Nannies, Maids, and Sex Workers in the New Economy*, edited by Barbara Ehrenreich and Arlie R. Hochschild, 39–54. New York: Henry Holt.

Phoenix, Ann, and Pamela Pattynama. 2006. "Intersectionality." *European Journal of Women's Studies* 13: 187–192.

Purdie-Vaughs, Valerie, and Richard P. Eibach. 2008. "Intersectional Invisibility: The Distinctive Advantages and Disadvantages of Multiple Subordinate-Group Identities." *Sex Roles* 59 (5–6): 377–391.

Quiñones-Rosado, Raúl. 1998, Summer. "Hispanic or Latino? The Struggle for Identity in a Race-Based Society." *The Diversity Factor*: 20–24.

Reynolds, Amy L., and Raechele L. Pope. 1991. "The Complexities of Diversity: Exploring Multiple Oppressions." *Journal of Counseling and Development* 70 (1): 174–180.

Rollins, Judith. 1985. *Between Women: Domestics and Their Employers*. Philadelphia: Temple University Press.

Romero, Mary. 1992. *Maid in the USA*. New York: Routledge.

———. 1997. "Chicanas Modernize Domestic Service." In *Workplace/Women's Place*, edited by D. Dunn, 358–368. Los Angeles: Roxbury Publishing.

Sampaio, Anna. 2004. "Transnational Feminisms in a New Global Matrix." *International Feminist Journal of Politics* 6 (2): 181–206.

Scully, Maureen A., and Any Segal. 2002. "Passion with an Umbrella: Grassroots Activism in the Workplace." In *Social Structures and Organizations Revisited*, edited by M. Lounsbury and M. J. Ventresca, 125–168. Amsterdam: JAI.

Sheridan, Bridgette, Evangelina Holvino, and Gelaye Debebe. June 2004. "Beyond Diversity: Working across Differences for Organizational Change." *CGO Commentaries*, 3. Boston: Center for Gender in Organizations, Simmons School of Management.

Shields, Stephanie A. 2008. "Gender: An Intersectionality Perspective." *Sex Roles* 59: 301–311.

Smith, Zadie. 2009. *Changing My Mind: Occasional Essays*. New York: Penguin Press.

Sonia Sotomayor Biography. Biography.com. http://www.biography.com/articles/Sonia-Sotomayor. Accessed 15 July 2010.

Sotomayor, Sonia. 2002. "A Latina Judge's Voice. (Text of The Judge Mario G. Olmos Memorial Lecture delivered at the Berkeley School of Law, University of California.)" *Berkeley La Raza Law Journal* 13: 87–94.

Spelman, Elizabeth V. 1988. *Inessential Woman: Problems of Exclusion in Feminist Thought*. Boston: Beacon Press.

Spickard, Paul, and W. Jeffrey Burroughs, eds. 2000. *We Are a People: Narrative and Multiplicity in Constructing Ethnic Identity*. Philadelphia: Temple University Press.

Torres, Vasti, Susan J. Jones, and Kristen A. Renn, 2009. "Identity Theories in Student Affairs: Origins, Current Status and New Approaches." *Journal of College Student Development* 50 (6): 577–596.

Valocchi, Stephen. 2005. "Not Yet Queer Enough: The Lessons of Queer Theory for the Sociology of Gender and Sexuality." *Gender & Society* 19 (6): 750–770.

Ward, Jane. 2004. "'Not All Differences Are Created Equal': Multiple Jeopardy in a Gendered Organization." *Gender & Society* 18 (1): 82–102.

Warner, Leah R. 2008. "A Best Practices Guide to Intersectional Approaches in Psychological Research." *Sex Roles* 59 (5–6): 454–463.

Weber, Lynn. 1998. "A Conceptual Framework for Understanding Race, Class, and Sexuality." *Psychology of Women Quarterly* 22 (1): 12–32.

———. 2010. *Understanding Race, Class, Gender, and Sexuality: A Conceptual Framework*, 2nd ed. New York: Oxford University Press.

White, Katherine. 1987. "Panel on Women and Men in Organizational Life." In *Irrationality in Social and Organizational Life: Proceedings of the 8th A. K. Rice Institute Scientific Meeting*, edited by James Krantz, 91–96. Washington, D.C.: The A. K. Rice Institute.

Wichterich, Christa. 2000. *The Globalized Woman: Reports from a Future of Inequality.* London: Zed Books.

Wing, Leah, and Janet Rifkin. 2001. "Racial Identity Development and Mediation of Conflicts." In *New Perspectives on Racial Identity Development: A Theoretical and Practical Anthology*, edited by Charmaine L. Wijeyesinghe and Bailey W. Jackson III, 182–208. New York: NYU Press.

Yuval-Davis, Nira. 2006. "Intersectionality and Feminist Politics." *European Journal of Women's Studies* 13 (3): 193–209.

Zinn, Maxine B., and Bonnie T. Dill. 1996. "Theorizing Difference from Multiracial Feminism." *Feminist Studies* 22 (2): 321–331.

# 9

## The Enactment of Race and Other Social Identities during Everyday Transactions

WILLIAM E. CROSS, JR.

## Introduction

Within and across the discourses on social justice education, multicultural-ism, and ethnic studies (inclusive of Black Studies), content specificity and particularism define the primary points of departure. Native American Iden-tity, Women's and Feminist Identity, Gay and Lesbian Identity, and African American Identity, as cases in point, emphasize different content, unique predicaments, and distinctive life stressors. Textbooks used in counselor education typically include separate chapters on the identity dynamics, con-tent specificity, and family patterns for key social groups (Diller 2007). This is also true for texts used in social justice education (Adams, Bell, and Griffin 2007). Multiculturalism and social justice education make difference foun-dational in order to contest mainstream narratives that underplay, silence, and trivialize the concerns of multicultural groups in general and specific groups in particular (Banks 2004).

In the wake of the evolution of multiculturalism and social justice education, teachers, scholars, and laypeople alike now have a spectacular array of options from which to choose (films, handbooks, Internet sites, documentaries, history texts, novels, plays-dramas, poems, etc.), when they need to create specific narratives about specific groups. At the university level, there are even programs and departments dedicated to the study and analysis of select social groups (Women's Studies, Africana Studies, LGBT Studies, etc.).

Content-specific material tends by its very nature to be descriptive and somewhat atheoretical (Brekhus 2003). However, since about 2000, extensive progress has been made in linking case-specific content and issues with overarching theoretical questions and perspectives (Banks 2004). For example, in the study of what is called stereotype threat (Steele 2010), Claude Steele, his associates, and doctoral students have demonstrated that (otherwise competent) members from practically any social identity group can be made to *underperform* on important social-academic or athletic tasks, if before starting a task participants are reminded of a negative stereotype that society associates with their social group. Thinking about the negative stereotype seems to disrupt performance. The psychological dynamics of stereotype threat (reaction time, cognitions, affect and anxiety, etc.) are the same across all social identity groups, even though the content of the stimulus used to trigger the sense of threat *must be* specific to the social identity group under study. For example, the negative stereotype content used in a study with gay participants will be different from the negative stereotype content employed in a study involving African Americans, despite the fact that a generic explanatory model is applicable to all groups (Steele 2010).

In another example of a generic model explicating the lived experience of divergent groups, Jackson and Hardiman (1997) constructed a generic stage-model of identity development that incorporates dynamics commonplace to a number of social groups; working independently of Jackson and Hardiman, a similar Pan-Ethnic Identity Development Model was created by Atkinson, Morten, and Sue (1989). Jean Phinney's theorizing and research has resulted in an ethnic-identity model thought to be applicable to members of indigenous as well as immigrant populations (Phinney 1989). In an extremely important contribution, Sue and Capodilupo (2008); see also Sue, Capodilupo, Torino, Bucceri, Holder, Nadal, and Esquilin 2007) proffered a model of identity-related microaggressions that can be grafted to an analysis of the way stress operates in the lived experience of a broad range of social groups such as Gays and Lesbians, African Americans, Asian Americans, and so on.

As an extension of this line of theorizing, the current work seeks to explore a model of identity enactments to show that—despite obvious and important differences in identity content—divergent social groups are more alike than different in the way social identity is *enacted during critical everyday transactions*. An enactment is a performance or way of acting, and members of socially ascribed groups are taught to enact-perform identity in ways that match the demand characteristics of different situations (Cross, Smith, and Payne 2002; Fiske 1992; Upegui-Hernandez 2010; Verkuyten and deWolf 2002).

Oyserman and Destin (2010) make the point that "people use identities to prepare for action and to make sense of the world around them (and that) thinking (about identity) is for doing." Later in the same paragraph they continue by stating that "individuals are sensitive to the meaningful features of the environment and adjust thinking and doing to what is contextually relevant" (Oyserman and Destin 2010, 1015). Brekhus (2003) also stresses an "identity as doing" perspective, but adds another feature he calls *identity fluidity*:

> Recognizing the microtemporal and variability of identity requires that we see identity as mutable and fluid rather than static and permanent. Identity is enacted, accomplished, and managed in our daily interactions. Some theorists and researchers of identity have treated identity as something that is "essential" and fixed in the individual. They have treated identity as a "noun" and ... some individuals do experience their identity in that way. This treatment; however, ignores the way identity is accomplished in everyday interactions. Identity is not simply something one *has*, it is something one works on. Here I follow the tradition of researchers who have located identity as an interactional accomplishment rather than a fixed entity. (20–21)

In this essay I share much of Brekhus's emphasis on the doing, performance, and accomplishment aspects of identity but part company with his depiction of identity as ever changing and random. I take the position that the stable aspects of identity help a person be aware of and thus recognize and even *predict* which predicaments, situations, and contexts are identity-related (salient) and which are not. Furthermore, and unlike Brekhus, I believe what changes, from situation to situation, is not identity but the manner in which identity is expressed. From this perspective, a (stable) nonfragmented identity is linked to an *enactment repertoire,* such that the contingencies of a specific situation may trigger one enactment while the elements of another situation may trigger another enactment propensity (Cross, Smith, and Payne 2002). Most individuals remain reasonably coherent and stable from one situation to another, but the mode of identity expression will change from situation X to situation Z.

Proposed, here, is a conceptualization of identity management that is social (interactional), situated (context-ecologically sensitive), chameleonic (identity repertoire), intergenerational (each generation promotes awareness about predictable encounters), synergistic-diunital (stigma management and culture are often intertwined), holistic (identity integration), and identity focused (identity salience or importance):

1. Social, in that identity enactments generally involve communications and exchanges with other human beings who are members of one's group (intragroup) or external to it (intergroup);

2. Situated, in that the enactment of identity is context-sensitive. For example, threatening or oppressive situations will trigger an enactment meant to protect or shield while attendance at a cultural celebration will trigger a sense of belonging, pride and attachment to the group, etc.;

3. Chameleonic, in that an otherwise coherent identity reticulates a repertoire of enactments. This is nearly a restatement of point #2 in that multiple modes of expression are linked to the same identity. A coherent identity reticulates multiple modes of expression in weblike fashion;

4. Intergenerational, in that the previous generation has experienced most of the predicaments likely to be faced by the group's progeny and thus awareness and prediction are possible. Just as culture is passed down from one generation to another, so it is that awareness of predictable social identity-related situations can be inculcated as part of the socialization process. To say the obvious, awareness and consciousness of racism can be taught, as is true of awareness of sexism or awareness of antisemitism;

5. Synergistic-Diunital, in that the enactments simultaneously effectuate "stigma management" and cultural expression. For example, the lyrics of the "blues" and Black gospels may reference the pain of oppression but the performance of either genre by a person (solo or in a choir) may help release tension, affirm the culture, and make a person feel all the more attached to the group;

6. Holistic, in that a person can experience a sense of identity integration, even as the chameleonic aspects of self are performed, The model does not explicate multiple identities, rather it links *multiple modes of expression* to an integrated identity;

7. Identity focused, in that people who enact social identity accord the social identity in question importance, salience, or centrality, while those whose

identification with the group is at best only "nominal," are far less likely to enact identity in the ways to be described in this work.

With this general overview of enactment-transactional theory in hand, what follows is a presentation of two enactment models, one group specific and the other generic. In a collaborative effort involving myself, Dr. Kersha Smith from the University of New Rochelle, and Dr. Yasser Payne from the University of Delaware, we developed a "Black Enactment-Transactional Model" (Cross, Smith, and Payne 2002) based on the components discussed above. After explicating the BETM, I will argue that its features can be used to construct a generic model for application with a broad range of social groups.

### Black Enactment-Transaction Model BETM

The birth certificate of a newborn African American infant provides the first opportunity for the larger society to classify the child with the social ascription "Black." From the vantage point of the infant's parents, "Black" probably carries the double meaning of race (social status) and culture (new member of the Black community), and this is evident in the way most Black parents socialize their offspring in preparation for everyday life as a Black person (Bentley, Adams, and Stevenson 2009). The findings from empirical studies show that Black parents in particular, and the parents of a broad range of racial-ethnic groups in general, prepare their youth for positive and negative race- and culture-related experiences transacted outside as well as within one's racial-ethnic community (Bentley, Adams, and Stevenson 2009; Hughes 2003; Hughes, Rodriguez, Smith, Johnson, Stevenson, and Spicer 2006; Stevenson and Arrington 2009).

Boykin (1986) explains that Black youth must eventually develop identity competencies that allow them to transact discriminatory, oppressive, and racist encounters. He also points to the need for Black youth to be able to achieve success within the mainstream. Boykin's discussion of discrimination and the mainstream is readily translated into preparation for negative experiences with whites (i.e., discrimination and racism), at the same time as one develops identity flexibility in order to take advantage of and perform well within mainstream institutions, also heavily populated by whites. Boykin's third emphasis has to do with preparation for life within "the community"—that is, the Black community—and here again his analysis has a yin-yang quality in that aspects of one's community can be nurturing,

positive, and developmental, while other dimensions can be negative, patho-
logical, and intrusive.

A Black youth's quandary is the need to be adept, functional, and successful
in all three types of situations. Stated in the more formal language of social psychology, research and theorizing on racial-cultural socialization point to preparation for *intergroup* race-culture related encounters (i.e., positive and negative
experiences with people, places, and institutions populated and controlled by
persons who are not members of one's social identity group), as well as preparation for intragroup race and culture-related encounters (i.e., experiences with
people, places, and institutions nested within one's social identity community).

As discussed in a series of papers (Cross, Smith, and Payne 2002; Cross,
Parham, and Helms 1991; Strauss and Cross 2005), the enactment of racial-
cultural identity under conditions of racism is called *buffering;* the enactment of experiences within the mainstream is called *code-switching;* and the
transaction of cross-racial (out of race) friendships is called *bridging*. At the
intragroup level, the positive enactment of identity reflects the enactment
of *attachment-bonding,* within-group experiences that are negative trigger
the enactment of *within-group buffering,* encounters with same-race members who hold mainstream status can trigger *within-group code-switching,*
and positive relationships and intimacy between two Blacks from divergent
parts of the Diaspora (i.e., one from Harlem, the other from South Africa, or
one from Harlem and the other from Nigeria) may trigger the enactment of
*within-group bridging*. What follows is a description of these modalities.

### BUFFERING

Discriminatory, racist, and oppressive intergroup contexts trigger identity
enactments meant to provide psychological protection (buffering). Depending on the situation, protection may be achieved through confrontation-
contestation, avoidance, passivity, or passive-aggressive behavior. In the face
of a horrific offense that has the potential for generating hatred, Blacks will
sometimes buffer through religious and spiritual beliefs. This allows the person to avoid demonizing the culprit ("we are all God's children and it is not
for me to pass judgment or forgive her/his sin"), while signifying the sinful
behavior (racism). Most importantly, the internalization of hatred and the
concomitant psychological and physiological damage that can accompany it
are kept to a minimum. Buffering is performed at the level of the individual; however, Blacks have a long history of creating organizations designed
to carry out collective buffering, as in the NAACP, the Urban League, Black
Student Associations, the Black Panther Party, and others.

## CODE-SWITCHING

To satisfy and fulfill critical needs, wants, and desires such as employment, education, banking, shopping, and medical care, African Americans must exit the Black community and then enter, perform competently within, and ultimately exit mainstream institutions (Oyserman and Destin 2010). The protocol for how to enter, act, dress, speak, and perform within the mainstream institution are generally scripted by mainstream "norms" and Black identity must include the capacity to code switch. In point of fact, code-switching has less to do with the crossing of spatial-physical boundaries (although that is often part of the experience) than the enactment of a form of identity switching, perspective taking, and bicultural competence (Jones and Shorter-Gooden 2003).

### BRIDGING

In addition to identity protection (buffering) and identity shifting (code-switching), Blacks are often placed in situations that can lead to close friendships with persons who are not Black. Platonic or even intimate relationships with persons from another race or cultural group will not happen automatically or easily, because one must hold in check suspicion, lack of trust, and stereotypes about the "other," while letting curiosity, trust, and openness have the final say.

Although one's nominal association with the social category "Black" has its origins with the ascription and classification found on one's birth certificate, each Black person must become *existentially* Black. By way of comparison, one can be born Jewish in a genealogical sense, but each "nominal" Jew must evolve (or not) a Jewish identity. The same is true of Blacks; at birth one is accorded nominal membership into the Black community, whether one likes it or not. The intragroup aspect of the Black Enactment-Transactional Model attempts to capture the way Black identity is enacted with people, places, institutions, and things *within* the Black community. Explication of intragroup transactions requires discussion of the following modalities: Attachment-Bonding, Within-Group-Buffering, Within-Group-Code-Switching, and Within-Group-Bridging.

### ATTACHMENT-BONDING

The enactment of positive relationships and experiences within the Black community is called *attachment* or *bonding*. A sense of connection, affiliation, and affection can be expressed through one's dress, gait, worldview and values, religious sensibilities, partner choice, language style, aesthetics, musical tastes, personal names and nicknames, holidays, rituals, social network, and the like. In the hands of artists, it can be playing, listening to or creating jazz, hip-hop, gospels, as well as writing poetry, plays, novels, and historical texts. Examples of collective attachment are OBAC or the Organization of Black American Culture (Harris 2000), the Annual Soul Train Music Awards, and the Association of Black Psychologists.

### WITHIN-GROUP BUFFERING

The transaction of negative race-related experiences with another Black person is called within-group buffering or *WG-Buffering*. In order to classify as an exemplar of WG-Buffering, the conflict between two people must reflect racial-cultural conflict, as when a light-skinned Black person summarily dismisses the possibility of a friendship with another Black person because that person is too dark. Such intragroup divides are often driven by the operation of internalized racism in the mind-set of one or both parties. There are many forms of internalized racism, and Colorism-Physicality is but one (see Cross and Cross 2008). Some observers have theorized that slavery left permanent psychological scars and this so-called legacy of slavery exacerbates Black-on-Black relationships in the present, as evidenced by Black-on-Black crime and homicides as well as divorce and general conflict between Black males and females (Gump 2010; Hicks-Ray 2004; Leary 2005). Such a legacy could, theoretically, increase the frequency of WG-Buffering while undermining the enactment of attachment-bonding between Blacks.

### WITHIN-GROUP CODE-SWITCHING

Given advances in American race relations, it is possible for a Black person to enter a mainstream operation (i.e., bank, school, hospital, etc.) and be greeted by another Black person who is in charge; under such conditions the person may effectuate a code-switching relationship, as the person in charge is seen as a representative of the mainstream and not "just another brother or sister." Code-switching involving a within-group member is called *WG-Code-Switching*.

### WITHIN-GROUP BRIDGING

At first glance, intimate relationships between any two Blacks would seem to be covered by the attachment-bonding category, obviating any need for the *WG-Bridging* category. However, achieving intimacy and friendship between a Black person born and raised in the United States—whose heritage is slavery and Black life in the Deep South—and a Black person who is a recent immigrant from Africa, the Caribbean, or Central or South America may prove as challenging a relationship as that between two people from different races. *WG-Bridging* captures the enactment of friendship and intimacy across the intercultural divides that exist within the Black community. By way of summary, intragroup enactments of race and Black culture include: *Attachment-Bonding (inclusive of collective attachment), WG-Buffering, WG-Code-Switching, and WG-Bridging.*

Before moving on, a few words about the enactment of individuality are in order. In a fifteen-day daily-diary study conducted by Strauss and Cross (2005), a sample of Black college students reported carrying out the range of race- and culture-related enactments described above. However, in anticipation that the enactment of racial-cultural identity would not account for all of their interactions, the participants were allowed to narrate other forms of identity enactments, including the category "individuality" (meaning, interactions or activities unrelated to their being Black or, for that matter, unrelated to any other social identity that might apply to them). The inclusion of this additional transactional category proved critical because, at the end of the study, nearly three out of four enactments recorded by all students involved the enactment of individuality. The individuality category captures the enactment of personal identity. Because it helps sharpen the distinction between personal versus social identity, individuality will be included as one of our transactional categories even though (technically) it does not involve the transaction of social or collective identity.

## Multicultural Enactment-Transactional Model METM

During the creation (Cross, Smith, and Payne 2002) and empirical exploration (Strauss and Cross 2005) of the Black Enactment-Transactional Model, the author was in frequent (personal) correspondence with Dr. Maurianne Adams, a faculty member and former head of the doctoral concentration in Social Justice Education at the University of Massachusetts at Amherst. Early on Dr. Adams noted that when filtered of race and Black culture-specific content, the core features of the way Black identity is transacted in everyday life would probably be applicable to a transactional analysis of practically any social identity—Gay/Lesbian, Jewish, Native American, or otherwise. To explore this possibility, Adams, who taught a graduate course in the Social Justice Education concentration titled "Issues in Identity Development in Social Justice Education," assigned students the task of keeping a daily diary on whether or not the BETM modalities capture the way persons representing other social groups enact their social identity. Over the last ten years the course has attracted graduate students who are Jewish, Disabled, Muslim, Gay/Lesbian/Bisexual or Transgendered, African American, Mexican

American, White and White-Ethnic, as well as representatives from other social identity groups. The knowledge gained in reading the student diaries—in combination with class discussions—led Adams to conclude that the construction of a generic model would be feasible.

At the time of the production of the BETM, the author was a faculty member in the doctoral program in Social-Personality Psychology at the Graduate Center-CUNY, and in short order graduate students in the program incorporated aspects of the BETM in the scaffolding of their own theorizing and research about other social identity groups. For example, in her qualitative study of the phenomenon of passing among gays and lesbians, Rachel Verni (2009) shows how passing can be interpreted as a form of code-switching. Another doctoral student, Michelle Billies (2009), found the concept of buffering helped explain the protective strategies used by Transgendered persons, as uncovered in findings from a participatory action research project on violence against Transgendered (and LGBQ) persons that Billies helped coordinate (Billies, Johnson, Murungi, and Pugh 2009). Sabrica Barnett, also from the GC-CUNY and an emerging expert on biracial and multiracial identity development, conveyed to me that even in the case of persons holding intersectional identities, the enactment-transactional perspective held considerable explanatory promise. Consequently, the Multicultural Enactment-Transactional Model (METM) offered here is derived from pedagogical, observational, and experiential knowledge. My intent is a level of precision that will facilitate future empirical studies such as the one conducted on the BETM by Strauss and Cross (2005). The intergroup (i.e., Buffering, Code-Switching, Bridging), intragroup (Attachment-Bonding, WG-Buffering, WG-Code-Switching, WG-Bridging), plus individuality categories appear to have significant interpretative value when analyzing the everyday identity transactions carried out by a good many social groups, and as cases in point, the following groups are explored: Native American, LGBQ, and Physically Challenged.

The Enactment of Native American Identity in Everyday Life

The front of a popular T-shirt pictures a group of Native American men in circa nineteenth-century dress (stoic faced and cradling rifles) and beneath the picture the caption reads: "Defending against Terrorism since 1492." Across the centuries Native Americans have been subjected to wars of genocidal proportions, systemic deracination campaigns, as well as social-spatial isolation and this has made essential the honing of both individualized and collective buffering capacities. At the level of the individual, Native

American youth are taught how to detect, spot, and anticipate threat and discrimination during intergroup encounters with people, places, and things controlled by non-Native Peoples (LaFromboise and Dixon 1981; Lockhart 1981). The onslaught of life-threatening encounters ebbed at the turn of the twentieth century and from 1900 onward the sense of threat became increasingly existential, although violence against Native Americans for the period between 1900 and the early 1960s was far from uncommon. With the rise of the American Indian Movement (AIM) in the 1970s, many Native Americans replaced buffering with a prideful vigilance, but between 1980 and the present, vigilance has again been reconfigured as buffering (Trimble 2000b; Trimble 1988).

Collective buffering is critical to contemporary Native American life. For example, the rate of poverty on the reservations is the result of artificial conditions. Over the years, had the Federal Bureau of Indian Affairs (BIA) and the Federal Bureau of Land Management (BLM) transferred into Native hands fees due to them from mining interests, as payment for the extrication of raw materials and minerals from reservation property, the economic health of many reservation governments would be radically different from what currently is the case. To receive what is rightfully due, Native American groups have initiated class-action suits and worked with the Congress for passage of legislation guaranteeing restitution (H.R. 4783, the Claims and Resolution Act of 2010, signed into law by President Obama on December 8, 2010, known as Public Law 111-291). The Native American fight for social justice is a prime example of what we call *collective buffering* (Cobell 2010; Indian Trust: Cobell v. Salazar 2010; Little 2010).

Buffering among Native Americans does not always operate at an optimum level, and this can lead to instances of internalized oppression evidenced as depression and suicidal thoughts. One explanation, albeit a controversial one, points to the dynamics of intergenerational oppression. Native Americans have been the target of brutal and genocidal actions, resulting in intergenerational anxiety, repressed rage, feelings of hopelessness, and the malaise that results from the failure to bring to resolution unjust treatment. The *legacy of oppression* perspective theorizes that perturbations become embedded in the collective psyche of Native Peoples and this angst, transmitted from generation to generation, short-circuits one's capacity and competence for psychological buffering (Brave Heart and DeBruyn 1998; Evans-Campbell 2008; Morrissette 1994).

For Native Americans living off (and especially on) Native reservations, a sense of duality and biculturalism is critical to success in everyday life; consequently, code-switching is as foundational to Native American psychology as it is for any other group under scrutiny in this essay (Garrett 1996; Henze and Vanett 1993; Jaime and Rios 2007; LaFromboise 1999; LaFromboise and Medoff 2004; Moran and Bussey 2007; Moran, Fleming, Somervell, and Manson 1999). At the geopolitical level, maintenance of Native Treaties and agreements with the U.S. federal government requires that some representatives of Native American groups have a profound comprehension of the laws and customs of the U.S. government and society (Indian Trust: Cobell v. Salazar 2010). For Native Americans of less rarified status, needs and wants related to employment, financing, entertainment, and schooling may involve daily excursions off and on the reservation; consequently, the need for code-switching is ubiquitous (LaFromboise, Coleman, and Gerton 1993; LaFromboise and Rowe 1983; LaFromboise 1999; Phelen, Davidson, and Coa 1991).

Tourism and the production, exchange, and selling of Native American arts and crafts—on and off reservations—have made code-switching an essential dynamic of the Native American economy, both from a historical and contemporary perspective (Weaver and Brave Heart 1999). The phenomenal growth of the reservation-based Native-controlled gaming-resort industry has practically institutionalized Native American code-switching. For Native peoples living away from reservations and not *assimilated*, their narrations of everyday life are replete with instances of code-switching at school, the workplace, the neighborhood, and so on (Jaime and Rios 2007).

In light of the intense and frequent code-switching transactions, many Native Americans find themselves in a position that can lead to friendships that cross racial-cultural boundaries (bridging). The intermarriage rate for Native Americans has been high for many years and the ever-expanding census category biracial/bicultural includes a large number of Native Americans of mixed racial-cultural heritage. Consequently, as part of modern Native American life, the enactment of bridging is not uncommon.

Let us turn to the intragroup identity enactments commonplace to contemporary Native American life, starting with the enactment of belonging and collective attachment. Attachment and bonding are critical to the development of a positive Native American identity and this has been true across history (Bryant and LaFromboise 2005). Nevertheless, between 1870 and the late 1960s, Native peoples were the object of relentless "Americanization" schemes and educational programs carried out by agencies of the federal government. The resulting *deracination* was attacked and blunted by the American Indian Movement in the early 1970s. In addition to its economic and social-political agenda, AIM injected new energy into Native American institutions, revitalized traditional customs, and chipped away and in some cases dealt a crushing blow to stigmatization forces operative within Native

Americans themselves. The effects of the "new" pride movement from the 1960s continue to ripple through Native American communities. For example, a small but important percentage of Native Americans have experienced what I will awkwardly label "reverse" code-switching (Clifton 1989; Cornell 1988). Many Native American scholars, leaders, and members of the Native American bourgeoisie, who once seemed headed toward cultural deracination, have (in the aftermath of a cultural epiphany) been "reborn" (Eschbach 1993; Warrior 1999). Part of their rebirth has involved "going back" to recapture their lost ways and languages. In relearning the languages and traditional customs, these Native American spokespersons and scholars can now practice code-switching that is as much Native-Centric as Eurocentric (Cornell 1988; Shultz 1998). In an interesting twist, having Native American blood as part of one's heritage has even become a source of pride among White Americans, African Americans, and other social groups (Trimble 2000a).

Problems such as suicide, physical-sexual spousal abuse, family breakup, school dropouts, and alcoholism are found in many Native American quarters and at first glance call into question the operation of positive attachment dynamics for many Native Americans. However, these negative social indicators are better explained by poverty and the historical and planned underdevelopment of reservation economies. Being wretchedly poor can trump personal-cultural attachment. More commonly, Native Americans attain a solid sense of social attachment to their group and thus transact attachment-bonding on a daily basis. However, and this is especially true at the adult level, being proudly and securely attached to one's social group can be made extremely problematic, if not irrelevant, in the face of economic redundancy.

Native American communities can be sites of *internecine* conflicts that require their members to become competent at WG-Buffering. For example, children of mixed heritage may be accused of not looking "Indian" enough or being too "white" (Trimble 1988, 2000a). Likewise, being too white may be a slur hurled at the college educated. Many institutions located on the reservations are staffed by persons from the community and when community members seek out these leaders and managers to satisfy wants and needs (housing, banking, health care, schooling), they may discard their shared group identity and communicate through code-switching, as a sign of respect for the person and his/her position of authority. Finally, there are thick cultural and in some instances linguistic differences between tribes and friendship across tribal boundaries may trigger the same type of bridging transactions found in an emerging friendship between an African American and recent Black immigrant from Ghana or Nigeria, or between a Jew from Argentina and another from Poland.

The Enactment of LGBT Identity in Everyday Life

LGBQ individuals continue to be the target of extreme, compulsive, and generally hostile social scrutiny from multiple quarters of the larger society; consequently, buffering transactions are vigorously practiced both at the level of
the individual and the group. The need for vigilant buffering has ebbed—
especially in certain urban centers—even though the horrific murder of
Mathew Shepard in 1998 is a memory still vivid in the minds of many. Nevertheless, since Stonewall (the riots that started the Gay Liberation Movement
in 1969), a combination of social victories linked to the actions of progres-
sives both within and outside the gay community has expanded the social
space where gays can openly live their lives (Carter 2004). Consequently, the
buffering competence for many LGBQ persons is designed to protect against
daily homophobic microaggressions any one instance of which is hardly life-
threatening, but, if left unchecked, can have the cumulative effect of raising
one's blood pressure—a precursor to numerous types of physical illnesses. If
the level of crude and blatant violence against LGBQ seems on the decline in
some sections of the United States, Transgender individuals, especially those
who are poor and persons of color, continue to report being the target of violent acts (Billies, 2009; Billies, Johnson, Murungi, and Pugh 2009; NCAVP
2008).

LGBQ persons are well organized, and through what is called collective buffering, their efforts to expand the boundaries of their life space—to
include, for example, employment-related partner benefits and the right to
civil marriage—have met with relative success (Goodnough 2009). Earlier it
was noted that buffering can be expressed assertively, passively, or through
avoidance behavior and this is true of collective buffering as well. In 1987, in
the face of the raging AIDS crisis within the gay community, some leaders
concluded that the gay community's ongoing response was too passive and
ineffectual and from this self-critique emerged ACT-UP: the Aids Coalition
to Unleash Power, one of the most militant, aggressive, and effective direct
action advocacy groups in modern U.S. history. The need to sustain aggressive, well-funded, collective buffering entities will probably remain a vital
part of LGBQ psychology, even as vigilant buffering, at the individual level,
continues to diminish.

LGBQ communities have a long history of being competent at code-
switching (Brekhus 2003; Verni 2009; Valentine 1993; Woods 1993). LGBQ
persons enact code-switching on a daily basis as they service and are serviced by, attend school, work side by side, attend social functions, play sports,
and serve in the armed forces with heterosexuals. In most instances, sexual

identity is invisible; consequently, LGBQ persons can enact a form of code-switching not readily available to members of other stigmatized groups: *passing* (Verni 2009). In workplaces or educational institutions, the enactment of passing, masking, and disguise are transacted routinely (Woods 1993). In the past, passing reflected an absolute necessity against violence, extreme social isolation, and outright and immediate rejection (a dynamic still operative in most professional sports circles), yet it is performed perfunctorily in contemporary times. Within many urban contexts and college-university settings, where safe spaces have been declared, established, and protected, the strategies of coming-out and being "open" have practically replaced passing-masking forms of code-switching (Rhoads 1994; Savin-Williams 2001).

Close friendships between LGBQ persons and heterosexuals are fraught with far less perturbation than was true in the past (when, in the aftermath of an argument, the heterosexual friend could out the LGBQ person unceremoniously, resulting in a loss of employment and social status). Consequently, today it is relatively commonplace for LGBQ persons to include heterosexual men and women in their circle of close friends and bridging transactions are a daily occurrence.

In understanding attachment-bonding transactions experienced by LGBQ persons, it is necessary to be cognizant of the "double" socialization history that marks their personal identity and social identity development between infancy and early adulthood (Denizet-Lewis 2009; Omoto and Kurtzman 2006; Isay 2009; Leap 2007; Savin-Williams and Cohen 1996). For members of all *other* social groups subject to social stigmatization, the socialization received in preparation for transacting social identity in everyday life finds parents, guardians, and community organizations at the forefront of the process of helping to inculcate what must be learned, practiced, and enacted. This somewhat coordinated and linear model of socialization is very nonlinear, complicated, and subject to extreme disruption, contestation, and negativity in the case of the socialization of LGBQ individuals (Bernstein 2003; Griffin, Wirth, and Wirth 1997; D'Augelli 1996). Although the *ego and personality strengths* that result from their earlier socialization remain intact, LGBQ persons must turn away from guardians, church leaders, and community leaders and *toward* LGBQ peers and organizations to learn what is normative in the transaction of attachment-bonding with LGBQ partners and Queer groups and organizations (Ford 1996). The shift from one source of socialization to the other can be problematic (Hershberger and D'Augelli 1995; Savin-Williams 1998), but once the newly self-affirmed LGBQ person makes contact with other LGBQ persons, the expanded social space and collective strength of the LGBQ community offer the new member immense social capital to feed his or her psychosocial developmental needs (Halde-man 2007). They learn to *attach and bond* with their gayness in ways once thought unachievable. Given that the person's earlier socialization resulted in adequate character and *personality* development, the combination of one's personal identity (i.e., personality) and newly reshaped and liberated social identity can result in a formidable, positive, and stable self-concept (Savin-Williams 2001).

Like any social group, LGBQ persons experience ideological schisms as well as internalized homophobia that can result in conflicts between them. For example, in light of heterosexual liaisons, bisexuals may come under scrutiny from closed-minded gays and lesbians (Tomassilli 2007; Verni 2009), and some LGBQ persons may attack Transgendered persons as self-hating and inauthentic (Billies 2009). In her focus group study with LGBQ participants, Verni (2009) recorded the following:

> Catherine described her experiences attending college in Boston, where she felt everyone in the community had a shaved head and fit within spe-cific parameters of a "gay" appearance; this left her perpetually feeling that she was not lesbian enough. Many participants discussed ideas around specific manifestations of authentic gay identities as manifested in clothing and haircuts. Failure to meet these rigid criteria frequently left participants feeling that their level of commitment to the community and a GLBQ identity was questioned by GLBQ others (75).

For these reasons and more, developing the awareness and skills to trans-act WG-Buffering is as much a necessity for LGBQ individuals as it is for members of any stigmatized group (Billies 2009; Verni 2009).

LGBQ individuals are positioned throughout the worlds of government, fashion, mass media, industry, and so on; consequently, is it commonplace for a LGBQ person to transact code-switching with another LGBQ person. Being LGBQ does not level profound identity differences, as when a gay who is "out" befriends someone still in the closet. The transaction of WG-Bridg-ing will likely undergird any chance for friendship between the two.

## The Enactment of Disability Identity in Everyday Life

The author's only brother lost the use of both his legs at the age of twenty-nine and is now in his sixties. It bothers him to no end when people address him in an overly loud tone, as if loss of hearing accompanied loss of the use of his legs. He has become an expert at helping able-bodied persons get over the awkwardness they feel when first encountering his body-chair presence. As has been stressed in the previous exemplars, buffering is generally enacted in the face of discrimination and bias, but for many forms of Disability Identity, managing the startled looks, solicitous reactions, and awkward expressions of others requires a special buffering competence. Buffering can take on a sense of vigilance for those physically disabled, who, for want of steady employment and affordable housing, live on the street and are thus vulnerable to random violence; disabled persons who are Black, poor, and homeless are especially at risk. In the 1990s, collective buffering helped the disabled and their allies push through monumental disability legislation aimed at, among other things, the reconfiguration of the physical environment. The legislation resulted in easier access to public bus service, entrance and exit to stores and places of leisure and entertainment, access to government buildings, and access to places of employment. (July 26, 2010 marked the twentieth anniversary of passage of the Americans with Disabilities Act or "ADA".)

As is true with other socially stigmatized persons, the disabled are experts at code-switching; their ability to help people focus on their competencies rather than their limitations is legend (Banco 2010; Gill 1994). As might be expected, technology plays a critical role in code-switching among the physically challenged. In recent years, stimulated in no small measure by the need to service returning disabled veterans from the wars in Iraq and Afghanistan, advances in technology have resulted in a phenomenal array of ear implants, computerized limb and hand replacements and wheelchairs that are lightweight, durable, and flexible. These devices play a critical role in the way the disabled transact code-switching within mainstream contexts. Passing (as a form of code-switching) continues to be enacted by people with less visible disabilities such as dyslexia and other forms of learning disabilities, ADH, epilepsy, and mental illness (Epstein 1995).

For children born deaf and who receive a cochlear implant at an early age, it is not clear whether one should classify them as passing. Often such children do not learn sign language, setting the stage for a fascinating form of reverse code-switching. While not commonplace, some youth with cochlear implants will, when they reach late adolescence or early adulthood, experience an identity conversion that compels them to embrace a "Deaf Identity" (Gill 1997; Gill and Cross 2010). In the aftermath of their epiphany, they will master sign language, immerse themselves in deaf culture and history, and join with likeminded persons in advocacy activities. In 2006 the selection of a new president for Gallaudet University turned on the discourse of authenticity wherein deaf persons with less than a masterful competence of sign language were thought to be less qualified for the office of president (Schemo 2006).

For many advocates of Deaf Identity and Deaf Culture, signing trumps technology as the primary vehicle for transacting the mainstream. Advocates of Deaf Identity point out that when viewed from a global perspective, low-tech sign language is economical, efficacious, and revolutionary in the freedom it brings deaf persons from around the world (especially those who are poor and/or serviced by underdeveloped health care systems). Consequently, Deaf Identity advocates do not see themselves as being myopic and want (among other things) Gallaudet University to promote Deaf Culture on an international level, with sign language as the universal instrument for advocacy (Onken and Slaten 2000).

Bridging or the enactment of friendship and intimacy with the nondisabled is commonplace among the disabled. Such intimacies start with members of one's family and branch out to the different layers of one's social network.

Deaf Identity and attachment-bonding enactments can be very specific, as persons with similar forms of disability bond together. Bonding activities can take many forms and one of the most well-known is sport. With advances in technology, the level of competition in basketball as well as track and field has been phenomenal. Through federal, state, and municipal funding, all levels of higher education—from community colleges through universities—have well-organized and well-staffed advocacy and support centers that (among other things) facilitate communication and attachment-bonding activities between disabled persons.

WG-Buffering is enacted among the disabled at the intersection of disability, race, and social class (Fujiura and Drazen 2010). People of color (especially Blacks) who are poor and disabled perceive racism to be a more significant factor at all levels of disability services than is often perceived by service providers. This can lead to conflicts and the enactment of WG-Buffering between persons who otherwise are trying to advocate for each other. Conflicts can arise around Disability Identity, with one person claiming to hold a more authentic form of disability than another; advocates of Disability Culture can become impatient with the disabled who do not join advocacy groups and do not openly embrace a Disability Identity (Alston, Bell, and Feist-Price 1996).

## Summary

The Multicultural Enactment-Transactional Model (METM) is applicable to persons holding membership in social groups whose relationship with the larger society has been and (in most cases) continues to be marked by marginalization and stigmatization (Buffering), opportunities for success within the mainstream (Code-Switching), and intimate encounters across social boundaries (Bridging). In addition to explicating a range of intergroup enactments (Buffering, Code-Switching, and Bridging), the model also takes into consideration that each person is a *cultural being* whose everyday life is framed by a series of interactions with persons sharing the same social identity. These intragroup transactions can be affiliative and group-affirming (Attachment-Bonding), defensive and protective (WG-Buffering), power- and need-satisfaction oriented (WG-Code-Switching), or the focus of complex intercultural friendships and intimacies (WG-Bridging).

An enactment-transactional approach links social identity to all these enactments, rather than to one in particular, because social identity involves a *repertoire* of enactments. The way a person "reads" the situation determines how social identity will be expressed, because what changes from context to context is not the nature of the person's social identity (that remains coherent and intact) but the mode of expression that "fits" or matches the demand characteristics of the situation. The chameleonic nature of the enactments does not belie identity fragmentation but the ability to express identity differently in line with the contours of the situation.

A wonderful example of the application of an identity enactment perspective to an *intersectional experience* is the recent dissertation by Debora Upegui-Hernandez, titled "Because I'm neither Gringa nor Latina, because I am not doing one thing: Children of Columbian and Dominican immigrants negotiating identities within (trans)national social fields" (Upegui-Hernandez 2010). However, the social identities discussed in this work are boundary-thick and highly differentiated, thus the question of *Intersectionality* is delayed for another time. This critical limitation duly noted, the BEMT and especially the METM are positioned alongside Steele's concept of stereotype threat, Sue and Sue's microaggressions model, Brekhus's model of the microecology of identity, and Jackson and Hardiman's model on the psychology of oppression to illustrate that it is now possible to *bridge* the psychologies of specific cultural and stigmatized groups with generic models and conceptualizations that (in the words of Wayne Brekhus) reflect "analytic richness, conceptual clarity, and theoretical generalizability" (Brekhus 2003, 8).

REFERENCES

Adams, Maurianne, Lee Anne Bell, and Patricia Griffin. 2007. *Teaching for Diversity and Social Justice*, 2nd ed. New York: Routledge.

Alston, Reginald J., Tyronn J. Bell, and Sonja Feist-Price. 1996. "Racial Identity and African Americans with Disabilities: Theoretical and Practical Considerations." *Journal of Vocational Rehabilitation* 62: 11–15.

Atkinson, Donald R., George Morten, and Derald W. Sue. 1989. "A Minority Development Model." In *Counseling American Minorities,* edited by Donald Richard Atkinson, G. Morten, and Derald Sue, 35–52. Dubuque, Iowa: William C. Brown.

Banco, Erin. 2010, August 11. "Transitioning to College with a Learning Disability: Programs Help Students Make the Switch from High School Environment." *USA Today:* 3A.

Banks, James A. 2004. "Multicultural Education: Historical Development, Dimensions, and Practice." *In Handbook on Research in Multicultural Education,* 2nd ed., edited by James A. Banks and Cherry A. M. Banks, 3–29. San Francisco: Jossey-Bass.

Bentley, Keisha L., Valerie N. Adams, and Howard C. Stevenson. 2009. "Racial Socialization: Roots, Processes, and Outcomes." In *Handbook of African American Psychology,* edited by Helen Neville, B. Tynes, and Shaun Utsey, 255–281. Thousand Oaks, Calif.: Sage.

Bernstein, Robert A. 2003. *Straight Parents, Gay Children: Keeping Families Together.* New York: Thunder Mouth's Press.

Billies, Michelle. 2009. "Gender and Other Matters: Low Income LGBTGNC People Surviving Daily Violence and Discrimination." Unpublished paper, Social-Personality Psychology, Graduate Center of the City University of New York.

Billies, Michelle, Juliet Johnson, Kagendo Murungi, and Rachel Pugh. 2008. "Naming Our Reality: Low-Income LGBT People Documenting Violence, Discrimination, and Assertions of Justice." *Feminism and Psychology* 19 (3): 375–380.

Boykin, A. Wade. 1986. "The Triple Quandary and the Schooling of African American Children." In *The Schooling of Minority Children: New Perspectives,* edited by Uric Neiser, 57–92. Hillandale, N.J.: Lawrence Erlbaum.

Brave Heart, Maria Yellow Horse, and Lemyra M. DeBruyn. 1998. "The American Indian Holocaust: Healing Historical Unresolved Grief." *American Indian and Alaska Native Mental Health Research* 8: 56–78.

Brekhus, Wayne. 2003. *Peacocks, Chameleons, Centaurs: Gay Suburbia and the Grammar of Social Identity.* Chicago: University of Chicago Press.

Bryant Jr., Alfred, and Teresa D. LaFromboise. 2005. "The Racial Identity and Cultural Orientation of Lumbee American Indian High School Students." *Cultural Diversity and Ethnic Minority Psychology* 11 (1): 82–89.

Carter, David. 2004. *Stonewall: The Riots That Sparked the Gay Revolution.* Binghamton, N.Y.: St Martin's Press.

Clifton, James. A. 1989. *Being and Becoming Indian: Biographical Studies of Native American Frontiers.* Chicago: Dorsey.

Cobell, Elouise. 2010. "The Facts v. the Brochure: The Interior Department Attempts to Cover Up Incompetence and Fraud in Its Handling of Individual Indian Money Accounts in a Glossy New 'Progress Report.'" Online brochure produced by E. Cobell and Indian Trust. http://www.indiantrust.com/_pdfs/IndianTrustBrochure.pdf. Accessed November 12, 2010.

Cornell, Stephen. 1988. *Return of the Native.* New York: Oxford University Press.

Cross, William E., Jr., and Tuere B. Cross. 2008. "Racial-Ethnic-Cultural Identity Development [REC-ID]: Theory, Research and Models." In *Handbook of Race, Racism, and the Developing Child,* edited by Stephen M. Quintana and C. McKown, 154–181. Hoboken, N.J.: J. Wiley and Sons.

Cross, William E., Jr., Thomas Parham, and Janet Helms. 1991. "The Stages of Black Identity Development: Nigrescence Models." In *Black Psychology*, 3rd ed., edited by Reginald L. Jones, 319–338. Berkeley, Calif.: Cobbs and Henry.

Cross, William. E., Jr., Lakersha Smith, and Yasser Payne. 2002. "Black Identity: A Repertoire of Daily Enactments." In *Counseling across Cultures*, 5th ed., edited by Paul B. Pedersen, Juris G. Draguns, Walter J. Lonner, and Joseph E. Trimble, 93–107. Thousand Oaks, Calif.: Sage.

D'Augelli, Anthony R. 1996. "Enhancing the Development of Lesbian, Gay, and Bisexual Youths." In *Prevention of Heterosexism and Homophobia*, edited by Ester D. Rothblum and Lynne Bond, 124–150. Newbury Park, Calif.: Sage.

Denizet-Lewis, Benoit. 2009, September 27. "Coming Out in Middle School: How 13-Year-Old Kids Are Dealing with Their Sexual Identity and How Others Are Dealing with Them." *New York Times Magazine* 36–41, 52.

Diller, Jerry D. 2007. *Cultural Diversity: A Primer for the Human Services*. Belmont, Calif.: Thomas Brooks/Cole.

Epstein, Susie. 1995. "Am I Crip Enough Yet? Life with a Hidden Disability——Oppressed, Oppressing and Without Support or Community." *Mainstream* 19: 15–19.

Eschbach, Karl. 1993. "Changing Identification among American Indians and Alaska Natives." *Demography* 30 (4): 635–652.

Evans-Campbell, Teresa. 2008. "Historical Trauma and American Indian/Native Alaska Communities: A Multilevel Framework for Exploring Impacts on Individuals, Families, and Communities." *Journal of Interpersonal Violence* 23 (2): 316–338.

Fiske, Susan T. 1992. "Thinking Is for Doing: Portraits of Social Cognition from Daguerreotype to Laserphoto." *Journal of Personality and Social Psychology* 63 (6): 877–889.

Ford, Michael T. 1996. *The World Out There: Becoming Part of the Lesbian and Gay Community*. New York: New Press, 1996.

Fujiura, Glenn T., and Carlos Drazen. 2010. "Ways of Seeing." In *Race and Disability Research*, edited by Fabricio Balcazar, Yolanda Suarez-Balcazar, Tina Taylor-Ritzler, and Christopher B. Keys, 15–32. Boston: Jones and Bartlett.

Garrett, Michael T. 1996. "Two People: An American Indian Narrative of Bicultural Identity." *Journal of American Indian Education* 36: 1–21.

Gill, Carol J. 1994. "A Bicultural Framework for Understanding Disability." *Family Psychologist* 10: 13–16.

——. 1997. "Four Types of Identity Integration in Disability Identity Development." *Journal of Vocational Rehabilitation* 9 (1): 39–46.

Gill, Carol. J., and William E. Cross, Jr. 2010. "Disability Identity Development and Racial-Cultural Identity Development: Points of Convergence, Divergence, and Interplay." In *Race, Culture, and Disability*, edited by Fabricio Balcazar, Yolanda Suarez-Balcazar, Tina Taylor-Ritzler, and Christopher B. Keys, 33–52. Boston: Jones and Bartlett.

Goodnough, Abby. 2009, November 5. "Gay Rights Rebuke May Bring Change in Tactics." *New York Times*, A1, A24.

Griffin, Carolyn W., Marian J. Wirth, and Arthur G. Wirth. 1997. *Beyond Acceptance: Parents of Lesbians & Gays Talk about Their Experiences*. New York: St. Martin's Press.

Gump, Janice P. 2010. "Reality Matters: The Shadow of Trauma on African American Subjectivity." *Psychoanalytic Psychology* 27 (1): 42–54.

Haldeman, Douglas C. 2007. "The Village People: Identity and Development in the Gay Male Community." In *Handbook of Counseling and Psychotherapy with Lesbian, Gay,*

*Bisexual, and Transgender Clients,* 2nd ed., edited by Kathleen J. Bieschke, Ruperto M. Perez, and Kurt A. DeBord, 71–90. Washington, D.C.: American Psychological Association.

Harris, Michael D. 2000. "Urban Totems." In *Walls of Heritage of Pride: African American Murals,* edited by James Prigoff and Robin J. Dunitz, 24–43. San Francisco: Pomegranate Communications.

Henze, Rosemary, and Lauren Vanett. 1993. "To Walk in Two Worlds—or More? Changing a Common Metaphor of Native Education." *Anthropology and Educational Quarterly* 24: 116–143.

Hershberger, Scott L., and Anthony R. D'Augelli. 1995. "The Impact of Victimization on the Mental Health and Suicidality of Lesbian, Gay, and Bisexual Youth." *Developmental Psychology* 31: 65–74.

Hicks-Ray, Denyse. 2004. *The Pain Didn't Start Here: Trauma and Violence in the African American Community.* Atlanta: TSA.

Hughes, Diane. 2003. "Correlates of African American and Latino Parents' Messages of Children about Ethnicity and Race: A Comparative Study of Racial Socialization." *American Journal of Community Psychology* 31 (1/2): 15–33.

Hughes, Diane, James Rodriguez, Emilie P. Smith, Deborah J. Johnson, Howard C. Stevenson, and Paul Spicer. 2006. "Parents' Racial/Ethnic Socialization Practices: A Review of Research and Agenda for Future Study." *Developmental Psychology* 42 (5): 747–770.

Indian Trust: *Cobell v. Salazar.* 2010. Online website provides primary references, court briefs, and judicial summaries as well as decisions handed down related to *Cobell v. Salazar.* http://www.indiantrust.com/ . Accessed October 18, 2010.

Isay, Richard A. 2009. *Being Homosexual: Gay Men and Their Development.* New York: Vintage Books.

Jackson, Bailey, and Rita Hardiman. 1997. "Conceptual Foundations for Social Justice Courses." In *Teaching for Diversity and Social Justice: A Source Book,* edited by Maurianne Adams, Lee A. Bell, and Patricia Griffin, 16–29. New York: Routledge.

Jaime, Angela, and Francisco Rios. 2007. "Negotiation and Resistance amid the Overwhelming Presence of Whiteness: A Native American Faculty and Student Perspective." *Taboo* (Winter/Fall): 37–54.

Jones, Charisse, and Kumea Shorter-Gooden. 2003. *Shifting: The Double Lives of Black Women in America.* New York: HarperCollins.

LaFromboise, Teresa D. 1999. "The Living in Two Worlds Survey." Unpublished test instrument. Stanford, Calif.: Stanford University.

LaFromboise, Teresa, Hardin Coleman, and Jennifer Gerton. 1993. "Psychological Impact of Biculturalism: Evidence and Theory." *Psychological Bulletin* 114: 395–412.

LaFromboise, Teresa, and David Dixon. 1981. "American Indian Perceptions of Trustworthiness in a Counseling Interview." *Journal of Counseling Psychology* 28: 135–139.

LaFromboise, Teresa, and Lisa Medoff. 2004. "Sacred Spaces: The Role of Context in American Indian Youth Development." In *Community Planning to Foster Resilience in Children,* edited by Caroline Clauss-Ehlers and Mark Weist, 45–63. New York: Klumer Academic.

LaFromboise, Teresa, and Wayne Rowe. 1983. "Skills Training for Bicultural Competence: Rationale and Application." *Journal of Counseling Psychology* 30: 589–595.

Leap, William. 2007. "Language, Socialization, and Silence in Gay Adolescence." In *Sexualities and Communication in Everyday Life,* edited by Karen E. Lovas and Mercilee M. Jenkins, 95–106. Thousand Oaks, Calif.: Sage.

Leary, Joy D. 2005. *Post Traumatic Slave Disorder: America's Legacy of Enduring Injury and Healing.* Portland, Oreg.: Uptone Publishing.

Little, Andy. 2010. "Case of Disappearing Assets." http://revandylittle.com/2009/07/05/the-case-of-the-disappearing-assets/. Accessed October 19, 2010.

Lockhart, Barbetta. 1981. "Historic Distrust and the Counseling of American Indians and Alaska Natives." *White Cloud Journal* 2 (3): 31–43.

Moran, James R., and Marian Bussey. 2007. "Results of an Alcohol Prevention Program with American Indian Youth." *Child and Adolescent Social Work Journal* 24 (1): 1–21.

Moran, James R., Candice Fleming, Philip Somervell, and Spero M. Manson. 1999. "Measuring Bicultural Ethnic Identity among American Indian Adolescents: A Factor Analytic Study." *Journal of Adolescent Research* 14: 405–426.

Morrissette, Patrick. 1994. "The Holocaust of First Nation People: Residual Effects on Parenting and Treatment Implications." *Contemporary Family Therapy* 16: 381–392.

NCAVP. 2008. "Anti-Lesbian, Gay, Bisexual, and Transgender Violence in 2007: A Report of the National Coalition of Anti-Violence Programs." New York: National Coalition of Anti-Violence Programs. www.ncavp.org. Accessed September 10, 2010.

Omoto, Allen M., and Howard S. Kurtzman. 2006. *Sexual Orientation and Mental Health: Examining Identity and Development in Lesbian, Gay, and Bisexual People.* Washington, D.C.: APA Books.

Onken, Steven J., and Ellen Slaten. 2000. "Disability Identity Formation and Affirmation: The Experiences of Persons with Severe Mental Illness." *Social Practice* 2 (2): 99–111.

Oyserman, Daphna, and Mesmin Destin. 2010. "Identity-Based Motivation: Implications for Intervention." *Counseling Psychologist* 38 (7): 1001–1043.

Phelen, Patricia, Ann L. Davidson, and Hanh T. Coa. 1991. "Students' Multiple Worlds: Negotiating the Boundaries of Family, Peer, and School Cultures." *Anthropology and Education Quarterly* 22: 224–250.

Phinney, Jean S. 1989. "Stages of Ethnic Identity in Minority Group Adolescents." *Journal of Early Adolescence* 9: 34–49.

Rhoads, Robert. 1994. *Coming Out in College: The Struggle for a Queer Identity.* Westport, Conn.: Bergin & Garvey.

Savin-Williams, Ritch C. 1998. ". . . And Then I Became Gay." New York: Routledge.

———. 2001. *Mom, Dad, I'm Gay: How Families Negotiate Coming Out.* Washington, D.C.: American Psychological Association.

Savin-Williams, Ritch C., and Kenneth M. Cohen. 1996. *The Lives of Lesbians, Gays, and Bisexuals: Children to Adults.* Fort Worth, Tex.: Harcourt Brace College Publishing.

Schemo, Diana J. 2006, May 13. "Protests Shut Down University for Deaf for a 2nd Day." *New York Times.*

Shultz, Amy J. 1998. "Navajo Women and the Politics of Identity." *Social Problems* 45 (3): 336–355.

Steele, Claude. 2010. *Whistling Vivaldi: And Other Clues on How Stereotypes Affect Us.* New York: W. W. Norton.

Stevenson, Howard C., and Edith G. Arrington. 2009. "Racial/Ethnic Socialization Mediates Perceived Racism and Identity Experiences of African American Students." *Cultural Diversity and Ethnic Mental Health* 15 (2): 112–124.

Strauss, Linda, and William E. Cross, Jr. 2005. "Transacting Black Identity: A Two-Week Daily-Diary Study." In *Navigating the Future: Social Identity, Coping, and Life Tasks,* edited by Geraldine Downey, Jacquelynne S. Eccles, and Celina Chatman, 67–95. New York: Russell Sage Foundation.

Sue, Derald Wing and Christina M. Capodilupo, 2008. "Racial, Gender, and Sexual Orientation Microaggressions: Implications for Counseling and Therapy." In *Counseling the Culturally Diverse (5th ed)*, edited by Derald Wing Sue and David Sue, 105-130. Hoboken, NJ.: John Wiley & Sons.

Sue, Derald Wing, Christina M. Capodilupo, Gina C. Torino, Jennifer M. Bucceri, Aisha M. B. Holder, Kevin L. Nadal, and Marta Esquilin. 2007. "Racial Microaggressions in Everyday Life: Implications for Clinical Practice." *American Psychologist* 62 (4): 271–286.

Tomassilli, Julia. 2007. "Attitudes towards Bisexual Women and Men: Predictors in Lesbian and Gay Populations." *APA Division 44 Newsletter* 23(2):11–12.

Trimble, Joseph E. 1988. "Stereotypic Images, American Indians and Prejudice." In *Toward the Elimination of Racism: Profiles in Controversy*, edited by Phylis Katz and Dalmas A. Taylor, 181–202. New York: Pergamon.

———. 2000a. "Social Psychological Perspectives on Changing Self-Identification among American Indians and Alaskan Natives." In *Handbook of Cross-Cultural and Multicultural Personality Assessment,* edited by Richard H. Dada, 197–222. Mahwah, N.J.: Lawrence Erlbaum Associates.

———. 2000b. "American Indian Psychology." In *Encyclopedia of Psychology,* vol. 1A, edited by Alan E. Kazdin, 139–144. Washington, D.C.: American Psychological Association.

Upegui-Hernandez, Deborah. 2010. "Because I'm Neither Gringa Nor Latina, Because I Am Not Doing One Thing: Children of Columbian and Dominican Immigrants Negotiating Identities Within (Trans)National Social Fields." Ph.D. dissertation, Social-Personality Psychology, Graduate Center of the City University of New York.

Valentine, Gill. 1993. "(Hetero)sexing Space: Lesbian Perceptions and Experiences of Everyday Spaces." *Society and Space* 11(4): 395–413.

Verkuyten, Maykel, and Angela deWolf. 2002. "Being, Feeling and Doing: Discourses and Ethnic Self-Definitions among Minority Group Members." *Culture and Psychology* 8 (4): 371–399.

Verni, Rachel. 2009. "Queering Passing: An Exploration of Passing among GLBQ Individuals." *Intersections: Women's and Gender Studies in Review across Disciplines* 7: 67–81.

Warrior, Robert. 1999. "Native American Scholar: Toward a New Intellectual Agenda." *Wicazo Sa Review* 14 (2): 46–54.

Weaver, Hillary N., and Maria Yellow Horse Brave Heart. 1999. "Examining Two Facets of American Indian Identity: Exposure to Other Cultures and the Influence of Historical Trauma." *Journal of Human Behavior in the Social Environment* 2 (1–2): 19–33.

Woods, James. D. 1993. *The Corporate Closet: The Professional Lives of Gay Men in America.* New York: Free Press.

10

Pedagogical Approaches to Teaching about Racial
Identity from an Intersectional Perspective

DIANE J. GOODMAN AND BAILEY W. JACKSON III

Historically, few racial identity models have included or allowed for the
effect that other categories of difference (e.g., ethnicity, sex, gender, class,
sexuality, age, ability, religion, and nationality) have on an individual's racial
identity. Yet, how people develop and experience their racial identity is interconnected with the other aspects of their identity. It has become increasingly clear that racial identity cannot be understood apart from other social
identities. As evidenced in other chapters in this volume (see Gallegos and
Ferdman, Holvino, and Wijeyesinghe), racial identity theorists are updating
or creating conceptual models that capture this complex interrelationship
between race and other social identities and incorporate aspects of what is
generally termed Intersectionality.

Not only are racial identity theorists reconsidering their models in light
of a more intersectional perspective, but so are educators. Those who teach
about issues related to racial identity are also called to consider how race
interacts with all other social identities. This undertaking raises questions
about how to move from theoretical to applied Intersectionality in these

educational efforts. How is the *teaching* about racial identity informed and changed by intersectional theory? How does the student's level of awareness affect how and what we teach?

In this chapter we explore some of the issues and challenges that arise when teaching racial identity through the prism of Intersectionality. Many educators have long been teaching about multiple axes of identity and social inequality (most commonly race, class, and gender). They are now doing so in increasingly intersectional ways. However, there is little written about how to actually effectively *teach* about social identities and forms of oppression intersectionally, especially with learners at different points in the process.[1] We suggest some pedagogical approaches that may be more appropriate for learners with different degrees of racial consciousness and readiness to handle cognitive complexity. Exploring issues of social identity and structural inequality in developmentally appropriate ways requires rethinking our approaches, in theory and in practice. While both authors have decades of experience teaching about diversity and social justice in general, and race, racism, and racial identity in particular, we freely acknowledge that this is new terrain. Conceptualizing and then effectively teaching about racial identity using an intersectional lens is relatively uncharted territory. We therefore offer what we hope are helpful ways to think about teaching about racial identity, given the intersectional nature of our identities and lives and the varying needs of our students. Our focus is specifically on racial identity. Educators can consider if or how these approaches are applicable to teaching about other social identities or issues of social diversity and oppression more broadly.

## Pedagogical Underpinnings and Assumptions

First, let us be clear what we mean by Intersectionality. We have often heard people confuse *multiple* with *intersectional* when speaking about social groups and oppression. Intersectional theory maintains that we have many social identities which simultaneously interact and affect our experiences of power and privilege.[2] Our multiple social identities are not simply parallel or additive; it is not that each identity affects us but is relatively independent of the others. Intersectionality requires that we consider how individual dimensions of difference overlap and interrelate. As Dill and Zambrana explain, "there is no point at which race is not simultaneously classed and gendered or gender is not raced and classed" (2009, 280). Identities mutually shape or constitute each other. While some identities may be more salient at different times, all of them are part of who we are and how we experience the world.

Moreover, since social identities are shaped by the social, political, cultural, geographical, and historical context, they shift as contexts change.

Ultimately in the course of teaching about racial identity we may want students to be aware of how all of one's social identities interact to shape and affect racial identity and life experiences (and vice versa). However, in the development of critical consciousness, Paulo Freire (1994) reminds us that "You don't get *there* by starting *there,* you get *there* from starting from some *here*" (1994, 58). Therefore, our pedagogy for teaching about racial identity is grounded in the belief that we need to meet students where they are in terms of consciousness about race and other categories of difference and help them develop greater breadth, depth, and complexity of understanding. So, how do we teach racial identity from an intersectional perspective when students are starting from very different "heres"? What about students who have little consciousness of their racial identity? What about the White student who says what we have often heard, "I never really thought about being White," or the Black student who says, "Race doesn't really matter anymore," or the Latino student who says, "But in my home country, I'm considered White."

Understanding racial identity entails answering the question: "What does it mean to be a member of a particular racial group?" This question invites exploration of one's own racial identity as well as the identity of others. Therefore, education about racial identity can promote both self-awareness as well as an appreciation of other people's realities. Educators may be dealing with just one or both of these aspects at any given point.

There are also many factors which contribute to the development and experience of one's racial identity. Some aspects are more related to race, such as one's physical appearance and the culture and history of one's racial group(s). Other aspects are more connected to racism, such as being a member of a racial group within a system of racial inequality. While racial identity is not limited to the influence of race and racism, these two facets are central components that have a major role in one's racial identity. They impact how one views the world and is seen and treated by others. Therefore, as we discuss teaching about racial identity, we highlight the examination of race and racism and one's sense of self and life experiences. In keeping with the core value of social justice in an intersectional analysis, other identities in conjunction with race will also be examined within a context of structural inequality. Even though each individual social identity influences all the others, in this chapter we give greater attention to the effect of other social identities on race and the impact that race has on an individual's collective social identity.

A one-size-fits-all pedagogical approach may not make sense when students are coming in with very different understandings of race, racism, and racial identity. How can we expect students to grasp the complexity of how multiple identities simultaneously overlap and interrelate when they have a limited understanding of racial identity or are focused on only one dimension of identity and social oppression? While some students are more ready for multilayered analysis, many educators teach students who have less theoretical and experiential background in these topics. We have seen students, White students in particular, being unable to effectively integrate two dimensions of identity when they were still challenged to understand one. This occurs both when considering their own identities as well as when considering the identities and experiences of others. For example, while studying equity issues in education, students began to understand how race *or* sex could affect their own or others' experiences in school. However, it was difficult for many to conceive of how race *and* gender *together* shaped their realities. How does being a White female or Black male differ from being a White male or Black female?

We are therefore suggesting that an incremental framework for using an intersectional approach to teaching about racial identity may be useful. We explore how to build toward an intersectional understanding of racial identity, moving from a single focus on race toward an increasingly multidimensional integration of other social identities. In our teaching, we attempt to lay a foundation that is then continuously built upon. This developmental framework includes four pedagogical approaches:

1. A race-centered, single-identity focus,
2. A race-centered, limited intersectional focus,
3. A race-centered, intersectional focus, and
4. A full intersectional focus.

These four pedagogical approaches to teaching racial identity development increase in their integration of other social identities and increase in their incorporation of an intersectional paradigm.

Before describing each of these approaches, we want to elaborate on the reasons we believe that *as a pedagogy* having a single focus on race and racial identity can be useful and appropriate, even while maintaining that an intersectional lens more fully captures people's realities. Dill and Zambrana (2009) name one of the tensions in trying to value both an intersectional perspective and the distinctiveness of different social identities: "How do we benefit from comparisons and interrelationships without negating or undermining the complex and particular character of each group, system of oppression, or culture?" (2009, 280). This question is particularly relevant as we explore pedagogies with different students. Furthermore, as Luft (2009) recognizes, "the merit of Intersectionality as an analytic frame does not necessarily translate into the efficacy of operationalizing it as a methodology in all settings" (2009,103). For broad, group-based, and macro-level interventions—social justice research, advocacy, and policy—a more multidimensional analysis is needed (African American Policy Forum 2008). However, for educational consciousness-raising or in the early stages of a "micro-level intervention" (Luft 2009, 102), a single-issue focus may be an appropriate place *to start* for several reasons. First, as noted above, many students new to these topics have little understanding of racial issues or racial identity. It is therefore unrealistic to expect them to appreciate how racial identity interacts with other categories of difference. A stronger grounding in race, in its various manifestations, creates a foundation for students to appreciate and retain the significance of race and racism when adding other identities to the discussion and analysis. This is often true for White students, but even for Multiracial students or students of color who may not have had the opportunity to meaningfully analyze the myriad effects of societal racism, the history of race as a social construct, the meaning of race in different contexts and for different racial groups, or reflect on their own racial identity development process. A singular focus on race enables students to explore the similarities and differences between and among racial groups. It also allows them to acknowledge the distinctiveness of race and racism relative to other forms of social identities and social inequalities.

Second, it is our experience that White students have a strong tendency to move the focus off of race in class discussions. They frequently prefer to discuss other identities, especially ones in which they are part of the subordinated group. For example, White women may focus on their oppression as a female, or White gay men their experience with homophobia. Similarly, Luft (2009), despite being an intersectional theorist, has advocated "strategic singularity" in antiracism education (2009,101). She maintains that this approach is warranted given that White people tend to avoid discussing race and racism and that the prevailing racial logic is *color blindness* which denies the significance of race and the existence of racism.[3]

Even within a race-centered approach, we can still set a context which recognizes other social identities and forms of oppression, and the ways they interact and intersect. Educators can acknowledge the fact that students have many social identities that simultaneously intersect with race, and that these other identities may have varying degrees of salience and social power. A more race-centered approach is not race exclusive. We can affirm the relevance of other identities and their overlap with race while still choosing to focus on racial identity. For example, as an introductory activity, even in a class with a predominantly single-identity focus, students can be asked to think about their identities within numerous social categories (e.g., race, ethnicity, sex, gender, sexuality, class, ability, age, national origin, religion). They can consider which groups are most central to who they are and how these identities affect their experiences, opportunities, sense of self, and worldview. Reflections and discussions with others about their responses highlight not only that we all have multiple social identities but that the salience, impact, and ways these identities interact vary among individuals. This conversation can prompt further exploration about why this is the case. Throughout a class, while emphasizing race, we can note examples of how other identities and types of social inequality interact.

Even though the different pedagogical approaches suggest a progression, they are not intended to reflect a rigid sequence or the notion that one is better than another. Rather, they each have value when applied in the right situation. Instructors may shift approaches within the same class as students gain awareness or as other issues/identities are introduced. Our pedagogical framework offers options for educators to consider as they assess what would be most effective for meeting the needs of their students. We are also not suggesting that this is the only or the best way to teach about racial identity with an intersectional lens. As each pedagogical approach is described more fully, we consider the criteria (when), the rationale (why), the learning objectives (what), the challenges and cautions, and the activities (how) for implementing it. The activities listed within each approach include strategies that focus on understanding the racial identity of oneself as well as others.

## Pedagogical Approaches
### Race-Centered, Single-Identity Approach

A race-centered single-identity approach puts the social category of race at the heart of inquiry. The purpose of this approach is to help students gain a basic understanding of racial identity within the larger context of race and racism. This approach increases students' appreciation of the significance of racial identity and how it is influenced by many variables. Students explore how race is socially constructed and the differences between how one may self-identify and how one may be viewed by others and the broader society. They become more conscious of the role race plays in one's sense of self and social reality. The central question in this approach is: What does it mean to be a member of a particular racial group?

## CRITERIA FOR USE

This approach may be most appropriate for people with a limited understanding of race, racism, and racial identity. They may be early in the process of their own racial identity development, having given little thought to the meaning of racial identity for themselves or others. Students may have a limited awareness of the significance of race in affecting one's sense of self, worldview, experiences, and opportunities. They may need a better understanding of institutional and structural racism and how historical circumstances have shaped today's racial realities. Even if students have encountered racism, they may lack the conceptual frameworks to articulate or analyze their experiences or the experiences of others.

Students for whom this approach is useful may hold some common misconceptions which indicate that further examination of race and racism is warranted. These beliefs may include: (1) color-blindness—claiming that they don't notice race and that race should not and does not matter; (2) meritocracy—that there is basically a level playing field and that if you're smart and work hard you will succeed, regardless of race; (3) reverse racism—that White people can be oppressed by racism just like people of color; and (4) that racism consists of isolated incidents of individual prejudice and discrimination. These are some of the perceptions that suggest that a learner would benefit from further exploration of racial issues before adding other identities and forms of social inequality.

## RATIONALE

In order to develop an understanding of racial identity, students need to reflect on the meaning of being part of a racial group. They need a basic knowledge of the dynamics and implications of race and racism before they can understand how racial identity intersects with other social identities. Without this foundation, they will not be able to accurately grasp how race functions in conjunction with other categories of difference and may not be able to hold race salient while considering other social identities.

## LEARNING OBJECTIVES

The learning objectives in a race-centered single-identity pedagogy may be broad to provide students with an adequate basis for further study. This approach encompasses discussions of racial identity, as well as topics related to other aspects of race and racism. Learning objectives that would be appropriate for a race-centered single-identity pedagogy might include having students explore, in regards to racial identity, how:

- racial identity is shaped, and how it shifts and evolves over time and context.
- individuals define their racial identity and view the salience of their race, and how this may differ from the way they are seen by others.
- race affects one's attitudes, behaviors, values, and worldview.
- racial identity affects an individual's understanding of racism and approaches to social justice.

in regards to race and racism, how:

- racism is manifested on individual, institutional, societal, and cultural levels.
- race affects one's experiences, opportunities, and access to power.
- racism is a system based on an ideology which assumes the superiority and inferiority of people based on race, and how people internalize and enact the ideology of racism—internalized racial superiority and inferiority.
- ethnic and racial groups are defined and related.
- racial categories and classifications are socially constructed and why the definition and meaning of a racial group may change.
- the history of institutional racism affects current racial realities.
- throughout history people have created greater racial justice.

### CHALLENGES AND CAUTIONS

The challenges in teaching from a race-centered single-identity approach are similar to the possible struggles instructors may face whenever teaching about race, racism, and racial identity, regardless of whether or not they have an intersectional perspective. Many others have written about ways to effectively teach about race and racism (cf. Bell, Love, and Roberts 2007; Derman-Sparks and Phillips 1997; Goodman 2011; Okun 2010; Tatum 1992). Helping students question accepted beliefs and rethink their sense of self is a formidable task, since it is both cognitively and affectively challenging. Often there is resistance from students when educators ask them to examine deeply held assumptions and worldviews. They are expected to reevaluate how they make meaning of themselves, others, and the world. Learners may resist questioning some of the beliefs identified above (meritocracy, color-blindness, reverse racism) and the ideology that supports White supremacy. Students frequently try to avoid feelings that make them uncomfortable.

White students in particular may find it difficult to recognize the significance of being White. Given the normativity and invisibility of whiteness and White privilege, it can be especially challenging for White people to see how they are part of a racial group that is advantaged. Many White people feel that they are "just normal," do not view their race as an important part of their identity, or do not even think about belonging to any racial group. If White students are relatively unaware of their whiteness, how they enact it, and how they benefit from it, it may be challenging for them to see why it matters. As they confront the significance of race, White students may employ different strategies to deal with their discomfort such as rebutting the information, shifting the discussion to other social identities and forms of oppression (especially where they are part of the marginalized group), and shutting down intellectually and emotionally. Some learners may feel mired in guilt, shame, fear, or anger.

Students of color and Multiracial students may also resist the content and process. They may balk at seeing themselves as part of an oppressed racial group or as part of a racial group that they may primarily view in a negative light. They may minimize the significance of race given their investment in living the American Dream, belief in a color-blind society, or desire to assimilate into the White dominant culture. The possibility of resistance, in at least one of its many forms, is highly likely in this approach. Therefore, educators need to be prepared with strategies for minimizing and handling it lest they risk losing student engagement.[4]

Even while keeping the spotlight on racial identity, instructors cannot ignore or discount the significance of other social identities. There is a delicate balance of ensuring that the focus on race is not subverted while honoring the reality of the multiplicity of one's identity. As noted earlier, at the beginning of a class, even with a predominantly single focus on race, students can be asked to think about their identities within numerous social categories and consider which identities are most central to who they are and how they experience the world. In addition, examples of the intersection of race with another social identity can be noted in discussions of the class material and personal experiences. The relevance and interplay of other identities needs to be acknowledged without losing sight of the goals of this approach—developing a basic understanding of race, racism, and racial identity.

ACTIVITIES

The following activities are just a sampling of the myriad ways people educate about race, racism, and racial identity from a single-identity race-centered pedagogy. They include, in particular, ways to examine racial identity which are not always emphasized in teaching about race and racism. Students can:

- reflect on their racial socialization and their experiences learning about their own and others' race. For example, they can be asked to recount early racial messages and when they became aware of races being treated differently, or to develop a timeline of significant events in their learning about race, racism, and racial identity.

- look at how they think about and experience their racial identity in different contexts (e.g., their home communities, a workplace, college, recreational activity).
- create a time line of how their own or others' racial identity has evolved. How have they thought about their racial identity at different points in their lives?
- explore the culture of their own or another's racial group(s) and how this influences values, beliefs, patterns of behavior, and worldview.
- consider their experience of race and its significance by asking questions such as, What is it like being a _____ (racial identity) in this community, on this campus, in this workplace? How do you think your experience might be different if you were a member of a different race?
- be informed with concrete examples of racial differences in treatment and opportunities through a variety of sources, such as research studies, statistics, personal stories, films, and observations.
- participate in experiential activities that demonstrate the dynamics of racism and the effects of inequitable treatment on individuals.
- use their knowledge of and experiences with other social identities (both dominant and subordinated) to relate to race, racism, and racial identity development. How can understanding the experience and impact of marginalization, privilege, and identity development in a different form of oppression assist in understanding racial subordination, privilege, and identity development?
- read models of racial identity development or personal reflections on racial identity as points of reference to look at their own and others' experiences. Read personal narratives and identify themes related to racial identity.
- examine internalized racial inferiority and superiority—how people of color and White people internalize the messages from the dominant culture about their racial groups. How do these affect their own and others' sense of self and behavior and intra- and intergroup relations?
- consider the effects of differences in self-ascription of racial identity (how one defines oneself) and others' ascription of racial identity (how one is seen by others).
- learn about the reasons why and history of how racial categories and classifications were created and have changed. Discuss how this has affected people's racial identity and how this is still occurring.
- explore how racial identity has affected how people of color and White people have worked for racial justice and have students develop their own strategies to challenge racism.

In the race-centered, single-identity pedagogical approach, students have the opportunity to examine race, racism, and racial identity as it affects themselves and others. Of course, this is just a beginning step in the exploration of a vast topic. Yet it readies them to investigate racial identity more deeply, in a more multidimensional way.

### Race-Centered, Limited Intersectional Approach

A race-centered, limited intersectional approach begins to complicate racial identity by integrating other social identities into the content and discussion. By adding another layer of complexity, a more nuanced, intersectional picture is being formed. Racial identity remains the focus as other social identities are incorporated in a limited way; only one or two other identities are considered simultaneously with race. The social groups explored can be based on which identities are most salient for the student, the teacher feels are most appropriate, or fit the topic of the class. This approach assists students in developing a basic conceptual understanding of an intersectional perspective. The central question in a race-centered limited intersectional approach is: How is one's racial identity shaped by one or two other social identities? How does one's class, sex, sexuality, gender, ethnicity, religion, national origin, ability, or other social identity affect one's racial identity and lived experiences?

CRITERIA FOR USE

This approach is likely to be useful when students have a basic understanding of race, racism, and racial identity. (See learning objectives for the race-centered, single-identity approach above.) Students are able to recognize the significance of race and racism in people's lives and have done some reflection on their own and others' process of racial identity development. They can appreciate the variations in racial identity and social realities, and how context influences how racial identity is shaped and experienced. Through exploring race, students have become familiar with some key concepts and dynamics related to social identities and social inequalities more generally, such as culture, power, privilege, oppression, and internalized inferiority/superiority.

RATIONALE

Students for whom this approach may be useful are those individuals who are ready to build on their foundational understanding of race, racism, and racial identity. Since they have a sufficient grasp of race, they can hold that while also considering its interaction and intersection with another social identity. They are ready to develop the theoretical and cognitive capability to explore how two or more identities mutually affect and inform each other.

### LEARNING OBJECTIVES

In the race-centered, limited intersectional approach, some of the main goals are for students to understand how at least one other social identity affects racial identity and lived experiences. It encourages students to explore how racial identity evolves, shifts, and gets reconfigured. Objectives that would be appropriate for race-centered single-identity pedagogy might include having students explore how:

- the interrelationship of race and another identity may change over time and depend on the context and circumstances.
- the integration of race with another social identity is not simply additive but creates a new whole which is greater than the sum of the parts.
- different identities in conjunction with race may differently affect one's experience and meaning of their racial identity. For example, what is the difference in how one's racial identity is experienced when considered in conjunction with one's sex versus one's sexual orientation?
- different social identities may have different degrees of salience in intersection with race, which can change over time and context.
- the social status of other social identities (dominant or subordinated) affect one's racial identity and life experiences, including the experience of racial privilege and oppression.
- less salient identities still have an  impact on racial identity and lived experiences.
- one's racial identity in intersection with another social identity affects one's understanding of and strategies for racial and social justice.

### CHALLENGES AND CAUTIONS

Since this approach calls for greater knowledge and cognitive capability there can be numerous challenges. One potential obstacle is having difficulty or the willingness to consider the *intersectional* relationship among identities, not just that an individual has multiple identities. Often it is hard enough to recognize that people have numerous cultural influences and different degrees of privilege and oppression because of their various individual social identities, much less to see how these interact. Some learners may find it easier to look at the intersectional nature of their own racial identities but find it more challenging to see it in others; other students may find it easier to look at how others' identities interweave but cannot readily see it in their own lives.

The particular social identities that are being considered in relation to race also raise challenges. Students may have different degrees of *ability* to consider certain identities. If students do not have enough familiarity with an identity and form of oppression, it is difficult to appreciate its interaction with race. This lack of knowledge can impede their own self-awareness as well as their understanding of others. Therefore, students will have greater or lesser ability to comprehend the intersection of race with particular identities based on their level of awareness of those categories of difference.

In addition, students may have different degrees of *willingness* or *interest* in examining certain identities. They may only want to explore the ones that are most salient to them. People of color may resist looking at identities where they are in the dominant group, with the corresponding privileges, and how those affect their racial identity and experience. They may feel that this diminishes their identification with their race and minimizes the acknowledgment of the racism they face. Whites may overemphasize their subordinated identities in order to feel less uncomfortable with their dominant status as White people. Similarly, they may also resist including for study additional dominant identities. Furthermore, when people are deeply immersed in a subordinated identity, it can be particularly challenging for them to examine and integrate other identities. For example, in a group where people were being asked how their race affected their work, a White woman expressed apologetically, "I know my being White matters, but right now I'm in the process of coming out as a lesbian and just can't think of anything else!"

Given these challenges, there are a couple of cautions when using this approach. If only one or two social identities are considered in conjunction with race, students may feel that the ones omitted are being discounted or marginalized. Given the constraints of the class, it may be warranted to limit the areas of study since not everything can be considered in one class. The reason for the parameters of the class can be clearly explained. It is important that students do not infer that some social identities are inherently more important or significant than others or are more central to an individual's racial identity. There is also the danger of conflating differences among forms of identity and oppression. Students may struggle with appreciating both the similarities among axes of identity and forms of oppression as well as the differences. They may need assistance to see how each social category has its own unique contribution to one's racial identity and experiences.

ACTIVITIES

There are many ways students can be encouraged to gradually develop a more intersectional analysis of racial identity. Below we list some suggestions that can be adapted for different kinds of classes. The focus is on only one or two identities simultaneously with race. Even when looking at racial identity in a limited intersectional way, activities can have varying degrees of complexity and require different levels of cognitive ability. Educators need to consider the readiness of the students even when choosing strategies within this approach. If students have limited knowledge about a particular dimension of difference that they will be considering in relation to race, it might be helpful to review it first as a single identity before looking at its intersection with race. In a race-centered limited intersectional pedagogy, students can:

- think about the relationship of a particular social identity category in conjunction with race as they engage with different curriculum materials or self-awareness activities. The following questions can be used (if looking at class): How is one's race affected by one's experience of class and classism? How is one's race classed?
- identify the one or two social identities they currently feel most affect their racial identity. Have students discuss why they chose that identity(ies) and its impact on their racial identity.
- look at different contexts (e.g., their home communities, a workplace, college, recreational activity) and identify which social identity in conjunction with race is most significant in each of those contexts. Have them discuss why they chose the same or different social identity and how that identity affects their racial identity.
- use a Venn Diagram (two circles that overlap in the middle) to chart the intersection of race and another identity. In one circle, describe key qualities and experiences of one's racial identity, in the other circle indicate the key qualities and experiences of another social identity, and in the middle write the ways they overlap and interact. Ask: How does considering them together change the understanding of them individually?
- look at how the intersection of race and another social identity are experienced differently as the setting changes. How does the experience of oneself change depending on the context? As an example, what is it like being a Latina in a predominantly White women's organization versus in a Latino community meeting?
- create a time line to map how race and another identity have intersected at different times in their own or others' lives and how it has shaped their racial identity. For example, people can look at how their gender has affected

their sense of race at different points in their lives (e.g., elementary school, middle school, high school, college, and beyond). This can be further complicated by also considering contexts within those time periods. They can consider the impact of their age, context, the historical time period, and geographical setting on how their gender influenced their racial identity development.

- do the time line activity above, but instead of looking at the same social identity with race, explore which social identity in conjunction with race was more salient at different times and how it shaped one's racial identity.

- listen to the stories of others or read personal accounts of people's lives and identify ways those individuals' identities and experiences were shaped by the intersection of their race and another identity. Have students examine the forces which shaped their identities, including systems of inequality. Initially it may be useful to hear narratives where those links are more explicit until they can more easily do their own analysis.

- consider how self-ascription versus other ascriptions of racial and other identities affect one's experience of race and racial identity. For example, what happens when someone identifies as biracial but is seen as Asian, or an African American is heterosexual but is presumed to be gay?

- read historical accounts, descriptions of current events, and discussions of issues that reflect an intersection of race with another social identity or form of oppression. Analyze how each of these identities intersects to create different experiences. For example, the 2008 Democratic presidential race with Barack Obama and Hillary Clinton could be used to analyze how race and sex interacted to create some interesting personal and political dynamics.

- analyze or conduct research on an issue or social problem that involves race using an intersectional framework. Which intersecting identities and forms of oppression are most central to understanding and addressing this issue? How might this be addressed from an intersectional perspective?

- explore how the intersections of race and other social identities with dominant or subordinate statuses affect experiences of racial privilege and oppression and alter self-concept. What happens when a dominant or subordinated identity is considered along with a racial identity that is dominant or subordinated? How does this affect the experience of racial privilege or oppression?

- examine how the interconnections between race and another social identity create connections and barriers to working together for social justice. For example, explore the dynamics between Black men and Black women in the civil rights movement, or between White, middle-class, and low-income Black and Latino activists in the environmental justice movement.

Throughout the activities within this approach, students can have opportunities to deepen their discussion of the intersection of race and other social identities by looking at key dynamics. When students are asked to reflect on their own identities and experiences, they can compare their responses with others in order to notice the similarities and differences within and between racial identity groups and consider what accounts for these variations. They can explore the impact of different social identities, the status of identities (from privileged or oppressed groups), the impact of the particular context, and role of other personal and societal factors.

A race-centered limited intersectional approach provides extensive opportunities to explore and deepen the meaning of racial identity. It allows learners to understand what an intersectional approach entails and how it informs our understanding of the complexity of racial identity. Being able to grapple with the content draws on and develops cognitive skills and flexibility. These are expanded further in the next approach.

## Race-Centered Multidimensional Approach

A race-centered, multiple intersectional approach allows for a more complete exploration of how race intersects with other social identities. In this approach, any number or categories of social identity can be considered simultaneously in conjunction with race. This approach offers an opportunity to examine the shifting interplay of race and other social identities. It best captures the complexity of how racial identity develops, evolves, and shifts.

The central question in a race-centered multiple intersectional approach is: How is one's racial identity shaped by one's class, sex, sexuality, religion, ethnicity, national origin, gender, ability, and/or other social identity? How do these other identities interact with each other and with race to affect one's experience of race and racial identity?

### CRITERIA FOR USE

This pedagogical approach is most appropriate with learners who already understand an intersectional perspective, have sufficient grasp of racial issues, and have a strong grounding in other forms of social identities and social oppression. Students have the content knowledge as well as the cognitive capacity to conceptualize and wrestle with the interplay of multiple identities and social realities.

They are ready to engage in a more comprehensive examination of Intersectionality and racial identity.

LEARNING OBJECTIVES

Learning objectives that would be appropriate for race-centered multiple intersectional pedagogy might include having students explore how:

- various social identities simultaneously intersect and affect the experience of racial identity.
- the salience of different social identities in intersection with race may change over time and context.
- the meaning of race in conjunction with other social identities may change over time and vary based on context. For example, in the U.S., Muslim men from an Arab country are viewed differently now than before 9/11/2001.
- different combinations of social identities may have different effects on one's experience and meaning of racial identity. For example, how differently is racial identity conceived when considering sex, sexual orientation, and gender versus class, ethnicity, and national origin?
-  the experiences of privilege and oppression across various forms of inequality interact and affect one's racial identity and experience of racial privilege or oppression.
- less salient identities impact one's racial identity.
- the intersectional mix of social identities affects one's understanding of racism and strategies for racial and social justice.


CHALLENGES AND CAUTIONS

The main challenges of this approach are holding multiple, overlapping identities simultaneously. While not every identity needs to be considered in every situation, several will be explored at the same time. The ability to look at the intersection of several axes of identity as they relate to race is not a simple task. It requires students to have sufficient knowledge of many categories of difference and be able to retain their particular qualities as they contribute to an intersectional picture. Moreover, a race-centered multiple intersectional analysis entails being able to consider changes over time and context—to look at how racial identity shifts and evolves in conjunction with other identities.

As noted in previous approaches, there can be resistance to or difficulty examining social identities that are less salient, especially those in dominant groups. Students of color may see this approach as diluting the centrality of, or deflecting attention away from, racism and giving White people the comfort of focusing on subordinated identities. White students may in fact gravitate toward their other subordinated identities to the exclusion of other dominant identities. There can also be competition regarding which identities are really most significant or most oppressive.

ACTIVITIES

Many of the activities in the race-centered intersectional approach build upon and expand the educational strategies discussed in the race-centered limited intersectional approach. Additional identities are added to the analysis. Any social identity can be considered in conjunction with any other social identity, along with race. For reader ease, the relevant activities previously listed in the race-centered limited intersectional approach will be restated in their expanded form. To develop an understanding of racial identity from a broader intersectional perspective, students can:

- identify the various social identities they currently feel most affect their racial identity. Have them discuss why they chose these and how they affect their racial identity and lived experiences.
- look at different contexts (e.g., their home communities, a workplace, college, recreational activity) and identify which social identities in conjunction with race are most significant in each of those contexts. Have them discuss why they chose the same or different mix of social identities in the different contexts and how those identities affect their racial identity and lived experiences.
- examine how changes in one identity within a constellation of identities impacts one's experience of race and racial identity. For example: How might it be different being an Asian, working-class, able-bodied male versus an Asian, working-class, able-bodied female?
- create a time line to map how race and different social identities have intersected at different times in their own or others' lives and how those have shaped their racial identity. They can also consider the contexts within those time periods as well as their age, geographical location, and the historical time period.
- do a similar time line as described above but hold constant the other social identities. Have students consider how those social identities affected their own or others' racial identity at different points in their lives.
- analyze personal stories, historical accounts, biographies, or descriptions of current events that reflect an intersection of race with other forms of social identity or inequality. How do these identities intersect with each other and with race to affect racial identity and lived experiences?
- analyze or conduct research on an issue or social problem that involves race (e.g., employment opportunities, college experiences, or media images) using an intersectional framework. Ask students which mix of social identities and

forms of oppression in interaction with race are most central to understanding and addressing this issue. Have students propose solutions using an intersectional perspective.

- explore how the statuses of other social identities (dominant or subordinated) affect the experience of racial privilege or oppression.
- consider how one's racial identity in intersection with other social identities affects one's understanding of racism and other forms of oppression and strategies for social justice.
- examine how the intersections of one's racial identity and other social identities create connections and barriers to working together for social justice. For example, explore the dynamics of how White women and women of color with varying class backgrounds, sexualities, and religious/spiritual identities worked together in the women's movement.

### Full Intersectional Approach

A full intersectional pedagogical approach creates a more holistic picture of how social identities shape one's sense of self and lived experiences. It allows people to consider how all social identities are integrated and interact. Racial identity is no longer the focal point. Other social identities are not viewed in reference to or through the lens of race. Race is examined in the context of other social group memberships and as one component of a person's overall sense of self. While race remains part of the mix, its salience may fluctuate as other social identities take on varying degrees of significance at different times. This approach encourages students to consider how identities interplay, mutually shape each other, and affect experiences of privilege and oppression. While all social categories can be considered, not all will necessarily be examined simultaneously. Given the focus on racial identity, it may be appropriate to ask students to look at the influence of race in particular. In this approach, the question becomes, how is one's social identity shaped by one's race, ethnicity, sex, sexuality, gender, religion, ability, national origin, and other social identities? How do these social identities intersect and interact with each other, across contexts, to affect social identity and lived experiences? What role does race play in this integration?

CRITERIA FOR USE

This is a highly complex approach that will likely be most effective when students already have a strong understanding of not only race, racial identity, and racism but other social identities and forms of oppression. This approach requires an understanding of Intersectionality and experience using this framework. If learners are able to look at racial identity from an intersectional perspective, they may be ready to expand their analysis to include how all social identities, including race, interrelate to shape one's identity and how one experiences the world.

### LEARNING OBJECTIVES

Learning objectives that would be appropriate for a full intersectional pedagogy might include having students explore how:

- various social identities intersect and simultaneously affect one's collective social identity and lived experiences.
- the salience of different social identities may change over time and vary based on context.
- identities that are less salient shape other social identities and impact one's identity and experiences.
- the social locations (dominant or subordinated statuses) of one's various identities interplay and affect one's social identity and experiences of privilege and oppression.
- how one's social identity affects one's understanding of systems of oppression and strategies for social justice.

### CAUTIONS AND CHALLENGES

Since this approach is the most intersectional and complex, it is the most challenging. Students may struggle with keeping an intersectional perspective, not just a multiple identity perspective. It is easy to fall into examining how each social group membership contributes separately to one's identity and experience, not necessarily how they overlap and mutually shape each other. Learners may also start to lose the distinctiveness and significance of each social identity. It can be hard to acknowledge what each identity contributes while understanding their interplay. There may also be a tendency to overlook or minimize the significance of certain identities.

### ACTIVITIES

To keep a focus on racial identity, educators could specifically include exploring the role and influence of race within these activities. Students can:

- look at different contexts (e.g., their home communities, a workplace, college, recreational activity) and identify which social identities are most significant in each of those contexts. Have them discuss why they chose the same or different mix of social identities in the different contexts and how those identities interact to affect their social identity and life experiences.

- do the activity above but look at which identities are least salient. Have students consider how less salient identities may be relevant, in intersection with other identities, to how they experience the world and are seen and treated by others.
- create time lines to map how various social identities have intersected at different times in their own or others' lives and how those have shaped their collective social identity and lived experiences. For example, people can look at which mix of social identities most affected their sense of self and life experience at different points in their lives (e.g., elementary school, middle school, high school, college, and beyond). They can also consider the contexts within those time periods as well as their age, geographical location, and the historical time period.
- look at similarities and differences within the same intersectional identities. How does the addition of other identities affect one's social identity and lived experiences? For example, how is it different being a White, Jewish, heterosexual woman who is working class versus upper class? How does it further change if we consider age?
- use an intersectional lens to analyze personal stories, historical accounts, biographies, or descriptions of current events. How do multiple identity categories and social inequalities intersect with each other to affect one's experiences and social identity?
- use an intersectional framework to analyze or conduct research on an issue or social problem. Ask students which mix of identities and forms of oppression are most central to understanding and addressing this issue. Have students propose solutions or policies using an intersectional perspective.
- examine their own or others' lives, and explore how the intersection of social identities with different social statuses (dominant or subordinated) affect one's experiences of privilege and oppression.
- Analyze different social change movements. How have people's mix of social identities affected their ability to work in coalition with others for social justice?
- Ask students to identify ways their own social identity can assist them in working for social justice as well as the challenges, given their particular intersectional identities.

Conclusion

As these various pedagogical approaches indicate, an intersectional lens opens up exciting ways to broaden and deepen our understanding of social identities and social inequalities. In particular, it allows racial identity to be examined with greater breadth and depth. It better captures the complexity and variety of how people make meaning of and experience their racial group membership.

In proposing these pedagogical approaches to teaching racial identity from increasingly more intersectional perspectives, we hope to add to the conversation of how to practically apply intersectional theory. As educators try to put theory into practice, questions and challenges get raised, such as

- Is the pedagogical framework we are suggesting for racial identity appropriate for exploring other social identities?
- How can we help students grasp the intersectional paradigm as a theoretical framework?
- How can we best acknowledge the particularities of each category of difference while recognizing how they simultaneously intersect?
- How can we promote the use of an intersectional approach while being mindful of the needs and abilities of our students?
- How can an intersectional lens help foster commitment to and create strategies for addressing societal inequities?

We know that our own thinking about and experiences with teaching about race, racism, and racial identity using an intersectional approach will continue to evolve. We hope that as others examine the strengths and limitations of what we have proposed and continue to share their own thinking and practices, we will develop increasingly effective strategies for helping students understand and address not only issues of race but all social identities and forms of social inequality, the hallmark of Intersectionality.

## NOTES

1. For examples of efforts to incorporate a more intersectional perspective into teaching issues of social diversity and inequality, see Boucher (2011), Carlin (2011), Jones and Wijeyesinghe (2011), Longstreet (2011), and Naples (2009). There are also some collections of readings that address these issues from an intersectional perspective and offer teacher guides along with them, for example, Ferber, Jimenez, Herrera, and Samuels (2009), and Anderson and Collins (2010).

2. For a review of the origins, evolution, and core tenets of intersectional theory, see Berger and Guidroz (2009), Collins (2000), Crenshaw (1991), and Dill and Zambrana (2009).

3. However, Luft (2009) only recommends the use of a strategic singular methodology for race, not gender. She believes that since the current sex/gender formation has a different dominant logic system, rooted in gender essentialism, it requires an intersectional analysis.

4. See, for example, Goodman 2011 for strategies for dealing with resistance.

## REFERENCES

African American Policy Forum. 2008. *A Primer on Intersectionality.* http://aapf.org/wp-content/uploads/2009/03/aapf_Intersectionality_primer.pdf. Accessed March 31, 2011.

Anderson, Margaret, and Patricia Hill Collins. 2010. *Race, Class and Gender: An Anthology.* Belmont, Calif.: Wadsworth.

Bell, Lee Anne, Barbara Love, and Rosemarie A. Roberts. 2007. "Racism and White Privilege." In *Teaching for Diversity and Social Justice,* 2nd ed., edited by Maurianne Adams, Lee Anne Bell, and Pat Griffin, 123–144. New York: Routledge.

Berger, Michele, and Kathleen Guidroz, eds. 2009. *The Intersectional Approach: Transforming the Academy through Race, Class and Gender.* Chapel Hill: University of North Carolina Press.

Boucher, Michel. 2011. "Teaching 'Trans Issues': An Intersectional and Systems-Based Approach." In *New Directions for Teaching and Learning: An Integrative Analysis Approach to Diversity in the Classroom,* edited by Mathew L. Ouellett, 65–75. Wilmington, Del.: Wiley.

Carlin, Deborah. 2011. "The Intersectional Potential of Queer Theory: An Example from a General Education Course in English." In *New Directions for Teaching and Learning: An Integrative Analysis Approach to Diversity in the Classroom,* edited by Mathew L. Ouellett, 55–63. Wilmington, Del.: Wiley.

Collins, Patricia H. 2000. *Black Feminist Thought: Knowledge, Consciousness, and the Politics of Empowerment.* New York: Routledge.

Crenshaw, Kimberle. 1991. "Mapping the Margins: Intersectionality, Identity Politics and Violence against Women of Color." *Stanford Law Review* 43: 1211–1299.

Derman-Sparks, Louise, and Carol B. Phillips. 1997. *Teaching/Learning Anti-Racism.* New York: Teachers' College Press.

Dill, Bonnie Thorton, and Ruth Zambrana, eds. 2009. *Emerging Intersections: Race, Class and Gender in Theory, Policy and Practice.* New Brunswick, N.J.: Rutgers University Press.

Ferber, Abby, Christina Jimenez, Andrea Herrera, and Dena Samuels, eds. 2009. *The Matrix Reader: Examining the Dynamics of Oppression and Privilege.* New York: McGraw-Hill.

Freire, Paulo. 1994. *Pedagogy of Hope: Reliving Pedagogy of the Oppressed.* New York: Continuum.

Goodman, Diane. 2011. *Promoting Diversity and Social Justice: Educating People from Privileged Groups,* 2nd ed. New York: Routledge.

Jones, Susan, R., and Charmaine L. Wijeyesinghe. 2011. "The Promises and Challenges of Teaching from an Intersectional Perspective: Core Components and Applied Strategies." In *New Directions for Teaching and Learning: An Integrative Analysis Approach to Diversity in the Classroom,* edited by Mathew L. Ouellett, 11–20. Wilmington, Del.: Wiley.

Longstreet, C. Shaun. 2011. "The Trouble with Disciplining Disciplines." In *New Directions for Teaching and Learning: An Integrative Analysis Approach to Diversity in the Classroom,* edited by Mathew L. Ouellett, 21–29. Wilmington, Del.: Wiley.

Luft, Rachel. 2009. "Intersectionality and the Risk of Flattening Difference: Gender and Race Logics, and the Strategic Use of Antiracist Strategy." In *The Intersectional Approach:*

*Transforming the Academy through Race, Class and Gender*, edited by M. Berger and K. Guidroz, 100–117. Chapel Hill: University of North Carolina Press.

Naples, Nancy. 2009. "Teaching Intersectionality Intersectionally." *International Feminist Journal of Politics*, 11 (4): 566–577. DOI: 10.1080/14616740903237558. Accessed March 25, 2011.

Okun, Tema. 2010. *The Emperor Has No Clothes: Teaching about Race and Racism to People Who Don't Want to Know*. Charlotte, N.C.: Information Age Publishing.

Tatum, Beverly. 1992. "Talking about Race, Learning about Racism: The Application of Racial Identity Development Theory in the Classroom." *Harvard Educational Review* 62 (1): 1–24.

WILLIAM E. CROSS, JR. recently retired from the Graduate Center-CUNY where he directed the doctoral program in social-personality psychology as well as coordinated the certificate program in African American Studies. Currently he is Professor and Coordinator of Graduate Studies in the Department of Counselor Education in the School of Education at the University of Nevada Las Vegas.

BERNARDO M. FERDMAN is Professor in the California School of Professional Psychology (CSPP) at Alliant International University. As a teacher, writer, speaker, and consultant, he specializes in diversity, inclusion, and multiculturalism in organizations, ethnic and cultural identity, Latinos/as in the workplace, cross-cultural communication, and organizational behavior and development.

PLÁCIDA V. GALLEGOS is Professor at Fielding Graduate University in the Human and Organizational Development Program and has conducted research in the areas of transformational leadership, career development of women and people of color, and creating inclusive organizations. Her research and practice have continued to emphasize the unique challenges and opportunities Latinos present to society and organization. She is also an organizational consultant in the areas of strategic culture change, creating inclusion and maximizing organizational diversity, supervisory and management skills, leadership styles, career development, conflict management, and team building.

DIANE J. GOODMAN has been an educator in the areas of diversity and social justice for over twenty-five years. She was the Director of Human Relations Education and the Interim Affirmative Action Officer at the University of Rhode Island. As a trainer and consultant, Diane works with a wide range of organizations, community groups, schools, and universities. Her publications include *Promoting Diversity and Social Justice: Educating People from Privileged Groups,* 2nd ed. Her website is www.dianegoodman.com.

RITA HARDIMAN is Chief Diversity Officer and Executive Director of Human Resources at Greenfield Community College in Massachusetts. A pioneer in antiracism training and White racial identity development,

Hardiman authored one of the first models of White racial identity development in the country. She is President of R. Hardiman Associates, a training and consulting firm specializing in diversity and social justice in organizations throughout the United States.

EVANGELINA HOLVINO is President of Chaos Management, Ltd., a consulting, training, and research partnership specializing in collaborative approaches to organization and social change. She is also an affiliate faculty at the Center for Gender in Organizations at the Simmons School of Management in Boston. She designs and facilitates change interventions in four areas: global diversity and capacity building strategies; large group planning and problem solving meetings; conflict management and collaboration across differences; and career development for Hispanics and women of color in organizations.

PERRY G. HORSE began his professional career as a program specialist with the U.S. Office of Education (HEW) in Washington, D.C. Subsequently, he worked as a technical assistance advisor, instructor, and director of research for the American Indian Higher Education Consortium (tribal colleges and universities). He later served as a member of laboratory staff with Sandia National Laboratories, then a subsidiary of AT&T, Bell Labs. After serving as president of the Institute of American Indian Arts in Santa Fe, he worked until his retirement as an independent consultant to community colleges, private foundations, and nonprofit organizations.

BAILEY W. JACKSON III is currently Professor Emeritus in the Social Justice Education concentration, School of Education, University of Massachusetts, Amherst. Prior to his retirement, he served as Dean of the School of Education for eleven years. Jackson is recognized nationally and internationally as one of the leading theorists in the area of Racial Identity Development. His models have been used as the basis for helping educators, as well as social and behavioral scientists, to understand the identity development issues facing members of various racial groups in the United States.

MOLLY KEEHN is completing her doctoral studies in the Social Justice Education Program at the University of Massachusetts, Amherst. She has a background in higher education and her research specialties include White identity development, intergroup dialogues, and the role of personal storytelling in the classroom. Keehn currently teaches undergraduate courses on oppression and empowerment, and helps coordinate an intergroup dialogue program for faculty and staff as well as undergraduate students.

JEAN KIM, a native of Seoul, Korea, has worked in seven universities including Stanford University, and served as the chief student affairs officer at five universities. She is currently the Vice Chancellor for Student Affairs and Campus Life at the University of Massachusetts, Amherst. In addition to her work as a university administrator, Jean's professional background includes a career as speaker and consultant for a number of Fortune 500 corporations in leadership/organization development and diversity.

KRISTEN A. RENN is Associate Professor of Higher, Adult and Lifelong Education at Michigan State University. Her research focuses on mixed-race college students, gender, and the experiences of lesbian, gay, bisexual, and transgender people in higher education. She is the author of *Mixed Race Students in College: The Ecology of Race, Identity, and Community.*

CHARMAINE L. WIJEYESINGHE is a consultant in organizational development and social justice. Her professional career includes numerous positions in higher education administration at the University of Massachusetts, Amherst, and Dean of Students at Mount Holyoke College. As a member of the national program staff of the National Conference of Community and Justice she developed social justice programs for sixty-two regional offices around the country. Her Factor Model of Multiracial Identity has been used for two decades to understand the experiences of Multiracial people, and was adopted into the anti-bias curriculum of the Anti-Defamation League (ADL). Her writing currently focuses on the relationship between racial identity models and intersectionality.

# INDEX